Paul F. Bradshaw
Editor

Paul F. Bradshaw
Stephen B. Wilson
Walter D. Ray
G. J. Cuming
Maxwell E. Johnson
D. Richard Stuckwisch
Kent J. Burreson
John D. Witvliet
Raphael Graves
Robert F. Taft, S.J.

Essays on Early Eastern Eucharistic Prayers

A PUEBLO BOOK

The Liturgical Press Collegeville, Minnesota

Design by Frank Kacmarcik, Obl.S.B.

A Pueblo Book published by The Liturgical Press.

Library of Congress Cataloging-in-Publication Data

Essays on early eastern eucharistic prayers / Paul F. Bradshaw,
    editor.
        p.   cm.
    "A Pueblo book."
    Based on a series of seminars for doctoral students in liturgical
studies at the University of Notre Dame.
    Includes bibliographical references and index.
    ISBN 0-8146-6153-X
    1. Eucharistic prayers.   2. Liturgies, Early Christian.
3. Eastern church—Liturgy.   4. Orthodox Eastern Church—Liturgy.
5. Catholic Church—Oriental rites—Liturgy.   I. Bradshaw, Paul F.
BV185.E87   1997
264'.011036—dc21   97-14102
                                                              CIP

Contents

Preface

Like an earlier collection of essays that I edited (*Essays in Early Eastern Initiation,* Alcuin/Grow Liturgical Study 8, Nottingham: Grove Books, 1988), this one, too, had its origins in a series of seminars for doctoral students in liturgical studies that I led at the University of Notre Dame. At the conclusion of the semester, I realized that around that table were gathered people who, collectively, had read more of the relevant literature on the topic and given more thought to the future direction of research than almost anyone else living. It seemed a pity to let it end there and not to share that knowledge more widely with those who had not the time or opportunity to study the subject in as great a depth. Thus was born the idea of a sort of companion to the early Eastern liturgical texts published in Ronald Jasper and Geoffrey Cuming's *Prayers of the Eucharist: Early and Reformed,* 3rd ed. (New York: Pueblo, 1980). For texts are really only useful to the student of liturgy if they are accompanied by explanation that sets them within their context and explains their connection to one another.

Since it had not been possible to cover fully in the seminars all the ancient eucharistic prayers (or anaphoras, as they are often called) that arose in the East, I am deeply grateful to the scholars Maxwell Johnson (of St. John's University, Collegeville) and Robert Taft (of the Pontifical Oriental Institute, Rome) for agreeing to contribute essays on two highly significant prayers, and to Kenneth Stevenson (bishop of Portsmouth, England, and literary executor to Geoffrey Cuming) for permission to reproduce here Cuming's classic essay on the development of the Alexandrian anaphora of St. Mark, originally published in *Le Muséon* 95 (1982) 115–29. Johnson's essay also previously appeared in Robert F. Taft, ed., *The Christian East, Its Institutions & Its Thought: A Critical Reflection,* OCA 251 (Rome: Pontificium Institutum Orientale, 1996) 671–702; and again I am grateful for permission to include it here.

No attempt has been made to force the various essayists to adopt a common stance toward the manner in which eucharistic prayers evolved and various elements passed from one text or tradition to another. The reader will therefore find points at which there are at least minor disagreements between them, and this will serve as a useful reminder that the results of current research have not yet led to a consensus in every respect, but that there is still much more work to be done, both along the lines that the different contributors indicate and also in other ways.

Paul F. Bradshaw

Abbreviations

JTS	*Journal of Theological Studies*
LQF	Liturgiewissenschaftliche Quellen und Forschungen
NPNF	Philip Schaff and Henry Wace, eds., *A Select Library of Nicene and Post-Nicene Fathers of the Christian Church*
OC	*Oriens Christianus*
OCA	Orientalia Christiana Analecta
OCP	*Orientalia Christiana Periodica*
OS	*Ostkirchliche Studien*
PEER	R.C.D. Jasper and Geoffrey J. Cuming, *Prayers of the Eucharist: Early and Reformed*, 3rd ed. (New York: Pueblo, 1987)
PG	J. P. Migne, ed., *Patrologia Graeca*
PL	J. P. Migne, ed., *Patrologia Latina*
PO	Patrologia Orientalis
SC	Sources chrétiennes
SL	*Studia Liturgica*
SP	*Studia Patristica*
TS	*Theological Studies*

Paul F. Bradshaw

Introduction:
The Evolution of Early Anaphoras

One of the problems we encounter when studying early liturgical practice is that we often unconsciously read back into the descriptions and accounts that have come down us assumptions that are based on later practice and not on what is actually in the texts before us. For example, when reading Justin Martyr's second-century description of the regular weekly assembly "on the day called Sunday of all who live in town or country,"[1] we tend to assume that this gathering took place in the morning and did not involve the consumption of a full meal because that is what we find to be the case in later sources. Justin himself, however, says nothing about the hour of the assembly, and it could just as well have been in the evening, as seems to have been the original New Testament custom.

Furthermore, while the rites connected with the bread and cup certainly appear to be distinguished from any other eating and drinking here, it is not completely impossible that a more substantial meal still followed the ritual act, and this may even be alluded to in the brief statement which follows his description of a baptismal eucharist, with its appended explanation of the significance of the bread and cup, and precedes his account of the regular Sunday eucharist: "After this we constantly remind each other of these things. Those who have more come to the aid of those who lack, and we are constantly together. Over all that we receive, we bless the Maker of all things through his son Jesus Christ and through the Holy Spirit."[2] This is usually taken to be simply a summary of Christian life in general; but if the opening phrase "after this" (*meta tauta*) is taken more literally, it

---

[1] Justin Martyr, *First Apology* 67.3; see *PEER*, 29.
[2] Justin Martyr, *First Apology* 67.1–2.

1

could be interpreted as an outline of what followed the ritual act with the bread and cup on a Sunday evening—religious discourse between the participants, charitable donations, and a supper with blessings over all that was received—a pattern analogous to rabbinic meals within Judaism.[3]

What is even more doubtful about Justin's rite is whether there was yet a single unified eucharistic prayer. Jewish practice seems to have required that a short blessing would be said over each item of food and drink before it was consumed at a meal; and all the New Testament accounts of the Last Supper speak of a blessing over the bread and a separate blessing or thanksgiving over the cup. We find a similar pattern in the meal ritual of the ancient church order known as the *Didache*, where in chapter 9 there are separate brief prayers of thanksgiving over the cup and over the bread (in that order[4]), with the latter having appended to it a petitionary prayer for the gathering of the church, and then in chapter 10 a prayer of thanksgiving to be used at the end of the meal, which is also composed of three distinct units, thanksgiving for the holy name, praise for the gift of food and drink, and a petition for the gathering of the church. In each case, the prayer units have their own concluding doxological formula ("glory to you for evermore," or some variant of it).[5] The eucharistic prayer of Addai and Mari, which is generally thought to have very ancient roots, also displays a similar structure of shorter units concluded by doxological formulas.[6]

While it seems clear that in the practice known to Justin the bread and cup were brought at the same time to the one presiding over the assembly, it does not follow that a single prayer was then recited over both together. Separate prayers could still have been used, and it may be significant that Justin says that the president "sends up prayers and thanksgivings to the best of his ability."[7] Even his next statement that "the people assent, saying the Amen" could mean that

[3]I owe this particular suggestion to Taylor Burton-Edwards, a student at the Associated Mennonite Seminaries, Elkhart, Indiana.

[4]This apparently "inverted" sequence may not have been so unusual in early Christian circles as it appears to modern eyes accustomed to the later standardized "normal" sequence: see Andrew McGowan, "'First regarding the Cup . . .': Papias and the Diversity of early Eucharistic Practice," *JTS* 46 (1995) 551–55.

[5]For an ET of these texts, see *PEER*, 23–24.

[6]See the essay by Stephen Wilson, below, 19–37.

[7]Justin Martyr, *First Apology* 67.3; *PEER*, 29.

this was done after each prayer and not just once at the very end.[8] The persistence of such separate prayers may also explain the otherwise enigmatic direction in the third-century Syrian *Didascalia Apostolorum* that if a visiting bishop does not wish to accept the invitation to preside over the whole eucharistic offering, he should at least "say the words over the cup."[9]

Enrico Mazza has not only drawn attention to these two sources in this regard, but has also suggested that the unusual form of the narrative of institution in the later *Sacramentary of Sarapion*—where the account of the ritual of the bread is separated from that of the cup by the petition for the gathering of the church from the meal rite of *Didache* 9—may be the remnant of an archaic structure of the eucharistic rite itself, in which a thanksgiving over the bread was followed by this short petitionary prayer and then by a thanksgiving over the cup.[10] In his recent detailed analysis of the *Sacramentary of Sarapion*, Maxwell Johnson has concurred with Mazza's theory.[11]

If this was indeed the pattern that early eucharistic praying once took, it means that the process of adding further components—such as the *Sanctus* and narrative of institution—that we encounter from the fourth century onwards does not represent an alien intrusion into what were formerly unitary creations, but is simply continuing a tradition of combining smaller units together that was at the heart of the most ancient compositions. It also means that the connecting links that exist between parts of these later prayers are unlikely to have belonged to their earliest stratum, but were more probably introduced at a later stage in order to smooth out the original roughness of the juxtaposition of discrete prayer units. So, for example, the phrase in the Strasbourg Papyrus which links the petitionary material in the second half of the prayer to what precedes it, "over this sacrifice and offering we pray and beseech you," is unlikely to be as old as what

---

[8]Note that in two cases at the end of the *Didache* prayer-units, the text includes an Amen, and it may also have been intended for all the rest.

[9]*Didascalia Apostolorum* 2.58.3. See Michael Vasey & Sebastian Brock, *The Liturgical Portions of The Didascalia*, Grove Liturgical Study 29 (Nottingham: Grove Books, 1982) 16.

[10]Enrico Mazza, *The Origins of the Eucharistic Prayer* (Collegeville: The Liturgical Press, 1995) 59–60, 221–30.

[11]Maxwell Johnson, *The Prayers of Sarapion of Thmuis: A Literary, Liturgical, and Theological Analysis*, OCA 249 (Rome: Pontificium Institutum Orientale, 1995) 224–26. See also his essay in this present volume, below, 85–6.

follows it, "remember your holy and only catholic Church . . .," especially when we recall that the petitionary prayer in *Didache* 10 began simply: "Remember, Lord, your Church. . . ."[12]

SOURCES

Scholars have traditionally sought to locate the origin of eucharistic prayers in the Jewish tradition, especially its grace after meals, and Mazza's recent study, to which we have already drawn attention, is no exception. Mazza, however, is at least willing to widen the perspective a little. Although he does see some of the later prayers as emanating from the grace after meals, the *Birkat ha-mazon*, he traces the roots of the eucharistic prayer in *Apostolic Constitutions* 7 through its source in the *Didache* to the Jewish blessings over cup and bread earlier in the meal, and he posits the *Yotzer*, one of the blessings before the *Shema* in Jewish morning prayer, as the ultimate source of the eucharistic prayer of the Strasbourg Papyrus.[13] Both Jacob Vellian and Bryan Spinks had earlier suggested that the anaphora of Addai and Mari may also have its roots in these blessings preceding the *Shema*.[14]

Attempts to find the source of later Christian prayers in Jewish forms face at least two major problems. The first is that many Jewish scholars today would have serious doubts that prayers in their tradition had yet acquired fixed forms at the time when Christianity first emerged, and it seems improbable that Christians would have borrowed them at a later date.[15] Indeed, Tzvee Zahavy has suggested that the fully-fledged system of food-blessings was not formalized until at least the middle of the second century, and was built upon an older tradition of only saying blessings over wine and at the end of a meal.[16] Yet, even if such blessings were already in use in the first cen-

---

[12]For an ET of the Strasbourg Papyrus, see *PEER*, 53–54.

[13]Mazza, *Origins of the Eucharistic Prayer*, 12–61, 194–96.

[14]Jacob Vellian, "The Anaphoral Structure of Addai and Mari compared to the Berakoth Preceding the Shema in the Synagogue Morning Service contained in Seder R. Amram Gaon," *Le Muséon* 85 (1972) 201–23; Bryan D. Spinks, "The Original Form of the Anaphora of the Apostles: A Suggestion in the Light of the Maronite Sharar," *EL* 91 (1977) 146–61.

[15]See Stefan Reif, *Judaism and Hebrew Prayer: New perspectives on Jewish liturgical history* (Cambridge: Cambridge University Press, 1993) 22–87.

[16]Tzvee Zahavy, *Studies in Jewish Prayer* (Lanham, Md.: University Press of America, 1990) 14–16. See also Baruch M. Bokser, "Ma`al and Blessings over Food: Rabbinic Transformation of Cultic Terminology and Alternative Modes of Piety," *Journal of Biblical Literature* 100 (1981) 557–74.

tury, there are signs that there may have been considerable variation in their form and wording. Fragmentary texts of meal-prayers both from the synagogue at Dura-Europos[17] and from Qumran[18] suggest forms that are different both from one another and from what later became the standard version in Rabbinic Judaism.

The second difficulty that such attempts encounter when they try to explain how the various extant texts all derive from this single root is that they exhibit such wide diversity among themselves that it is often hard to see much connection between them. This raises the question as to whether we are right in looking for a common source for all these later forms, or whether at least some of them may not have arisen out of quite different contexts from meal-prayers.

The Strasbourg Papyrus provides a very good example of a prayer that seems not to be closely connected with that tradition. Indeed, if we were simply to examine the text as it stands, without any prior supposition as to what sort of prayer it was or to what liturgical rite it belonged, would we easily come to the conclusion that it was eucharistic? Its first section blesses God for creation, but makes no explicit mention of the gift of food and drink, still less of the spiritual food and drink of the eucharist. Nor is the theme of redemption treated here, or elsewhere in the whole prayer, or any mention made of the death and resurrection of Christ. Similarly, the last part of the prayer is a substantial block of intercessions for all sorts of people, but again without any direct connection to the eucharist, without any epiclesis or petition for the uniting of the communicants in the hope of their future gathering into the kingdom such as we find in the prayers of the *Didache* and of the *Apostolic Tradition*.

This leaves only the central portion of the prayer, which reads:

"giving thanks through him to you with him and the Holy Spirit, we offer the reasonable sacrifice and this bloodless service, which all the nations offer you, 'from sunrise to sunset,' from south to north, (for) your 'name is great among all the nations, and in every place incense is offered to your holy name and a pure sacrifice.'"

[17]See Jacob Neusner, *A History of the Jews in Babylonia* I (Leiden: Brill, 1969 = Chico, Calif.: Scholars Press, 1984) 161, n. 3.

[18]See Moshe Weifeld, "Grace after Meals in Qumran," *Journal of Biblical Literature* 111 (1992) 427–40.

The first phrase, "giving thanks . . . Holy Spirit" has the appearance of a secondary linkage, possibly re-working what had previously been the doxological conclusion of the first part of the prayer.[19] The citation of Malachi 1:11 may also be a later expansion, since it has become a widely accepted principle of liturgical scholarship that the substantial quotation of biblical passages tends to be the mark of later compositions: earlier prayers instead generally allude more indirectly to scriptural texts.[20] If correct, this would simply leave the statement: "we offer the reasonable sacrifice [an allusion to Rom 12:1] and this bloodless service." While this might appear to have obvious eucharistic reference, we should note that expressions like this were used by Christians in the second and third centuries to refer both to the offering of specifically eucharistic worship and equally to the offering of the non-eucharistic sacrifice of praise.[21]

One might have expected that a prayer text which supposedly originated and was used for a considerable period of time within the context of the Christian eucharistic meal would have picked up rather more clearly eucharistic themes and references. This, therefore, raises the possibility that what we have here is a prayer of blessing for creation and of intercession for the church and the world that had previously been used in a non-eucharistic context, as for example the hours of daily prayer, and was only later taken over into eucharistic usage, either by the addition of the reference to the offering of the reasonable sacrifice and bloodless service, or conceivably by the reinterpretation of that statement as eucharistic in intent.

Maxwell Johnson's reconstruction of the earliest form of the anaphora in the *Sacramentary of Sarapion* bears a remarkable likeness to the Strasbourg Papyrus, as he himself points out.[22] Once again, we have a substantial praise section, a brief reference to the oblation of "this living sacrifice, the unbloody offering," and a lengthy series of

---

[19]See Mazza, *Origins of the Eucharistic Prayer*, 194; and also Walter Ray, "The Strasbourg Papyrus," below, 42.

[20]Indeed, this was one of Anton Baumstark's "liturgical laws." See Anton Baumstark, *Comparative Liturgy* (London: Mowbray/Westminster, Md.: Newman Press, 1958) 59; and also Eric Segelberg, "The Ordination Prayers in Hippolytus," *SP* 13 (1975) 397.

[21]See the examples cited in G. J. Cuming, *The Liturgy of St.Mark*, OCA 234 (Rome: Pontificium Institutum Orientale, 1990) 107–8.

[22]See Johnson, *The Prayers of Sarapion of Thmuis*, 255–9, 271–6; and his essay in this collection, below, 75.

intercessions. And once again, there is nothing in the praise or intercessions that would particularly imply a eucharistic setting. Was this prayer, too, converted in a similar way from earlier use in a quite different context?

PARAMETERS

A further difficulty associated with attempts to trace the early evolution of eucharistic prayers arises in defining what constitutes a legitimate piece of evidence for the structure and contents of such prayers. The prayers in the *Didache* provide a very good illustration of this problem. Many scholars earlier this century—among them R. H. Connolly, Gregory Dix, and Josef Jungmann—excluded these texts from consideration because they judged them not to be genuine eucharistic prayers but rather table prayers for some other sort of Christian community meal.[23] Even Louis Duchesne, who did regard *Didache* 9 and 10 as a eucharistic rite, still dismissed it from serious consideration because he thought it had "altogether the aspect of an anomaly; it might furnish some of the features which we meet with in later compositions, but it is on the whole outside the general line of development both in respect of its ritual and style."[24] More recently Willy Rordorf has maintained the older point of view, that this church order contains "not a eucharistic liturgy in the strict sense, but prayers spoken at table before the eucharist proper," and has claimed that this is "the most common view today."[25] The truth is, however, that the majority of scholars in the last thirty years have taken the opposite view, that it is a eucharist, and that therefore theories about the evolution of eucharistic prayers must take this particular form into account in some way.[26]

---

[23]See for example R. H. Connolly, "Agape and Eucharist in the Didache," *Downside Review* 55 (1937) 477–89; Gregory Dix, *The Shape of the Liturgy* (London: Dacre, 1945) 48, n. 2 and 90ff.; Josef Jungmann, *The Mass of the Roman Rite* (New York: Benzinger, 1951) 1:12.

[24]Louis Duchesne, *Christian Worship: Its Origins and Evolution* (London: SPCK, 1903) 54.

[25]Willy Rordorf, "The Didache," in *The Eucharist of the Early Christians* (New York: Pueblo, 1978) 6.

[26]See for example Louis Bouyer, *Eucharist* (Notre Dame: Notre Dame Press, 1968) 115–9; Louis Ligier, "The Origins of the Eucharistic Prayer: From the Last Supper to the Eucharist," *SL* 9 (1973) 177–8; Mazza, *Origins of the Eucharistic Prayer,* 12–97; Thomas J. Talley, "The Eucharistic Prayer of the Ancient Church According to Recent Research: Results and Reflections," *SL* 11 (1976) 146–50.

Obviously, this major shift of opinion has had a profound effect on the way in which the history of eucharistic prayers is understood, and the same would be true if other pieces of evidence were either included or excluded from the picture. For instance, it has been customary only to give attention to prayers which conform, broadly speaking, to those that later became standard in the mainstream Christian tradition, and to ignore those that have a very different appearance (e.g., lack an opening "praise" section), especially if they are known to us solely from sources that appear to reflect less conventional forms of early Christianity, such as Syrian apocyphal texts.[27] But to pick from the remains of history only those pieces that fit the pre-conceived pattern and to ignore those that do not is to distort the picture. It may well be true that it is the pieces which most closely resemble the later forms that are best able to explain where those particular shapes came from, but they do not necessarily tell the whole story, nor do they accurately portray the situation in the earlier centuries. It would be rather like explaining later Rabbinic Judaism solely in terms of the Pharasaic traditions of the first century: while Pharasaism may have had the greatest influence in shaping what survived the destruction of the Temple, we do not understand Judaism properly or fully if we ignore the Sadducees, Essenes, and other groups within the earlier Jewish world.

Moreover, such an approach has another methodological weakness. It presumes that a sharp distinction can be drawn between "orthodox" and "heretical" groups in the Christianity of the second and third centuries, so that the eucharistic practices of the one were totally unlike those of the other. Yet this flies in the face of recent historical scholarship,[28] and indeed differs from the approach taken towards early baptismal practice, where Syrian apocryphal texts constitute the principal source for the liturgical traditions of the

[27]See G. Rouwhorst, "Bénédiction, action de grâces, supplication: Les oraisons de la table dans le Judaïsme et les célébrations eucharistiques des chrétiens syriaques," *Questions liturgiques* 61 (1980) 211–40; Cyrille Vogel, "Anaphores eucharistiques préconstantiniennes: Formes non traditionelles," *Augustinianum* 20 (1980) 401–10.

[28]See for example the essays by Rowan Williams, "Does it make sense to speak of pre-Nicene orthodoxy?" and by Richard Hanson, "The Achievement of Orthodoxy in the Fourth Century AD," in Rowan Williams, ed., *The Making of Orthodoxy* (Cambridge: Cambridge University Press, 1989) 1–23, 142–56.

region.[29] We need, therefore, to cast the net much more widely, to draw in all potential sources of evidence from the first three centuries, if we are to have a full and proper appreciation of the formation of the so-called "classical" eucharistic prayers of the fourth century onwards.

A COMMON STRUCTURE

Although in his 1945 study *The Shape of the Liturgy*, Gregory Dix effectively drove the last coffin-nail into what had earlier been the dominant theory, that all eucharistic prayers were ultimately descended from a single apostolic archetype, that has not stopped scholars since then from trying to find some common denominator to link together all later eucharistic texts to their presumed apostolic and/or Jewish roots. Dix himself, as the title of his book suggests, located the commonality in the structure of the whole rite and did not pursue connections between eucharistic prayers beyond what he saw as their shared characteristic of thanksgiving, or more precisely a series of thanksgivings.[30] Others, however, have gone further in seeking to discern a standard shape or pattern beneath their apparent diversity.

Thus a tripartite structure—usually defined in terms of two thanksgivings and a petition and alleged to mirror the profile of the Jewish *Birkat ha-mazon*—has been a popular choice. Mazza has reasserted this position in his recent study, though it requires considerable ingenuity to make all extant forms fit within this framework, as we shall shortly see when we consider the case of the anaphora of the *Apostolic Tradition*. Other scholars, recognizing the difficulties posed by such an approach, have preferred to look instead for an original bipartite structure, encouraged by Cesare Giraudo's contention that the Old Testament prayer form *todah* had such a pattern, composed of remembrance and supplication (anmnesis-epiclesis), into which an embolism explaining the grounds for the act might also be inserted.[31] Thomas Talley in particular, in attempting to do justice to the variety

[29]See for example Gabriele Winkler, "The Original Meaning of the Pre-Baptismal Anointing and Its Implications," *Worship* 52 (1978) 24–45; Baby Varghese, *Les onctions baptismales dans la tradition syrienne* (Louvain: Peeters, 1989).

[30]Dix, *The Shape of the Liturgy*, 216–37.

[31]Cesare Giraudo, *La struttura letteraria della preghiera eucaristica* (Rome: Biblical Institute Press, 1981). For a critique of the whole idea, see Paul F. Bradshaw, "*Zebah Todah* and the Origins of the Eucharist," *Ecclesia Orans* 8 (1991) 245–60.

of extant anaphoral structures, has envisaged a quite complex process of development taking place, from an initial bipartite pattern, still visible in some ancient forms, to a later tripartite shape, normally resulting from the prefixing to the prayer of an act of praise for the Creator that culminated in the *Sanctus*.[32]

Many of the difficulties involved in such evolutionary hypotheses disappear, however, if we allow for the possibility that not all eucharistic prayers belong to the same family and have the same ancestor, but that variety was inherent in them from the start. Some may have exhibited a tripartite structure from early times, others may have always been bipartite, while some ancient forms may even have been unitary in construction, consisting of the expression of praise alone,[33] as simple Jewish blessings over items of food appear to have been. Any of these—as Talley has suggested—may have mutated from one shape to another through the later addition of a new element to the prayer. We have no reason to suppose that any one specific pattern was laid down from the beginning—whether in Jewish circles or by Jesus himself—and if it was, then later Christians were very lax in adhering to it, if we are to judge from the variety of literary forms that they left behind. A twofold movement from praise to petition is certainly a natural shape for prayer to take, but a redactor may well want to combine two themes of praise within the same prayer or to add a further section to the prayer, whether copied from another tradition or created to give expression to developing theological ideas within the local church.

THE APOSTOLIC TRADITION OF HIPPOLYTUS
Attempts to trace the evolution of eucharistic prayers have always had to take into account the anaphora found in the ancient church order usually identified as the *Apostolic Tradition* of Hippolytus (AT) and dated to the early third century.[34] This prayer presents a well-developed appearance. It seems to flow in a coherent and unified fashion from beginning to end, and although it does not include the

[32]See in particular his essays, "The Eucharistic Prayer: Tradition and Development," in Kenneth Stevenson, ed., *Liturgy Reshaped* (London: SPCK, 1982) 48–64, and "The Literary Structure of the Eucharistic Prayer," *Worship* 58 (1984) 404–19.

[33]Geoffrey Cuming, developing a suggestion made by Louis Ligier, put forward this idea in his "Four Very Early Anaphoras," *Worship* 58 (1984) 168–72.

[34]ET in *PEER*, 34–5.

Sanctus, it does incorporate a narrative of institution, an anamnesis, and an epiclesis. That such an apparently "advanced" prayer existed in the early third century has generally led scholars to assume that all eucharistic prayers—or at least all "orthodox" eucharistic prayers—must have reached more or less the same stage of development by this time.

This conclusion is questionable on at least two grounds. First, it presupposes that eucharistic traditions everywhere were marching in step and exhibiting similar characteristics and changes at roughly the same time as each other. But this is not necessarily so, and what we know of early Christianity in general suggests the opposite: that local churches tended to preserve quite different practices and theologies from one another until the fourth century, when the changed situation of Christianity caused them to begin to come more into line with one another.[35] Second, there are doubts whether the document in question really is the *Apostolic Tradition* of Hippolytus and whether it had acquired its definitive form by the early third century.[36] Since all the textual witnesses to it belong to the fourth century or later, it is possible that its eucharistic prayer did not assume its present appearance until the middle of that century. That is not to say, of course, that it does not contain material that is very much older than that: it may be composed of several strata from widely differing periods.

Enrico Mazza's analysis of the text supports the contention that it is composed of more than one layer. He seeks to demonstrate that material in the first part of the prayer has striking parallels with passages in two ancient Easter homilies: *Peri Pascha* of Melito of Sardis and *In Sanctum Pascha* of Pseudo-Hippolytus. He is not suggesting that there is any direct literary dependence on these two works, nor even that there is any similarity of structure:

"Rather, our conclusion will be that this anaphora depends *generally* on material contained in the Easter homilies, that is, on particular kinds of terms (for example, Christological titles), idioms, typological

[35]See further Paul F. Bradshaw, "The Homogenization of Christian Liturgy—Ancient and Modern," *SL* 26 (1996) 1–15.

[36]See Paul F. Bradshaw, "Redating the Apostolic Tradition: Some Preliminary Steps," in John Baldovin & Nathan Mitchell, eds., *Rule of Prayer, Rule of Faith: Essays in Honor of Aidan Kavanagh, OSB* (Collegeville: The Liturgical Press, 1996) 3–17.

expressions, biblical quotations and so on that are essential character-istics of the literary genre of the Easter homilies. Our anaphora in question depends not on the homilies of Melito or Pseudo-Hippolytus as such but, as we shall see, on the material that is typical and consti-tutive of the literary genre of the Easter homilies such as one finds in the homilies of Melito and Pseudo-Hippolytus and in many other texts as well."[37]

After a detailed examination of the text, Mazza arrives at the conclu-sion that the author inserted this "paschal" material into an older, simpler structure, one that was like that of *Didache* 10.

This last assertion may be going too far. In order to sustain the claim, he has to resort to the argument that in that transition the first thanksgiving of *Didache* 10 disappeared and was "replaced by the ac-count of salvation in Christ such as it was presented in the literary genre of the Easter homilies."[38] Moreover, the parallel between the supposed second thanksgiving of AT ("giving you thanks because you have held us worthy to stand before you and minister to you") and that of *Didache* 10 (praise for creation, the gift of food and drink, and "spiritual food and drink and eternal life through your child Jesus") is hardly close. Mazza tries to resolve this problem by draw-ing into the argument the prayer in the *Martyrdom of Polycarp* and the grace from the intertestamental *Book of Jubilees* in an attempt to show that all four texts belong to one family in which the second thanks-giving is always in some way for the gift of the present moment.[39] Similarly, he seeks to establish a link between the final, petitionary sections of the anaphora of AT and of *Didache* 10 by setting them within what he believes to be an evolving process, beginning from the supplication in *Didache* 10 for God to perfect the church in his love and bring it into his kingdom. This request, he alleges, devel-oped into different but related petitions in certain other liturgical texts. Thus AC 7.26 asks God to "free [the church] from every evil and make it perfect in your love and your truth and unite us, all of us, into your kingdom"; E-BAS asks God to "preserve us . . . in your faith and lead us into your kingdom"; and the *Sacramentary of Sara-*

---

[37]Mazza, *Origins of the Eucharistic Prayer*, 102–76; quotation from 103 (emphasis in original).

[38]Ibid., 176.

[39]Ibid., 153–61.

pion prays "for the destruction of evil and for the the confirmation of the Church," and later asks God to give the departed "a place of rest in your kingdom." Mazza claims that the petitionary section of the anaphora of AT belongs to this family because it shares the phrase "for the confirmation" with *Sarapion*, "of faith" with E-BAS, and "in truth" with AC 7.26.[40]

Nevertheless, even if there are weaknesses in Mazza's line of reasoning, that does not necessarily invalidate his fundamental point that the material in the first part of the anaphora of AT appears to belong to a quite different world from the rest. He would include within this "first part" the narrative of institution itself, even though it does not contain the same sort of parallel language to the Easter homilies that characterizes what precedes it. His grounds for doing so are that (a) it is grammatically connected to the preceding material, and (b) the homily *In Sanctum Pascha* not only recounts the events of the Last Supper (though in a different form from AT) but introduces that narrative with a passage which bears some similarity to that found in AT in the same position.[41]

Against this, however, one may note that E. C. Ratcliff believed that the narrative in AT followed awkwardly upon the reference to the harrowing of the underworld and the resurrection, and so thought it possible that "the want of smoothness and order at this point indicates that the older tradition has here been remodelled and stabilized in accordance with later fashion."[42] Furthermore, Mazza himself goes on to claim that the theology of the anamnesis section of the prayer, in linking death and resurrection together on the same plane, belongs to a different world of ideas and a later historical period than the so-called preface, in which it is Christ's death that is the salvific act *par excellence*.[43] Since other scholars generally accept that narrative and anamnesis have always formed a single liturgical unit,[44] it would seem more reasonable to conclude that both the narrative and the anamnesis/oblation section were subsequent additions to the material in the first part of the prayer. These additions were perhaps not made

[40]Ibid., 161–6.

[41]Ibid., 134–9.

[42]E. C. Ratcliff, "The Sanctus and the Pattern of the Early Anaphora," *JEH* 1 (1950) 32.

[43]Mazza, *Origins of the Eucharistic Prayer*, 167–9.

[44]See for example Ligier, "The Origins of the Eucharistic Prayer," 180; Talley, "The Eucharistic Prayer of the Ancient Church," 151.

until about the middle of the fourth century, when the *Sacramentary of Sarapion* was also apparently experimenting with the novelty of inserting an institution narrative into the eucharistic prayer, while in other regions the older tradition was still being maintained: both Cyril of Jerusalem and Theodore of Mopsuestia, for example, seem to have known eucharistic prayers that lacked such a development.[45]

In spite of Bernard Botte's spirited defence of the authenticity of the epiclesis as part of the third-century text of the prayer,[46] there seems to be merit to Mazza's suggestion that only the second part of it, which asks for the bestowal of the Holy Spirit on the communicants, belongs to an older layer of the prayer, and that the first part, the invocation of the Spirit on the eucharistic gifts, to which the second is not very smoothly connected, is a later addition, made at the same time as the anamnesis/oblation section (and, we would add, the narrative of institution).[47] The original prayer, therefore, would appear to have been created by the combination of a somewhat lengthy hymn of praise for redemption, arising out of the world of the second-century paschal homilies, with a short petition for the Holy Spirit and a concluding doxology. Everything else was probably added in the course of the fourth century, to which we now turn.

FOURTH-CENTURY LITURGICAL COMPOSITION
If the approach taken so far in this essay has any validity, it suggests that:

1. Early Christian prayers—eucharistic and non-eucharistic alike— were more often formed by combining small pre-existent units as the situation required than by the creation of unitary compositions.

2. While some of these may well have had their roots in Jewish meal-prayers, others are likely to have arisen out of quite different contexts, both Jewish and Christian.

3. Both bipartite and tripartite (and perhaps even more complex) patterns are likely to have existed in various local traditions and to have been subject to at least a measure of improvisation and adaptation.

---

[45]See E. J. Cutrone, "Cyril's Mystagogical Catecheses and the Evolution of the Jerusalem Anaphora," *OCP* 44 (1978) 52–64; Mazza, *Origins of the Eucharistic Prayer,* 302–9.

[46]Bernard Botte, "L'épiclèse de l'anaphore d'Hippolyte," *Recherches de théologie ancienne et médiévale* 14 (1947) 241–51.

[47]Mazza, *Origins of the Eucharistic Prayer,* 169–74.

In most cases, these prayers probably circulated orally rather than in written form until the first half of the fourth century. The increasing use of written texts at that time would have been encouraged by the desire to provide more elevated and polished forms appropriate to the new surroundings created by the building of large city churches, in place of what had no doubt often been short and simple formulas used in the relatively domestic settings experienced by many—though not all—earlier Christian communities. Thus those responsible for leading prayer are likely to have cast around for what they regarded as suitable models, regardless of whether these originally belonged to eucharistic or non-eucharistic contexts, and to have discarded some traditional forms that did not meet contemporary needs. In other words, a measure of selective evolution was taking place.

Such a process would help to explain not only the emergence in eucharistic usage of forms that seem to have something in common with Jewish texts belonging to morning prayer as well as of forms that have no obvious Jewish ancestry, but also the appearance of the *Sanctus*. The commonly held view that this text was not used in Christian liturgy prior to the fourth century is not as firmly grounded as has been supposed. Great reliance is usually placed on W. C. van Unnik's celebrated essay on the subject,[48] but he only argued that there was no evidence for the liturgical use of the *Sanctus* in the First Letter of Clement: his conclusions do not exclude the possibility of its use in other ancient Christian traditions elsewhere than at Rome. Scholars who have envisaged a rigid separation in the minds of early Christians between forms belonging to eucharistic usage and those intended for non-eucharistic worship have always had difficulty in imagining how the *Sanctus* could suddenly emerge in fourth-century prayers. If, however, the division between different types of prayer forms was not as sharply defined by early Christians as it tends to be by modern observers, and if there were already a tradition among some Christian communities in the first three centuries of using the *Sanctus* either as part of their daily prayers or within initiatory rites,[49] its migration into eucharistic texts of the fourth century does not

[48]W. C. van Unnik, "I Clement 34 and the Sanctus," *Vigiliae Christianae* 5 (1951) 204–48.

[49]See Gabriele Winkler, "Nochmals zu den Anfängen der Epiklese und des Sanctus im Eucharistischen Hochgebet," *Theologische Quartalschrift* 174 (1994) 214–31.

seem so very surprising: its style made it a very suitable component for such compositions.[50]

The further expansion of eucharistic prayers in the fourth century was thus simply continuing a tradition of combining short units to form longer prayers that was already well established. What was probably new, however, was the copying of units from one local tradition into the eucharistic prayers of another. While some imitation of patterns of prayer may have gone on between some local churches prior to this time, the fourth century provided a more conducive environment for such a process, for several reasons.

First, it was much easier to transfer written texts from one region to another than to reproduce a composition only existing in oral form. Second, Christian leaders travelled much more widely at this period than they had done in earlier times—attending ecumenical councils and making pilgrimages to saintly figures and holy places—and so more often came into contact with liturgical patterns very different from their own. Third, the pressure to ensure the doctrinal orthodoxy of what was prayed in public liturgy in the face of the perceived threat from what were regarded as heretical groups within Christianity not only contributed towards the emergence of fixed and written forms and discouraged continuing improvisation, but it also encouraged conformity between different regional traditions. To have been out of step liturgically might have raised questions about one's orthodoxy. Hence the eucharistic prayers of the different regional centers of Christianity begin to look more and more like one another as elements from one tradition are adopted by others.

Thus the presanctus/*Sanctus* and the narrative of institution/anamnesis units gradually spread, and were eventually adopted everywhere. Prayers that originally lacked a substantial block of intercessions had them inserted from a neighboring tradition. As structures stabilize, awkward joints are smoothed over and linking phrases inserted so that a more unified appearance results in most Eastern anaphoras, in contrast to the Roman canon, where the individual building blocks remain more clearly visible, especially since several units—proper preface, *Memento*, *Communicantes*, and *Hanc igitur*—continue to vary on different occasions.

[50]For further details see Robert F. Taft, "The Interpolation of the *Sanctus* into the Anaphora: When and Where? A Review of the Dossier," *OCP* 57 (1991) 281–308; 58 (1992) 83–121.

It was doctrine, too, that was partially responsible for the further expansion of eucharistic prayers during this period, and especially the development of the epicletic element. As the Strasbourg Papyrus shows, there were early eucharistic prayers that did not ask God to do anything in particular in relation to the eucharistic feast, but simply interceded for the needs of the world. Other prayers, however, did invoke the divine presence on the assembled community, but traditions seem to have varied as to the manner in which this was done. Gabriele Winkler has recently argued that in the earliest Syrian tradition the customary form was an imperative, "Come," addressed to the Messiah and/or his Spirit.[51] In Greek circles, on the other hand, it seems to have been the Logos who was generally seen as the agent of the action: the only two apparently pre-fourth century references to the Holy Spirit in this context come from the *Didascalia Apostolorum*, which doubtless reflects the Syrian rather than the Greek tradition, and from AT, the date and provenance of which are very uncertain.[52] Since the doctrine of the Trinity had not yet fully developed, Christians did not distinguish clearly between Christ, the spirit of Christ, and the Holy Spirit. However, the pneumatological debates of the second half of the fourth century caused Eastern Christians to be more precise in their use of language and to adopt an explicit invocation of the Holy Spirit in their eucharistic prayers, if they had not already got one. This invocation was no longer addressed directly to the Holy Spirit or to Christ, but was increasingly in the form of a request to God to "send" the Holy Spirit upon the eucharistic elements as well as upon the gathered community, and often with an explicit request for them to be transformed into the body and blood of Christ.

What prevented a dull uniformity in eucharistic prayers emerging, however, was that while their architects certainly seem to have been eager to include units that they found elsewhere, they do not appear to have been concerned that they located them in exactly the same position in their own anaphora that they had occupied in the source

[51]Winkler, "Nochmals zu den Anfängen der Epiklese und des Sanctus im Eucharistischen Hochgebet"; see also idem, "Weitere Beobachtungen zur frühen Epiklese (den Doxologien und dem Sanctus). Über die Bedeuteung der Apokryphen für die Erforschung der Entwicklung der Riten," *OC* 80 (1996) 1–18.

[52]See Robert F. Taft, "From Logos to Spirit: On the Early History of the Epiclesis," in A. Heinz and H. Rennings, eds., *Gratias Agamus. Studien zum eucharistischen Hochgebet. Für Balthasar Fischer* (Freiburg: Herder, 1992) 489–502; Johnson, *The Prayers of Sarapion of Thmuis*, 233–52.

from which they came. Thus, at least in part, the rest of the essays in this volume attempt to show how elements that arose from different prayers originating in different geographical regions were copied, adapted, and inserted into other prayers in a variety of ways to produce the distinctive yet related anaphoras of the Eastern churches.

Stephen B. Wilson

1. The Anaphora of the Apostles Addai and Mari

Historically, Syria is a region that has been typified by its heterogeneous character. Gregory Dix describes this area as a "mosaic of different races, cultures, religions and languages, which no political framework has ever held together for long."[1] Even the spread of Hellenism in the wake of Alexander's conquest of the region failed to bring cultural uniformity, as it had done in much of the ancient world. Many Syrians maintained their Semitic culture, which often resulted in conflict with the hellenized portions of the population. Because of its location on the fringes of the empire, the Romans could do little more than bring nominal unity to the region. Syrian Christianity would tend to reflect these wider cultural differences and would thus be marked by a pluriformity of belief and practice. This tendency would result in three main branches of Christianity there: (1) West Syrian, centered in Antioch; (2) South Syrian, which had Jerusalem as its center; and (3) East Syrian, which was focused in Edessa.

These cultural distinctions became overt theological divisions following the christological controversies of the fifth century. At the Council of Ephesus, the teachings of Nestorius, a pupil of Theodore of Mopsuestia, were condemned. In 436 Hiba (Ibas), who had Nestorian sympathies, became the bishop of the East Syrian church, and under the leadership of Narsai the school at Edessa became a center of Nestorianism. But in the latter part of the fifth century the Monophysites gained control of Edessa. Consequently, the East Syrians who followed the teachings of Theodore relocated to Nisibis in Persia. As a result of its relative isolation from Christendom, the East

[1]Gregory Dix, *The Shape of the Liturgy* (London: Dacre, 1945) 173.

Syrian church continued to develop its own particular form of Christianity, which it spread through missionary efforts as far east as Tibet, China, and India. The liturgical language of this church was the highly Semitic Syrian tongue. The three main eucharistic prayers went by the names of the anaphoras of the Apostles Addai and Mari (hereafter AM),[2] *Theodore*, and *Nestorius*. While AM was from its beginnings a Syriac text, both *Theodore* and *Nestorius* were translated from Greek. In addition to the particularities of its cultural and historical context, the anaphora itself presents several distinctive characteristics. For example, one of the central paragraphs in the prayer lacks a main verb. The anaphora, moreover, oscillates between addressing God as Trinity, Father, and Son in way that is at times quite confusing. Another peculiarity of this prayer is that it lacks what many Christians consider one of the definitive elements of a eucharistic prayer—the institution narrative.

Before proceeding to an overview, however, it is necessary to define some of the terms that one encounters frequently in the study of AM:

cushapa—private intercessory prayer of the celebrant;
gehanta—"inclination," intercessory prayer said in low voice;
qanona—audible conclusion to a *gehanta;*
kuddasha—"sanctification," "hallowing," or "consecration," used as a
    title of whole eucharistic liturgy and of the anaphora itself;
Hudra—Nestorian service book;
Sharar—"confirm" or "strengthen," the opening word of a prayer in
    the pre-anaphora of the Third Anaphora of St. Peter.

R. H. CONNOLLY

The work of R. H. Connolly in 1914 provides us with a suitable starting point for our discussion of modern considerations of AM.[3] By means of a detailed concordance, Connolly was able to demonstrate that AM was the same liturgy as that used by the Malabar church in India. He thus opened up a new avenue for the study of AM: the history of the development of the Malabar liturgy was now seen as ca-

---

[2]English translation in *PEER*, 42–4. The most recent edition of the text is A. Gelston, *The Eucharistic Prayer of Addai and Mari* (Oxford: Clarendon, 1992).

[3]R. H. Connolly and E. Bishop, "The Work of Menzenes on the Malabar Liturgy," *JTS* 15 (1914) 396–425, 569–89. Bishop is cited as co-author because he presents an addition to the second part of the study.

pable of providing insight into AM. One of the principle observations of this study was that the institution narrative was present in the Malabar text, yet missing in the manuscripts of AM. Connolly proceeded to show that an institution narrative was inserted by Antonio de Gouvea into the Malabar liturgy between the anaphora and the fraction ("Menezian" rite, published in 1606) following the synod of Diamper, which had made suggestions concerning revisions within the liturgy. He further noted that the Synod revised a Malabar rite which contained an institution narrative that was probably located outside the anaphora. Connolly summarized this position by stating: "It must be, I think, set down as an assured conclusion that before Menezes touched the Malabar liturgy of the Apostles it had a formula of Institution *after* the Invocation of the Holy Spirit."[4] The remaining question was whether or not the Malabar liturgy restored a lost narrative which was originally found within AM. Because of the absence of the narrative from any extant manuscripts, Connolly cautioned against any conclusion as "unsafe."

EDWARD RATCLIFF

The most significant early study of AM is an article published by Ratcliff at the end of the 1920s.[5] Though not stated until near the end of his article, Ratcliff's working hypothesis is that AM was a "εὐχαριστία pure and simple." This classification means that the structure of AM should reflect a stage of development of the liturgy somewhere between the "agape" and the "mass." Working with this idea in mind, Ratcliff analyzed the extant structure of AM to see which elements were interpolations. Using two of Narsai's *Homilies* (XVII and XXI) as a gauge, he excised the *cushapa* prayers and also the *gehanta* prayers, because, though earlier in date than the *cushapa*, they have no connection with the surrounding material. He thus deleted all the intercessions from the anaphora. The *Sanctus* and accompanying material were to be removed because they interrupted flow of thought between the material which proceeds and follows (before: praise to Creator and Redeemer; after: thanksgiving for salvation). The epiclesis was the next element to be omitted because it also interrupted the flow of thought of material immediately before

[4]Ibid., 583.

[5]E. C. Ratcliff, "The Original Form of the Anaphora of Addai and Mari: A Suggestion," *JTS* 30 (1928–1929) 23–32.

and after it (before: commemoration of Christ's work; after: "And for all thy wonderful dispensation . . ."). Ratcliff's excisions lead to a threefold structure of the original version of AM:

"(a) An address of praise to the name of the Creator and Redeemer;
(b) A thanksgiving for what he has done for men;
(c) A solemn following of Christ's example and a special commemoration of his redemptive death and resurrection, for which again praise and thanks are offered to the divine name."[6]

In addition to structural concerns, Ratcliff also asserted that the anaphora was originally directed to Christ. He based this conclusion on several factors, one of which was his reading of the phrase "Worthy of praise from every mouth . . ." as being reminiscent of Philippians 2:9-11. Another factor was that several of the post-anaphoral prayers were addressed to Christ. Though these prayers were from a later period, Ratcliff thought that they reflected a tendency in the tradition of East Syrian prayer to address prayers to the Son, and cited the Syrian *Acts of Thomas* as an example of this tendency, where in four passages "we have descriptions, with prayer-forms, of the Eucharist as celebrated by Thomas. The rite is directed to Christ."[7]

HIERONYMOUS ENGBERDING
Engberding's principal contribution to the study of AM was his comparison of the text with that of the other two East Syrian anaphoras and with the anaphora of the Maronite church mainly located in Jordan and Israel.[8] This Maronite anaphora is called the Third Anaphora of St. Peter or simply *Sharar*.[9] Engberding came to the conclusion that the Maronite rite is, on the whole, more ancient than AM, and also asserted that AM and *Sharar* are derived from a common source which was later subject to a Chaldean redaction that resulted in AM.[10] From this insight Engberding was able to draw fur-

---

[6]Ibid., 29.

[7]Ibid., 31.

[8]Hieronymous Engberding, "Urgestalt, Eigenart und Entwicklung eines altantiochenischen eucharistischen Hochgebetes," *OC* 29 (1932) 32–48; "Zum anaphorischen Fürbittgebet der ostsyrischen Liturgie der Apostel Addaj und Mar(j)," *OC* 41 (1957) 102–24.

[9]The text of this prayer is in *PEER*, 46–51.

[10]Engberding, "Urgestalt," 46–7.

ther inferences about the *gehanta* intercessions, "anamnesis," and institution narrative.

Unlike Ratcliff, Engberding thought that the *gehanta* intercessions were part of the original form of AM, their presence within *Sharar* forming the basis of this conclusion. Engberding also disputed the classification of the paragraph that commences with the phrase "We also, Lord" as an anamnesis. According to Engberding, this paragraph is a continuation of the previous *gehanta* for the living. The foundation for this assessment is that in the intercessions of other anaphoras, particularly *Nestorius,* there are prayers for the living following prayers for the dead which begin with the phrase "We also." Because this paragraph is not an anamnesis, it does not provide the basis for the location of an institution narrative, and its omission would make clearer the nature of the intercession. This led him to postulate that the narrative was not originally in *Sharar.*[11] Following his suggestions would lead to a twofold structure of AM, centering on praise and petition.

BERNARD BOTTE

Botte published an article in 1949 (which he revised and republished in 1969) that proved very influential on the study of AM.[12] He began by noting that the style of the prayer was highly Semitic, exhibited by its use of features such as parallelism.[13] His analysis of the anaphora accepts many of the points made previously by Ratcliff. For instance, he agreed with Ratcliff about the *Sanctus,* the intercessions, and the epiclesis. Botte differed from Ratcliff, however, on several key points.

The first area of contention centered on the address of the anaphora. Botte did not think that the prayer was initially directed consistently to Christ. Rather, AM addressed both the Father and Son in such a way that it betrayed a latent monarchianism. But the most significant distinction between the analyses of Ratcliff and Botte concerned the narrative of institution. Botte considered the lack of both an institution narrative and an epiclesis to be problematic. He then

[11]Engberding, "Zum anaphorischen," 107–9.

[12]Bernard Botte, "L'anaphore chaldéenne des Apôtres," *OCP* 15 (1949) 259–76; "Problèmes de l'anaphore syrienne des Apôtres Addaï et Mari," *L'Orient Syrien* 10 (1965) 89–106; cf. "L'épiclèse dans les liturgies syriennes orientales," *Sacris Erudiri* 6 (1954) 48–72; "Problèmes de l'anamnèse," *JEH* 5 (1954) 16–24.

[13]Botte, "Problèmes de l'anaphore syrienne," 89.

analyzed the central paragraph ("And we also, Lord . . ."), which revealed some interesting features. First, the sentence lacks a main verb, which renders it rather difficult to translate. Botte thought that the opening line in the paragraph required a prior statement to give it some context. Second, the last phrase in the paragraph parallels the conclusion of the anamnesis of *Theodore*, which is preceded by an institution narrative. Botte therefore classified this paragraph as an anamnesis which was originally preceded by a narrative along the lines of that found in *Theodore*. He accounted for the textual omission of the narrative by asserting that it was recited from memory by the celebrant.

W. F. MACOMBER

The study of AM was taken to a new level in 1966 when Macomber published a manuscript of the anaphora dating from the tenth or eleventh century.[14] Previously, students of AM had been handicapped by a lack of adequate tools for analyzing the prayer because there were only six manuscripts available, and these were of a late date, two being from the 1500s and four from the 1600s. The text published by Macomber is commonly referred to as the Mar Eshaya text after the church in which Macomber found the *Hudra* that contained the anaphora. The most obvious difference between the Mar Eshaya text and the later manuscripts is that the earlier document does not contain the *cushapa* prayers. This omission seems to confirm Ratcliff's thesis that these were later interpolations. No such answers, however, were provided by the Mar Eshaya text on the questions concerning the *Sanctus* and the narrative of institution. As with later manuscripts, the Mar Eshaya anaphora contains the *Sanctus* and lacks the narrative of institution.

Macomber followed up his 1966 article with one in 1971 in which he contrasted *Sharar* with the Mar Eshaya text of AM.[15] He focused his comparison on three areas: (1) the prefatory dialogue, (2) the address of the anaphora, and (3) the institution narrative. In analyzing the preface, Macomber noted that it does not correspond with either of the other two Chaldean anaphoras. By comparing the dialogue of

[14]W. F. Macomber, "The Oldest Known Text of the Anaphora of the Apostles Addai and Mari," *OCP* 32 (1966) 335–6.

[15]W. F. Macomber, "The Maronite and Chaldean Versions of the Anaphora of the Apostles," *OCP* 37 (1971) 55–84.

AM with that of three other rites (two baptismal rites and *Sharar*), he was able to assert that the dialogue of AM had been influenced by the catachetical homilies of Theodore of Mopsuestia at some point in its development. He then proceeded to suggest a possible reconstruction of the dialogue of AM that omitted the Pauline phrase "The grace of our Lord. . . ." He also stated that the last portion of the dialogue ("The offering is offered . . . fitting and right") should be moved to the opening of the section.[16]

Macomber observed that *Sharar* was addressed consistently to the Son, which led him to conclude that it reflects an earlier stage in the development of AM; given the anomalous character of addressing the Son, it is unlikely that someone would have altered a prayer originally addressed to the Father or to the Trinity so that it addressed the Son.[17] With regard to the institution narrative, Macomber thought that *Sharar* had preserved both the form and location of the narrative that was originally in AM "because the Narration is inserted in the Maronite version precisely at the first of two places of the third *gehanta* where the Chaldean version shows a vacillation with regard to the person addressed, that is, in a part of the prayer where the Chaldean version gives clear signs of having been tampered with."[18]

BRYAN SPINKS

Spinks has done some of the most significant work on AM in recent years, and the results of his research have been published in several articles and in an English translation of AM.[19] In his first substantial treatment of the anaphora,[20] Spinks pointed out that Ratcliff's suggestions for the reconstruction of AM were based on two assumptions: he classified this prayer as a "eucharistia," and he saw the natural form of this "eucharistia" to be one complete prayer characterized by

[16]Ibid., 64–5.

[17]Ibid., 67, 69.

[18]Ibid., 72.

[19]Bryan Spinks, "The Original Form of the Anaphora of the Apostles: A Suggestion in Light of the Maronite Sharar," *EL* 91 (1977) 146–61; "Priesthood and Offering in the Kussape of the East Syrian Anaphoras," *SL* 15 (1982/1983) 104–17; "Addai and Mari and the Institution Narrative: The Tantalising Evidence of Gabriel Qatraya," *EL* 98 (1984) 60–7; "Eucharistic Offering in the East Syrian Anaphoras," *OCP* 50 (1984) 347–71; *Addai and Mari—The Anaphora of the Apostles: A Text for Students*, Grove Liturgical Study 24 (Nottingham: Grove Books, 1980).

[20]Spinks, "The Original Form."

a coherent sequence of thought. In contrast, Spinks argued for a bipartite structure to the anaphora, and claimed that AM reflected a prayer tradition in which bishops formulated prayers "modelled . . . on the developing Synagogue *Berakoth*."[21] Specifically, Spinks claims that nascent forms of *Yotzer* and the *Ahabah,* the two *berakoth* which precede the *Shema,* are the basis for the tradition in which AM stands. On this basis, Spinks suggests the following structure for the anaphora:

Berakah 1 (a) dialogue ("Let your mind be on high")
         (b) blessing ("Worthy of Glory from every mouth")
         (c) *Sanctus* ("A thousand thousand")
         (d) anamnesis of the work of Christ ("And with these heavenly armies")
         (e) doxology.

Berakah 2 (f) *gehanta* ("You, Lord, through your many mercies")
         (g) *gehanta* ("That all the inhabitants")
         (h) anamnesis? ("We also,Lord")
         (i) epiclesis
         (j) doxology.[22]

Spinks notes that this bipartite prayer underlies both AM and *Sharar.* The differences between these two anaphoras can be accounted for by the work of two redactors—one East Syrian (AM) and the other Maronite *(Sharar).* The first of these inserted an institution narrative, marking its position by means of an anamnesis. Subsequently, the narrative was dropped. The Maronite redactor placed the narrative in a different position based on the theme of commemoration and employing the phrase "you have taught us" as a point of connection. A minor point of distinction between AM and *Sharar* is the twofold occurrence of the phrase "weak, frail, and miserable servants" in the East Syrian anaphora. Because of its presence within both *Theodore* and *Nestorius,* Spinks states that this was a Nestorian devotional phrase that was added to AM. Since this phrase occurs within the anamnesis, Spinks thinks that this lends credence to the possibility that the whole of the anamnesis was an interpolation.

[21]Ibid., 150.
[22]Ibid., 151–2.

WALTER RAY

Ray has argued that the structure of the anaphora is marked by a "chiastic flow" such as we find in many biblical passages.[23] According to Ray, the text of AM readily falls into an A B C X A' B' C' pattern, in which the letters denote major parallel pairs that have "X" as their central focus. The first group of parallels (A and A') is found in the opening and closing paragraphs of the prayer, both of which serve to praise God for God's works of grace. The second parallel group (B and B') is found in the third *gehanta* and is constructed by the mention of the "fathers" and "eucharist" and a similar reference to "sons" and "baptism." The third primary group of parallels (C and C') center on the phrases "pure and holy"/"purity and holiness" and "taught us" in third *gehanta*. If this structural pattern is the true form of the prayer, then the focus of the prayer ("X") is the petition for peace and eternal life at the beginning of paragraph seven.

TEXTUAL STUDY

Having examined these major scholarly treatments of AM, we are now prepared to take a look at the text in an informed manner. One of the common threads in contemporary scholarship on AM has been the awareness of the strongly Semitic stamp of this prayer. The first and most obvious signal as to the Semitic style of the anaphora is its abundant use of parallelism. One of the effects of this literary device is to allow for unity and progression within a text in a manner that is quite different from that created by means of linear progression. Whereas the latter creates coherence by a logical, thematic, or narrative progression from one point to another, parallelism creates a much more musical effect in that its use allows a text to "move" by means of subtle variations on a theme which eventuate in a kind of crescendo and then recede back towards the point of departure. Accordingly, when parallelism is employed within an anaphora, it emphasizes the poetic quality of the prayer.

In addition to its parallelism, the Semitic flavor of AM is betrayed by the prayer's economy of expression. In this respect, AM is like many of the narrative portions of Scripture that use a minimum of detail in chronicling the events of salvation history. This tendency within AM can be seen most readily by comparing it to the closely

---

[23]Walter Ray, "The Chiastic Structure of the Anaphora of Addai and Mari," *SL* 23 (1993) 187–93.

related, though much longer, *Sharar*. For example, when AM addresses God, it does so in a restrained manner, generally preferring the simple title "Lord." By way of contrast, *Sharar* will often string together a number of descriptive epithets when referring to God (e.g., "Lord, God of Abraham, savior of Isaac, strength of Israel"). The effect of such restraint is that it allows the central elements within a text to remain prominent by not obscuring them with secondary or tertiary considerations.

As we turn our attention to AM's modes of addressing God, we come to one of the text's most prominent peculiarities. Because of its continual variations in address, the prayer can seem quite ambiguous. In the opening doxology of the anaphora, God is referred to in the third person using the trinitarian phrase "the adorable and glorious name of the Father and of the Son and of the Holy Spirit." In the following paragraph the simple title "Lord" is employed in the second person as a direct address to either the Godhead or the Father. In the second *gehanta* "Lord" is again used in a direct address but this time it seems that it is Christ who is being addressed. The third *gehanta* starts out with the second person use of "Lord" which would appear to have the Father as the referent because of the use of the phrase "your Christ" later in the paragraph. However, the ensuing phrase "as you taught us," which is an oblique reference to Jesus' actions at the Last Supper would appear to indicate that it is Christ who is being addressed.

So what are we to make of these varying forms of address? It is possible that, like the present form of *Sharar,* AM at one time had a consistent form of address. Those who favor this approach tend to argue that the original addressee was Christ. There are several points which supporters of this position accentuate. First, as we noted above, there is a precedent within the East Syrian tradition for prayers addressed to Christ, the most prevalent examples coming from the *Acts of Thomas*. Second, it is unlikely, so the assumption goes, that the clear address to Christ in the second *gehanta* would have been modified from an address to the Father. Those who argue against the position that the prayer was originally addressed uniformly to Christ point out that it is probable that if a redactor had changed the prayer from addressing Christ to addressing the Father or Trinity, then the redactor would have done so consistently in order to render the prayer less ambiguous. This perspective can be countered, however, by arguing that the redactor left the clear reference to

Christ in the second *gehanta* because the material within this section is uniquely applicable to Christ.

Given the paucity of information available, the acceptance of either of the two perspectives is one that is predicated more on logic than on textual evidence. Accordingly, what position one finally decides upon will depend almost exclusively on how convincing one finds a particular argument. With that idea in mind, dogmatic acceptance of either position should be cautioned against.

In the remainder of our study we will undertake an analysis of the text which focuses on its structure. Such an approach to the text is helpful, especially for those unacquainted with Syriac, because it offers insights on the text that do not require special linguistic training. Another advantage to this form of analysis is that allows one to discern the skeleton of a text. In what follows, moreover, we will limit ourselves to a consideration of the body of the prayer and will thus omit a consideration of the introductory dialogue. Since our study will focus on the basic structure of the text, a consideration of the material in the preface adds little to our project.

First Gehanta

As we begin to look at the body of the prayer we are assisted in our efforts to analyze the text by a comparison with *Sharar*. The primary difference between the two anaphoras in this *gehanta* is that AM addresses God in the third person singular and *Sharar* uses the second person singular, as it does throughout the prayer. Other differences in this section are few and minor, involving AM's expansion of the first line of the *gehanta* and a slight shift in terms in the last line by *Sharar*. This suggests that this portion of the prayer has undergone little alteration. Where differences do occur, they are so slight it is difficult to determine which anaphora maintains the better reading. Given the relative insignificance of these differences, however, such a determination is not essential for our purposes.

Presanctus and Sanctus

As may be recalled from our discussion of the studies of AM, one of the focal points of the analyses of the prayer has been the originality of the *Sanctus* and its accompanying material. The strongest indication of the antiquity of this material is that it is found with subtle variations in both AM and *Sharar*. Though the best editions of AM only contain the *incipit* of the *Sanctus* proper, making comparisons a suspect endeavor, the material in the presanctus reveals only minor differences between the two texts. Arguments against the originality of the *Sanctus* and presanctus have stressed two points. First, the introductory clause in the presanctus ("Your majesty, O Lord . . .") seems to have no connection with the preceding material. Second, this material appears to "interrupt" the anaphora's twofold description of the gift of God's grace in creation (first *gehanta*) and redemption (second *gehanta*). Counter arguments focus on a broad understanding of the term "inhabitants" from the first *gehanta* that would include both earthly and heavenly beings such that the angelic figures mentioned in the *Sanctus* seem to fit logically into the sequence of thought. However, it should be noted that the statements that follow "inhabitants" in the first *gehanta* ("he saved men through his mercy, and gave great grace to mortals") definitely present an anthropological interpretation of that word.[24]

In bringing together these divergent views on the originality of the *Sanctus*, we can say that because of its presence within both AM and *Sharar*, this material is indeed very old. Yet, the discontinuity between the *Sanctus* and the surrounding material still demands that the "originality" of the *Sanctus* needs further argumentation. Put simply, the *Sanctus* is unquestionably an early part of the prayer but the antiquity of this material does not preclude the possibility that it is an addition to a preexisting text. If the *Sanctus* was an interpolation, then the chiastic structure of the original would have been much tighter than in the present form of the text. Nevertheless, the *Sanctus* does not obscure the chiasmus of this portion of the anaphora.

Second Gehanta

The closest parallels between AM and *Sharar* can be found within the postsanctus. Accordingly, commonalties between the two anaphoras can be expected to be traceable to their common source. Despite their similarities, there are some differences in the wording of the two prayers. In analyzing these differences, Spinks correctly noted that *Sharar* probably presents the more faithful transmission of the core material.[25] A close reading of the texts shows that the two anaphoras contain twenty-eight common Syriac words. The Mar Eshaya text of

---

[24]At this point it is also important to note the use of "inhabitants" in the third *gehanta,* which clearly refers to humans.

[25]Spinks, "The Original Form," 157–8.

AM contains forty-five Syriac terms and *Sharar* has only thirty-one Syriac words. Thus the Maronite prayer presents only three terms that are not in the common core of material. Consequently, *Sharar* seems to preserve the better reading.

Much of the additional material within AM is minor, involving items such as conjunctions and synonyms. There are, however, several substantial discrepancies that are worthy of further consideration. The first of these passages is the opening clause of the paragraph in AM, "And with these heavenly armies." The purpose of this phrase is to connect this *gehanta* with the preceding *Sanctus*. In *Sharar* the connecting of the earthly and heavenly praise is made by a clause that comes awkwardly before the recitation of the *Sanctus*: "Let us also, Lord . . . 'Holy, Holy, Holy.'" Because the arrangement of *Sharar* is somewhat clumsy, it is possible that a redactor of AM has smoothed out the earlier version for a more fluent reading. A second significant distinction between the two anaphoras is in AM's use of the phrase "lowly, weak, and miserable servants," where *Sharar* uses the succinct "sinful servants." Spinks has argued that AM's formulation could be a liturgical phrase distinctive of the East Syrian tradition.[26] Credence is lent to this position by the fact that it can also be found in both *Nestorius* and *Theodore*. A third peculiarity of AM is the paraphrase "our Lord and our God" from John 20:28. The insertion of the passage here is logical because the preceding statement from the anaphora refers to enlightenment and the text of John 20:28 is part of the confession of Thomas. A final major contrast between AM and *Sharar* is found in the concluding sentence in which AM has added the term "lowliness" and the clause "through the abundant mercy of your grace" to the construction.

Third Gehanta

In this section the major differences between AM and *Sharar* begin to emerge. Both texts begin in similar manner but from *Sharar*'s quotation of John 6:55 onward the anaphoras are markedly different. Our first concern, however, is with their parallel openings. On the whole, *Sharar* better preserves the opening core material. A redactor of AM has added terms at this point in order to clarify thought. For instance, where *Sharar* has the simple construction "great mercy," AM has the expanded "many mercies which cannot be told." Likewise,

[26]Spinks, *Addai and Mari*, 6.

AM has added the phrase "in your sight" after the reference to the pleasing actions of the fathers.

After *Sharar* adds the Johannine quotation, the wording of the two prayers diverges and does not converge until the epiclesis. Immediately following the gospel passage in *Sharar* is an institution narrative which is addressed to Christ. Some scholars have suggested that *Sharar* preserves the original location, if not the wording, of AM's "lost" narrative. This position, however, faces several obstacles. The best argument against the missing narrative thesis is that the current text of AM does not contain one and it is unlikely that one would have dropped out with the increasing use and valuation of the narrative in later liturgical texts. A second argument in favor of the present form of AM is that its current structure has a certain structural and theological flow to it. As may be recalled from our summation of the work of Ray, the heart of the chiastic structure of AM is located within this *gehanta*. This characteristic can best be discerned by looking at the text in a format which emphasizes the parallel elements:

B You, Lord, through your many mercies be graciously mindful
      for all the pious and righteous **Fathers** who were pleasing
         in the **commemoration of the body and blood of your Christ**,
C   which we offer to you on the **pure and holy** altar, as you
         taught us. And grant us your tranquillity and your
         peace for all the days of the world.
X   That all the inhabitants of the earth may know
           that you alone are the true God and Father, and
         you sent our Lord Jesus Christ, your beloved Son,
C'   and he **taught us** through his life-giving gospel all
      the **purity and holiness** of the prophets, apostles,
   martyrs, confessors, bishops, priests, deacons, and all
B' the **sons** of the Holy Catholic Church who have been sealed
with the living seal of holy **baptism**.[27]

Looking at the *gehanta* from this perspective readily reveals the logical ordering of the present state of the material. The addition of an institution narrative would obviously distend this structure of this section to the point where it would not be as readily discernible. That

---

[27]Text adapted from *PEER* in light of previous discussion.

a narrative was excised from the text is improbable because structural features such as we have discerned within AM are more difficult to impose on preexisting material. Yet, such a deletion cannot be ruled out summarily.

"Anamnesis"

We now come to what has been the most discussed section within AM. Undoubtedly, this portion of the prayer presents us with the most problematic material. Except for the Mar Eshaya manuscript, this sentence does not contain a main verb. Analysis of this section is further complicated by the lack of parallels in the Maronite text. With these considerations in mind, it is easy to see why this part of the anaphora has received so much attention. Scholarly discussions have tended to gravitate towards two specific areas—the classification of the material and the location of its main verb.

The dominant trend has been to classify this material as an anamnesis. The use of the terms "tradition" and "commemorating," as well as the mention of Christ's saving work, gives this interpretation a good deal of textual support. Unquestionably, this part of the anaphora contains anamnetic material. A problem arises, however, when scholars apply the category of "anamnesis" in a formulaic manner in which certain related elements are presupposed. Botte, for instance, defines this paragraph as an anamnesis proper that requires an accompanying institution narrative. The problem with this approach is that it puts the typological cart before the textual horse. Because we have certain presuppositions about what an element is and ought to entail, we then assume that if an item which is constitutive of the classification is not present, then it has "dropped out." It may be that we need to revise the category. Thus what we have in AM can be considered an anamnesis because of its memorial statements; it is not an anamnesis, however, if we assume that this category presumes an institution narrative.

The second and more significant area of concern with this paragraph is its lack of a main verb. In playing "find the verb," we are faced with three possibilities as to its location. First, we can look for the verb within the sentence as it now stands. Second, we can assume that the text has been corrupted and it has thus dropped out. Third, we can look for it outside of the sentence.

The first option finds support in Macomber's observation that in Syriac a participle at times can function as an indicative verb in the present tense.[28] In applying this insight to AM we find ourselves with problem. All of the participles in this section are "occupied" by their use in a series of parallel relative clauses which describe "we." Because of the symmetry and tightness of the construction, it is difficult to come up with criteria for discerning which of these participles can be dislodged from its present use in a manner that does not appear arbitrary. Though such a determination cannot be ruled out summarily, we should first see if either of the other two alternatives presents us with a less capricious decision.

Our second possibility is that of textual corruption. This position is best described as a kind of default category in which we are forced to retreat if neither of the other two positions are tenable. In and of itself, the theory of textual contamination cannot be proved nor disproved. If a cogent argument cannot be made for finding a verb somewhere within the text, this position wins by default. But let us first proceed to the third possible solution.

This notion, that the main verb of the paragraph may be found elsewhere in the anaphora, actually presents us with two possible locations. The "we also" at the beginning of the paragraph seems to indicate that we are to look at the preceding sections in attempting to find the verb. Accordingly, the word "know" from the previous *gehanta* becomes a likely candidate. At first glance this solution is satisfactory because it provides linkage with material closest to it. However, it also presents us with a problem in that it leads to an awkward construction that is out of keeping with the economic style of AM. If one is looking at the preceding material for the verb, another possibility is that it could be found in the now lost institution narrative, presupposing, of course, that there was one there in the first place. On the other hand, there is one last possibility that we have yet to entertain, namely that the verb can be found in material which follows the sentence. Therefore, we will bracket further consideration of this topic until we have discussed the ensuing sections.

Epiclesis
As we begin to consider the epiclesis of the anaphora, our analysis is made easier because *Sharar* once again presents parallels with AM. Accordingly, we will commence our discussion with a comparison of the two prayers in order to discern their core material. In the initial

[28]Macomber, "The Maronite and Chaldean Versions," 70, n. 4.

portion of the epiclesis AM has added the phrase "bless and sanctify it," which imparts a consecratory understanding to the Holy Spirit's activity at the eucharist. Since the phrase is also found in *Theodore* and *Nestorius,* we can assume that it is an interpolation that has been employed to bring AM into conformity with the other two East Syrian eucharistic prayers. Another element that finds no accompaniment in *Sharar* is the phrase "with all who have been pleasing in your sight," which duplicates a statement from the third *gehanta* that also finds no parallel in *Sharar.* It follows, then, that the expression is an East Syrian addition to the core text.

If we omit the aforementioned consecratory phrase from AM, the focus of the epiclesis is similar to that which we find in the so-called *Apostolic Tradition* of Hippolytus. In both of these texts the emphasis is on the advantages that are received from participation in the eucharist (e.g., forgiveness of sins). This parallel with Hippolytus may indicate that the epiclesis that we see in the common text of AM and *Sharar* is an early form since later variations tend to be consecratory. An early dating of the material is also implied by the verb that is employed in this epiclesis. Spinks has argued that an epiclesis which describes the Spirit as "coming," rather than being "sent," indicates an early date.[29] An example of the "primitive" form is that found in the Egyptian version of BAS while a later adaptation of BAS—JAS—has the "send" formulation.[30]

Doxology

The last portion of the prayer is doxological in orientation and thus mimics the second *qanona.* In addition to a common motif, the resemblance between these two sections is further exhibited in their shared *incipit.* In the Mar Eshaya manuscript the text of the first doxology contains only the *incipit,* though the other manuscripts supply the congregational parts. The Mar Eshaya text, however, does contain the whole of the final doxology and shows that it is God's "dispensation" that is the reason for the praise. The term translated as "dispensation" is the Syriac equivalent to *oikonomia,* which implies a christological focus to God's saving actions. This contrasts with the more generic "helps and graces" which some manuscripts show as the

[29]Bryan Spinks, "The Consecratory Epiklesis in the Anaphora of St. James," *SL* 11 (1976) 19–38.
[30]For texts see *PEER,* 71, 93.

purpose of the first doxology. In addition, the second concluding doxology has an explicit use of the term "church," whereas the first doxology implies church with the pronoun "us," again supplied from later manuscripts.

In comparing this section with its parallel in *Sharar*, we find that the latter text uses the phrase "we your sinful servants," where AM has the abbreviated "we." It may be recalled that *Sharar* employed this phrase previously in its version of the second *gehanta* where AM had the threefold "we, your lowly, weak, and miserable servants." Other points of distinction between the two anaphoras are relatively minor and need not concern us.

Having contrasted the final doxology with those of the second *qanona* and *Sharar*, we are left with three topics that warrant further consideration. Why the use of "economy"? Why the explicit mention of the church? And why does *Sharar* employ the phrase "sinful servants"? All three inquiries can be assisted by reference back to the "anamnesis" and the second *gehanta*. In so doing, the term "dispensation" seems to be a reference to the phrase discussing the Incarnation in the "anamnesis" ("this great mystery of the passion, death, and resurrection of our Lord Jesus Christ"). This linkage of the terms "mystery" and "economy" recalls Ephesians 1 in which the two words are used together as an elaboration on Christ's saving activity. The use of the term "church" in the final doxology should be understood as "those who have been sealed with the seal of holy baptism" (end of the second *gehanta*) and, more specifically, those "who have gathered and stand before you" (beginning of the anamnetic material). In terms of the third aspect of our present investigation, it is interesting to note that AM's equivalent of *Sharar*'s term "sinful" is also found at the beginning of the "anamnesis."

In his treatment of the anaphora, Jean Magne suggested that the "missing" verb of the anamnetic paragraph is the "give thanks" from the concluding doxology.[31] The linkage between the two sections is further exhibited by the three points we have just highlighted. Of course, the current positioning of the epiclesis presents us with a dilemma in that it obscures the connection. Ratcliff and Macomber, among others, have argued that the epiclesis was an interpolation. A stumbling block for this position is that, as we noted above, AM's

[31]Jean Magne, "L'anaphore nestorienne dite d'Adée et Mari et l'anaphore maronite dite de Pierre III. Étude comparative," *OCP* 53 (1987) 145–7.

epiclesis appears to be an early form of this aspect of the eucharistic prayer. However, even if AM's epiclesis is fairly "primitive," it does not necessarily preclude the possibility that it was still an interpolation. After all, "early" and "original" are not synonyms. If we leave open the possibility of several major stages of development, then it is quite conceivable that the epiclesis made its way into the text of the prayer quite early, yet in such a way that the primal chiasmus of the section was stretched.

CONCLUSION

In this essay we have attempted to provide the previously uninitiated student with some rudimentary knowledge that could be of assistance for an informed reading of AM. As with all tools, such a device is intended as a heuristic helpmate for those who seek more adequately to understand what the text of the prayer itself has to say. After becoming familar with *how* one can read the prayer, then, the next step is to learn *what* the prayer states about God, creation, and their relationship. It is this responsibility and opportunity that we leave with the student.

Walter D. Ray

2. The Strasbourg Papyrus

INTRODUCTION

The so-called Strasbourg Papyrus consists of six tattered papyrus fragments comprising a single leaf measuring perhaps 8 by 5 3/4 inches, the top third of which is missing, and catalogued as Papyrus Gr. 254 in the Bibliothèque Nationale de l'Universitaire de Strasbourg. Its editors, Michel Andrieu and Paul Collomp, date the writing on the papyrus to the fourth or fifth century.[1] When Andrieu and Collomp copied out and pieced together the fragments in 1928, they discovered what they took to be "fragments on papyrus of the Anaphora of St. Mark" six or seven hundred years older than the next oldest witness to the Alexandrian anaphora. The papyrus covered the part of the anaphora before the *Sanctus*, including praise, offering, and intercessions, and ended in a doxology. "The *Sanctus*, anamnesis, etc.," they surmised, "came on the following leaves, and after the doxology, which doubtless marked the end of the great supplication."[2] Andrieu and Collomp's assessment held sway for nearly fifty years. Beginning in the 1970s, however, scholars began to think that the Strasbourg Papyrus, rather than just a part of the anaphora of St. Mark (hereafter MARK), was in itself a complete eucharistic prayer. This new interpretation, which is now the consensus opinion, has great significance for the history not only of MARK, but of the eucharistic prayer in general.

A COMPLETE ANAPHORA?
HISTORY OF THE SCHOLARSHIP

Andrieu and Collomp, believing they had an early fragment of MARK, saw the value of their papyrus for chronicling the development of that anaphora, at least for the first part. "In spite of their

---

[1] M. Andrieu and P. Collomp, "Fragments sur papyrus de l'anaphore de saint Marc," *Revue des sciences religieuses* 8 (1928) 491. ET of Strasbourg Papyrus in *PEER*, 53–4.

[2] Andrieu and Collomp, "Fragments sur papyrus," 514.

short length" they wrote, "our fragments permit us to observe in the manuscripts numerous interpolations and serious alterations."[3] Further systematic comparisons of the papyrus with later manuscripts of MARK were carried out in 1959 by Klaus Gamber[4] and the 1960s by Hieronymous Engberding (for the intercessions)[5] and R.-G. Coquin (for the rest of the anaphora).[6]

In 1974, Edward Kilmartin seemed to suggest that the Strasbourg Papyrus was a complete anaphora "correspond[ing] to the later prayer of St. Mark but . . . shorter."[7] He located the prayer at a third-century stage of development of the eucharistic prayer. Geoffrey Cuming made a similar suggestion at the 1979 Oxford Patristics Conference, which was later included in his own study of the development of MARK.[8] Cuming begins with the problem of the placement of the intercessions. Most scholars had considered these to be an interpolation. Using a measure of linguistic analysis, which we will take up later, Cuming observes that in the Strasbourg Papyrus and the Coptic version of MARK, unlike the later Greek manuscripts, the intercessions are "carefully dovetailed" into the preceding offering. The implication is that the intercessions were always there. Their position, moreover, does not seem unusual if the papyrus is viewed as a complete prayer. It is only when the other usual elements of an anaphora are added—*Sanctus,* institution narrative, anamnesis, epiclesis—that their placement becomes problematic. Cuming suggests that the Strasbourg Papyrus "is in effect a Christian *berakah,* beginning with praise and thanksgiving, passing on to intercession, and ending with a doxology," similar to the *Birkat ha-mazon,* the Jewish blessing after a meal, which Louis Ligier had suggested as a likely

[3]Ibid., 515.

[4]"Das Papyrusfragment zur Markusliturgie und das Eucharistiegebet im Clementsbrief," *OS* 8 (1959) 31–45.

[5]"Die anaphorische Fürbittgebet der griechischen Markusliturgie," *OCP* 50 (1964) 396–446.

[6]"L'anaphore alexandine de Saint Marc," in *Liturgies d'Orient et d'Occident,* Lex Orandi 47 (Paris: Cerf, 1970) 51–82. A later version appeared in *Le Muséon* 82 (1969) 307–56.

[7]"Sacrificium Laudis: Content and Function of Early Eucharistic Prayers," *TS* 35 (1974) 280.

[8]"The Anaphora of St. Mark: A Study in Development," *Le Muséon* 95 (1982) 115–29; reproduced in this volume, 57–72. His argument is resumed in his edition of *The Liturgy of St. Mark,* OCA 234 (Rome: Pontificium Institutum Orientale, 1990) xxiii–xxvii.

source for the Christian eucharistic prayer. He notes that "this possibility is much enhanced if the single leaf which the fragments constitute was complete in itself when new."[9]

Independently of Cuming, H.A.J. Wegman arrived at a similar conclusion, though from a different direction. Beginning with the *textus receptus* of MARK, Wegman stripped away everything which appeared to be borrowed from JAS, which he believed was everything from the *Sanctus* to the end of the anaphora, to arrive at its "most ancient layer." This leaves him with the praise, offering, and intercessions. By good fortune, "the papyrus Str. gr. 254 corresponds exactly to this most ancient layer of the anaphora of St. Mark," which both shows to his satisfaction that his reconstruction of the early state of MARK is correct and suggests that the Strasbourg Papyrus is in itself a complete prayer. His "provisional" conclusion is that the Strasbourg Papyrus is not an anaphora in the technical sense of the word but "a complete eucharistic benediction in three strophes." The origin of this kind of prayer Wegman finds in the rites after the early Christian eucharistic meal, such as in *Didache* 10, and ultimately in the Jewish family meal ritual.[10]

In a 1984 article[11] Bryan Spinks challenged the arguments of both Wegman and Cuming. Any attempt to trace the history of MARK, he says, must deal squarely with its peculiar *Sanctus* unit, which comes right at the point where the Strasbourg papyrus ends. Moreover, the presence of a doxology at this point in the papyrus is no proof that the prayer has ended. He points to *Didache* 10 and Addai and Mari as examples of prayers which have internal doxologies. It is possible, he suggests, that at Alexandria at the time of the Strasbourg Papyrus the anaphora consisted of a series of prayers, each ending in a doxology, which would have been found on different leaves. Spinks does not conclude that the papyrus is not a complete anaphora, but only that the case has not been proved.

The following year Enrico Mazza entered the discussion. After reviewing the arguments of Cuming, Wegman, and Spinks, he sides with the first two scholars. Mazza acknowledges the problem of the

[9]"The Anaphora of St. Mark," 119–20 (below, 63).

[10]H.A.J. Wegman, "Une anaphore incomplète? Les Fragments sur Papyrus Strasbourgh Gr. 254," in R. van den Broek and M. J. Vermeseren, eds., *Studies in Gnosticism and Hellenistic Religions* (Leiden: Brill, 1981) 432–50.

[11]Bryan D. Spinks, "A Complete Anaphora? A Note on Strasbourg Gr. 254," *Heythrop Journal* 25 (1984) 51–5.

Sanctus, but he notes that in MARK the *Sanctus* is more securely connected to what follows it than to the intercessions which precede it, implying that it belongs more to the second part of the anaphora. "Consequently," he concludes, "in the reconstruction of the genesis of the Alexandrian anaphora it is possible to reach some conclusion on the origin of the *Sanctus* without this changing the elements of the problem in evaluating the Strasbourg Papyrus as a complete anaphora." As for the question of the doxology, Mazza agrees that doxologies are often found between strophic elements of eucharistic prayers, but also observes that such doxologies frequently drop out, as they do in the reworking of *Didache* 9 and 10 in *Apostolic Constitutions* 7. MARK provides another example. The doxology which we find in the Strasbourg Papyrus has disappeared in the received text; in its place we find the *Sanctus.* An examination of the text of the Strasbourg Papyrus itself, moreover, seems to indicate that it has already undergone a process in which internal doxologies were suppressed. Mazza notes what appears to be the remnants of a doxology at the end of the first strophe: "through whom to you . . .," and conjectures that the short expression which serves as a transition between the second and third strophes—"over which sacrifice and offering . . ."—replaced a doxology which had fallen out. The remaining doxology, then, must have concluded the whole prayer.[12]

In a subsequent book into which he incorporated this article, Mazza compares the Strasbourg Papyrus with other tripartite prayers which are known to be complete prayers: the *Eucharistia mystica* of *Apostolic Constitutions* 7, the eucharistic prayer of the *Apostolic Tradition,* and *Didache* 10, all of which he sees as a development of the Jewish *Birkat ha-mazon.* The structure of the Strasbourg Papyrus, he argues, is analogous to these other prayers: three strophes: two eucharists and a petition. From this he concludes that "nothing prevents our holding that the Strasbourg Papyrus is an anaphora, or better, a 'paleoanaphora,' that is complete in itself and is not just part of an anaphora needing further strophes to be complete."[13]

The growing recognition that the Strasbourg Papyrus represents a complete eucharistic prayer should be sufficient to dispel the long

[12]Enrico Mazza, "Una Anafora incompleta? Il Papiro Strasbourg Gr. 254," *EL* 99 (1985) 425–36.

[13]Mazza, *The Origins of the Eucharistic Prayer* (Collegeville: The Liturgical Press, 1995) 177–94.

held notion that the "normal" anaphora has all the elements of the West Syrian type, Wegman's and Mazza's reluctance to accord the papyrus the title of anaphora notwithstanding. Elements once considered obligatory—institution narrative, anamnesis, etc.—can be considered so no longer. The current tendency is to view the Strasbourg Papyrus as a stage in the development of the the anaphora, and scholars have tried to show the prayer's development from its Jewish origins. The papyrus is often ranged with *Didache* 10 as a Christianized development of the Jewish meal benediction, the *Birkat ha-mazon*, as we saw above with Cuming, Wegman, and Mazza. Mazza also tries to show an influence from the synagogal *Yotzer*.[14] Thomas Talley finds in the prayer an example, not of the tripartite structure of the *Birkat ha-mazon* but of the bipartite structure of the Old Testament "tôdâ" prayer forms analyzed by Cesare Giraudo: "anemnetic" thanksgiving and "epicletic" supplication.[15] At the same time, several scholars have taken the papyrus as a starting point from which to explore later anaphoral development. David Tripp, though he only briefly considers the Strasbourg Papyrus, finds in it a representative of a second-century anaphoral pattern which he thinks should be considered "the ground-plan of several later anaphoral traditions."[16] Cuming thinks that the Strasbourg Papyrus represents the primitive layer not only of MARK, but also of the Jerusalem JAS.[17] Recently, Mazza has attempted to show a similar direct relationship between the Strasbourg Papyrus and the Roman Canon, whose verbal affinities with MARK have long been noted.[18]

In this essay we will examine the prayer in itself, as the product of a particular worshiping community at a particular time and place, which expresses that community's theological concerns and outlook. The community itself, of course, has a history and tradition. It is

[14]Ibid., 334, 194–8.

[15]Thomas J. Talley, "The Literary Structure of the Eucharistic Prayer," *Worship* 58 (1984) 417; cf. Cesare Giraudo, *La Struttura letteraria della preghiera eucaristica*, Analecta Biblica 92 (Rome: Biblical Insitute Press, 1981). Giraudo does not apply his analysis to the Strasbourg Papyrus, which he still takes as a fragment of MARK.

[16]David Tripp, "The Prayer of St. Polycarp and the Development of Anaphoral Prayer," *EL* 104 (1990) 118–9.

[17]"The Anaphora of St. Mark," 128–9 (below, 72); cf. idem, "Egyptian Elements in the Jerusalem Liturgy," *JTS* 25 (1974) 117–24.

[18]*The Origins of the Eucharistic Prayer*, 240–86.

shaped by the prayer traditions it inherits. It may well be that, as W. H. Bates says, "the Strasbourg Papyrus may be seen as a classic example of a Christian *eucharistia* deriving from the Jewish *berakhah* model."[19] But it is not presently possible to discover a precise genetic link with any particular Jewish prayer. While we will note evidence in the text of earlier prayer traditions, our primary focus will be the tradition presented by the papyrus itself. It is hoped that in this way, the contributions which the community of the papyrus brought to the prayer will stand out clearly.

AN EXAMINATION OF THE TEXT
'It is meet'—Justification for Praise
"to bless [you] . . . [night] and day, [you who made] heaven [and] all that is in [it, the earth and all that is in the earth,] seas and rivers and [all that is] in [them], [you] who made the human [according to your own] image and likeness. You made everything through your Wisdom, the Light [of?] your true Son, our Lord and Savior Jesus Christ, through whom to you and with him, with the Holy Spirit, giving thanks, we offer the reasonable sacrifice and this bloodless worship. . . ."

The first part of the prayer provides the motive for praise and thanksgiving. It is one of the hallmarks of the Alexandrian anaphora that the thanksgiving is centered solely on God's act of creation, and not at all on his act of redemption in the incarnation of Christ. Implied in this is a particular understanding of the eucharist as the means of returning thanks to God for the things he has made, which we find in Origen: "We must not refuse to enjoy those things which have been created for our use, but must receive them with thanksgiving to the Creator. . . . We give thanks to the Creator of all, and, along with thanksgiving and prayer for the things which we have received, we also eat the bread presented to us, which becomes by prayer a sacred body, which sanctifies those who sincerely partake of it."[20]
The idea that it is the duty of the world to give thanks to its Maker is, of course, already present in Philo. In the incense of the temple sacrifice, for example, Philo sees a symbol of "the world fashioned by the divine wisdom which offers its whole self as a burnt offering

[19]"Thanksgiving in the Liturgy of St. Mark," in Bryan D. Spinks, ed., *The Sacrifice of Praise* (Rome: C.L.V.—Edizioni Liturgiche, 1981) 113.
[20]*Against Celsus* 8.33; ET from *ANF* 4.

morning and evening. For the life which is proper to the world is to give thanks continually and without ceasing to the Father and Creator. . . ."[21] Here we find many parallels to the ideas of our prayer: The world is made by divine wisdom; its duty is to give thanks to its Creator; this thanksgiving is a sacrifice, the offering up of itself, which it performs morning and evening. Origen and the prayer, however, add another dimension to this cosmic offering: Christ. The whole action of the prayer hinges on Christ. Creation, for which we give thanks, comes through Christ, the Wisdom of God, and it is through Christ that we give thanks for what God has created. "We offer first fruits" to the Creator, Origen says, "and to Him to whom we offer first-fruits we also send up our prayers, 'having a great high priest, that is passed into the heavens, Jesus the Son of God' [Heb 4:14]."[22] It is the cosmic activity of Christ as God's Wisdom in creation and High Priest in redemption which the prayer implies and on which it depends.

A pre-Christian origin for this section of the prayer is suggested by its kinship with the Old Greek recension of Daniel 4:37(34), where Nabuchodonosor prays: "I will confess (anthomologoumai) the Most High and praise the One who created heaven and earth and the seas and the rivers and all that is in them." We find here not only the unusual reference to the creation of rivers—which Wegman[23] thought was especially Egyptian—but also the rare verb anthomologeisthai, which of all anaphoras is found only in MARK. We may assume that it also belonged to the Strasbourg Papyrus: It fits neatly into the lacuna after "to bless," and the dative case of the participle requires some such verb. The Old Greek recension of Daniel, however, was quickly supplanted in the Church by the "Theodotion" translation, which differs markedly in this section of chapter 4.[24] This reduces the

---

[21]Quis Rerum Divinarum Heres Sit 196–200.

[22]Against Celsus 8.34. Henri Crouzel, Origène (Paris: Lethielleux, 1985) 297, wonders why "the link between the passion of the Savior and the eucharist is insinuated often enough, [but] rarely expressed clearly." Perhaps this lack of clear expression is not so much the disciplina arcana, which Crouzel suggests, as the expression of a eucharistic spirituality nourished by a eucharistic prayer in which this link is not expressly stated but only implied.

[23]"Une anaphore incomplète?" 440.

[24]Hippolytus uses Theodotion for his commentary (c. 204). And Origen quotes the Theodotion version of this very verse in Against Celsus 7.31, though in his Homilies on Numbers (18.3) he indicates that the Septuagint is still the version used in the church in Caesarea in the mid-third century.

chances that the phrase entered the prayer text through Christian borrowing of a biblical text. It suggests rather that it belongs to a living prayer tradition which pre-dates its Christian use, to which the biblical text is also beholden.

The lacuna is not big enough to fit also another long verb, such as *proskunein*, "to worship," or *eucharistein*, "to give thanks," which appear in manuscripts of MARK here. It is probable that the verb "to give thanks" did not appear here at all. Origen, possibly with the eucharistic prayer in mind, argued that confession *(anthomologēsis)* was the same as thanksgiving *(eucharistia)*.[25]

The recounting of the creation of humanity is a straight-forward paraphrase of Gen 1:26, and requires little comment. Its presence at this point in the anaphora is unique to Alexandria. There is a similar reference to Gen 1:26, though without the mention of "likeness," in the postsanctus of BAS (where it is conflated with Gen 2:7) and JAS, where it serves as a prelude to the history of redemption. In our text it indicates the centrality of humanity in the cosmic activity of thanksgiving and offering which is now accomplished through Christ.

Wegman thinks that the identification of the creative Wisdom of God with Christ points to the Prologue of the Gospel of John as the basis of the prayer. "It is there that we find combined creation by the Word, the true light, and the incarnation of the unique Son of God. It is above all by reading the Prologue that we understand our passage."[26] Missing from the prayer, however, is the key term which characterizes the Prologue of John: Word. In its place we find Wisdom. Scholars have long sought a source for John's prologue in Jewish Wisdom theology.[27] It is likely that the prayer has a similar source. A Wisdom milieu in fact evidences itself in the whole cluster of ideas which make up the prayer: the central significance of the act of creation, the mediation of personified Wisdom, the spiritualized conception of sacrifice, and the need for and possibility of petitionary prayer.[28] That the prayer was later influenced by John is clear from

---

[25]*De oratione* 14.2.

[26]"Une anaphore incomplète?" 442.

[27]See Michael E. Willett, *Wisdom Christology in the Fourth Gospel* (San Francisco: Mellen Research University Press, 1992) 3–4, 32–4.

[28]On these themes in biblical wisdom literature see James L. Crenshaw, "Studies in Ancient Israelite Wisdom: Prolegomenon" and "The Restraint of Reason, the Humility of Prayer," in idem, *Urgent Advice and Probing Questions: Collected Writings on Old Testament Wisdom* (Macon, Ga.: Mercer, 1995) 90–140, 206–21.

the expansion it has undergone in MARK, in which "true" now clearly modifies light, and Son has acquired the modifier *monogenēs*, "only." But the use of Wisdom in the papyrus suggests not a dependence on John, but a common outlook. The word itself probably belongs to an early, pre-Christian, recension of the prayer. In Alexandria, Wisdom was being eclipsed by Word already in Philo.[29] The prayer later received a christological expansion, possibly under the influence of the Gospel of John, but just as likely from another source which also may have influenced John.

Wegman, Cuming, and Mazza have all suggested that the relative clause that ends this section originally led into a doxology, which Cuming suggests may have concluded an original "mini-anaphora."[30] We can compare it, without the apparent trinitarian interpolation, to the doxology at the end of the papyrus: "through whom to you glory to the ages of ages." With the apparent interpolation, we can compare it to the almost identical doxology at the end of Polycarp's prayer: "through whom to you with him and the Holy Spirit be glory both now and for the ages to come."[31] In its present form it serves as a point of transition, linking a new prayer action—offering—with the preceding section. At the same time, it stands in parallel to the preceding clause to form the pivot of the central drama of the prayer, the coming of creation from God and the return of creation to God in thanksgiving through Christ:

"All things you made through your Wisdom . . . Jesus Christ, through whom to you . . . giving thanks, we offer. . . ."

It is quite possible that the driving vision of the cosmic activity of Christ the High Priest supplied the motive for the transformation of this clause from a simple concluding formula.

'Giving thanks, we offer'—Thanksgiving/Offering
"giving thanks, we offer the reasonable sacrifice, this bloodless worship, which all the nations offer you, from the rising of the sun to its setting, from the north to the south, for your name is great among all

[29]See Willet, *Wisdom Christology,* 19–20.

[30]G. J. Cuming, "Four Very Early Anaphoras," *Worship* 58 (1984) 169, 170.

[31]*Martyrdom of Polycarp* 14.3. This prayer also has a strong sense of the mediating activity of Christ: "I praise you, I bless you, I glorify you, through the eternal and heavenly High Priest, Jesus Christ, through whom to you . . . glory."

the nations, and in every place incense is offered to your holy name and a pure offering, over which sacrifice and offering we pray and beseech you. . . ."

If the relative clause of the preceding section originally belonged to a doxology, this section of the prayer would have opened with a verb. Quite possibly this verb was "we give thanks" (*eucharistoumen*), as it is in the prayers of the *Didache*. Here the main verb is "offer" and *eucharistein* has been reduced to a participle. The main action, however, is still thanksgiving. The participle expresses the means by which the offering is accomplished: "By giving thanks, we offer." The main verb and the quotation from Malachi which follows serve to define for the community what it is accomplishing in its worship, which is still understood as an act of thanksgiving. We can contrast this to the inversion of the terms which we find in, for example, the Byzantine anaphoras BAS and CHR: "offering . . . we give you thanks. . . ." Here the focus is on the liturgical action of offering, and hence on the eucharistic gifts, the offering of which is understood as a means of giving thanks. We should not push the contrast too far, however. For already in Origen the eucharistic bread is a symbol of thanksgiving.[32] And in *Didache* 14, the pure sacrifice (again referring to Mal 1:11) is both the giving of thanks and the breaking of bread in the gathered community. The idea of thanksgiving as offering is not new, but it obtains explicit expression in the papyrus.

Thanksgiving is here called a "reasonable sacrifice" and "bloodless worship." Possible scriptural sources for this idea include Romans 12:1, where the self-offering of Christians is termed a "living sacrifice" and "reasonable worship," and Hebrews 13:15: "through him [Christ] we offer the sacrifice of praise, which is the fruit of lips which confess his name." Here again we find no direct quotation, but a confluence of ideas which points to a common intellectual background. The term "bloodless" in connection with sacrifice and worship appears in several late second-century texts. In Athenagoras (c. 177), who was possibly head of the catechetical school in Alexandria, the offering of "a bloodless sacrifice and the reasonable worship" to the Creator of all things by the Christians is contrasted with the

[32]*Against Celsus* 8.57: "We say that he truly discharges the duties of life who is ever mindful who is his Creator. . . . We are . . . concerned lest we should be ungrateful to God. . . . And we have a symbol of gratitude to God in the Bread which we call the Eucharist."

bloody sacrifices of the pagans.[33] In *Acts of Apollonius* 8, the martyr (d. 185) is quoted as saying that Christians offer "a bloodless and pure sacrifice, which is through prayer" to God Almighty, "Lord of heaven and earth [the Armenian version adds "and seas"] and everything that breathes." Both these texts may be citing the liturgy, as Origen certainly is when he says that the true way to celebrate a feast is to "pray always, continually offering bloodless sacrifices in prayers to the Divinity."[34] It is clear from the context that he has in mind a spiritualized version of the material worship of the church. A much earlier occurrence, possibly suggestive of a source tradition, is found in the Testament of Levi (3:5-6) where the propitiations which the archangels make in the highest heaven "for the sins of ignorance of the righteous ones" are described as "a rational and bloodless offering."

We find here the only certain quotation of scripture in the prayer, from Mal 1:11. This verse is a common second-century *topos* in discussions on the eucharist. We find it in *Didache* 14.3, Justin,[35] and Irenaeus.[36] Talley[37] and Mazza[38] have both suggested that the verse functions in the prayer as an institution narrative, an "embolism" in Giraudo's terminology, the "formal citation in direct style of the scriptural *locus theologicus* of the event which is celebrated."[39] It both defines and provides the warrant for the eucharistic celebration. At the same time, it serves to distinguish the Christian sacrifice from that especially of the Jews, as the arrangement of the text and its introduction make clear: this is the sacrifice "which all the nations (the Gentiles) offer."

'We pray and beseech'—Intercessions
"over which sacrifice and offering we pray and beseech you: Remember your holy and only Catholic Church, all your peoples and all your flocks. Provide the peace which is from heaven in all our hearts, and grant us also the peace of this life. The . . . of the land peaceful things towards us, and towards your [holy] name, the prefect of the province, the army, the princes, councils . . .

[33]*Legatio* 13.
[34]*Against Celsus* 8.21.
[35]*Dialogue with Trypho* 41, 117.
[36]*Against the Heresies* 4.17.5.
[37]"The Literary Structure of the Eucharistic Prayer," 417–8.
[38]*The Origins of the Eucharistic Prayer,* 191–2.
[39]Giraudo, *La struttura letteraria della preghiera eucaristica,* 384.

[lacuna of 15–20 lines]

". . . [for seedtime and] harvest, for the poor of [your] people, for all of us who call upon [your] name, for all who hope in you. Give rest to the souls of those who have fallen asleep; remember those of whom we make mention today, both those whose names we say [and] whose we do not say . . . [Remember] our orthodox fathers and bishops everywhere; and grant us to have a part and lot with the fair . . . of your holy prophets, apostles, and martyrs. Receive (?) [through] their entreaties [these prayers] . . .

[three corrupt lines]

". . . grant to them through our Lord and Savior, through whom be glory to you through the ages."

Cuming made the introduction to the intercessions the *crux interpretationis* of the papyrus, using it to argue for the integrity of the prayer. The medieval manuscripts of MARK treat the first three words in the papyrus (*eph' hē thusia*, "over which sacrifice") as one word (*epithusia*, "a sacrifice") and make the first part of the transition an appendix to the citation from Mal 1:11: "'. . . in every place . . . is offered . . . a pure offering,' *a sacrifice and offering*." The next sentence then begins abruptly "And [*kai*, or "Therefore," *dio*] we pray and beseech you: Remember. . . ." It was this abrupt transition which among other things led Coquin and others to conclude that the intercessions were an interpolation.[40] Cuming, however, noted that the Strasbourg Papyrus lacks the "And," and that instead of *epithusia*, it reads *eph' hē thusia*. *Epithusia* is, moreover, otherwise unattested (as is *ephēthusia*), and its verbal form *epithuein* is rare and, when used in Christian contexts, as in *Martyrdom of Polycarp* 4.1, carries the negative connotation of sacrifice to idols. It is, therefore, best to read it as a prepositional phrase with a relative pronoun, "over which sacrifice." Such a reading is confirmed by the Coptic, which has "and over this sacrifice and offering we pray and beseech you."[41]

Mazza suggests that this transitional phrase supplanted an original doxology. It is just possible that the preposition-relative pronoun construction is in fact the remnant of such a doxology. In its present form

[40]See, for example, Coquin, "L'anaphore alexandrine," 313; Gregory Dix, *The Shape of the Liturgy* (London: Dacre, 1945) 218.

[41]Cuming, "The Anaphora of St. Mark," 119–20 (below, 61–2); idem, *The Liturgy of St. Mark,* xxv.

it has exactly the same structure as the other possible doxological remnant we encountered: a relative clause linking a new action with the preceding section. And the construction as it stands is not without difficulties, which Cuming notes: The use of the relative pronoun, "which," as a demonstrative is unusual, as is the use of the preposition *epi* plus the dative case to mean "over."[42] A more common use of *epi* with dative is to show ground or motive, especially with verbs for expressing emotion, including verbs of thanksgiving and praise.[43] The *eph' hē* clause may have included a resumption of the thanksgiving, something like the "For all these things we give thanks to you" of APSyr and CHR, which both Ligier and, following him, Cuming think may have originally been a concluding formula.[44] In one third-century papyrus we even find the construction used in a doxology: ". . . through your only beloved Child, Jesus Christ, our Lord and the Healer of our souls; because of (or "through") him to you be glory *(eiē soi ep' autō doxa)*. . . ."[45] In any case, the relative clause is better understood as the concluding formula of a strophe than as the introductory formula of the succeeding strophe, as the later manuscripts of MARK in fact understand. The more abrupt break between the thanksgiving and the petitions which results is what one would expect whether one attached the prayer to Giraudo's bipartite "tôdâ"—in which the epicletic section begins "And now"[46]—or to a

[42]"The Anaphora of St. Mark," 119–20.

[43]This usage better accounts for its use in the one example Cuming provides (Luke 15:7): *chara . . . epi heni hamartōlō*, "joy . . . *on account of* one sinner who repents" (though the English, too, often expresses this idea as "over"). We find an example with thanksgiving in 1 Cor 1:4: "I give thanks to my God always for you because of the grace *(epi tē chariti)* of God which was given you in Christ Jesus." In Origen, *On Prayer* 14.2., we find the same construction in a passage which we have seen before: "Thanksgiving *(eucharistian)* is confession *(anthomologēsin)* with prayer for blessings received *(epi tō teteuchenai agathōn)* from God." Examples of its use in expressions of praise include Luke 2:20: "The shepherds returned, glorifying *(doxazontes)* and praising *(ainountes)* God for all *(epi pasin)* they had heard and seen"; and this sentence from a prayer in a papyrus fragment of the apocryphal *Acts of John*: "We praise *(ainoumen)* you and worship *(proskunoumen)* and give thanks *(eucharistoumen)* because of your every gift *(epi pasē sou dōrea)*" (Charles Wessely, ed., *Les plus anciens monuments du christieanisme écrits sur papyrus* 2, PO 18/3 [Paris: Firmin-Didot, 1924] 484).

[44]Louis Ligier, "The Origins of the Eucharistic Prayer: From the Last Supper to the Eucharist," *SL* 9 (1973) 179; Cuming, "Four Very Early Anaphoras," 168.

[45]Berlin Papyrus 9794, in Wessely, ed., *Les plus anciens monuments* 2:430.

[46]Giraudo, *La struttura letteraria*, 164–5.

tripartite prayer such as we find in *Didache* 10—in which the petition begins abruptly after a doxology with "Remember (*Mnēsthēti*)," which is also the opening word of the petitions in the Strasbourg Papyrus.

In fact, though Cuming found it necessary to show that "the intercessions are carefully dovetailed into the preface"[47] to justify their presence at this point in the prayer, no such justification is necessary. We have many examples of Jewish and early Christian prayers in which thanksgiving and intercessions are thus juxtaposed without any attempt at "dovetailing," including *Didache* 10 and 1 Clement 59–61.[48]

What led scholars to question the integrity of this pattern for Christian eucharistic prayer were false expectations based upon a false evolutionary schema according to which the original eucharistic prayer was a "spiritual *eucharistia*," a pure thanksgiving with no room for intercession. Petitions came in only when the focus of the prayer had shifted to the offering of the eucharistic gifts themselves. But these petitions, on this theory, had to come after the consecration of the gifts, whether this was through the words of institution or the invocation of the Holy Spirit.[49] Their presence in another location, therefore, demanded justification.

What this theory misses is that, at least for the Alexandrian tradition, thanksgiving itself was early understood as sacrifice, as we have seen, and sacrifice is always "for" something. Joseph Heinemann has suggested that public prayer, which originated in second-temple Judaism, was from its inception understood as sacrifice, either paralleling the sacrifices of the temple, or after the temple's destruction, replacing them.[50] Further, "it was customary from the earliest times

---

[47]"The Anaphora of St. Mark," 119 (below, 61).

[48]Gamber, "Das Papyrusfragment zur Markusliturgie," uses these prayers to argue for the originality of the intercessions in MARK.

[49]Josef Jungmann, who is perhaps most responsible for putting this schema forward, summarizes it thus (*The Mass of the Roman Rite* [New York: Benzinger Brothers, 1955] 2:109): "By degrees the viewpoint changed, and the celebration was no longer looked upon as an altogether spiritual *eucharistia*; over and above this there was the offering of the gifts, the *anaphora*, the *oblatio* . . . and this, too, had to be clearly kept in view; naturally, then, there developed a provision for putting this oblation of gifts forward in an intercessory sense, a thing not easily done in a 'thanksgiving prayer.'"

[50]*Prayer in the Talmud: Forms and Patterns* (Berlin/New York: de Gruyter, 1977) 14–5.

to insert brief petitions into benedictions of praise and thanksgiving."[51] This pattern of prayer—praise-petition—fully accounts for the pattern which we find in the Strasbourg Papyrus.

The papyrus in fact exhibits many of the characteristics which Heinemann finds in Jewish statutory prayer.[52] This is the prayer of the community, hence in the first person plural: "*We* pray and beseech. . . . Provide peace in all *our* hearts, grant *us* peace in this earthly life. . . ." And it is prayer for the community: "Remember your Church" is the first petition in the papyrus. It is possible that originally this was the only petition, as it is in *Didache* 10, to which others were added. Such intercessory petitions for specific persons were not a significant part of the synagogue prayers,[53] but it is not difficult to view them as extensions of the core petition for the community. The first four especially are consistent with the command that "supplication, prayers, intercessions, and thanksgivings be made for all men, for kings and all who are in high positions, that we may lead a quiet and peaceable life, godly and respectable in every way" (1 Tim 2:1-2). At his trial, Apollonius is able to protest that "I and all Christians offer a bloodless sacrifice to God . . . on behalf of the spiritual and rational images who have been appointed by the providence of God to rule over the earth,"[54] but in the prayer to which he refers the chief aim of the petition for the rulers is no doubt the peace of the community.

The petitions end in a now largely lacunose request that the prayers be accepted through the intercessions of the saints. David Tripp, based on his study of the prayer of Polycarp, thought that this was the original petition and that the other petitions were inserted sometime before 200 C.E.[55] But W. H. Bates is probably correct to see

---

[51]Ibid., 239.

[52]Ibid., 243-50.

[53]Ibid., 250.

[54]*Martyrdom of Apollonius* 8.

[55]"The Prayer of St. Polycarp," 128. In Polycarp's prayer we find a progression of ideas which parallels the concluding petitions of the papyrus: mention of being granted "a share in the number of the martyrs" followed by a petition for the acceptance of the sacrifice. Polycarp's prayer, however, is a literary production tailored to his situation. He is the sacrifice and he now has a share in the number of the martyrs. What we find, therefore, as a petition in the Strasbourg Papyrus—for "a part and lot with the fair"—becomes a thanksgiving in Polycarp's prayer. The petitionary section in Polycarp then continues from this point with a petition for acceptance, followed by a concluding blessing.

this as an *inclusio* which frames the petitions by returning to the theme of thanksgiving, this time the thanksgiving of the saints at the heavenly altar, and leads into the final doxology. "In the intercessions themselves the thread of the *eucharistia* is not lost, but is carried right through to the conclusion of the prayer. It ends where we have been taught to seek its ending, in the prayers of the saints and the worship of heaven."[56] The orientation toward the heavenly worship begins with the petitions for "those who are asleep" and for "a part and a lot" with the saints. This concluding eschatological focus culminating in thanksgiving may also have a precedent in Jewish public prayer. In the Eighteen Blessings, for example, in both Palestinian and Babylonian recensions, the final petitions ask for the coming of the messianic age: for the rebuilding of Jerusalem, for the restoration of the reign of David, that the prayers of the worshipers may be heard, and for the restoration of the liturgy on Zion. Each petitionary blessing in these prayers had to end with praise, and the whole prayer with thanksgiving.[57]

CONCLUSIONS

The community which prayed the prayer of the Strasbourg Papyrus was steeped in Jewish Wisdom tradition and thoroughly familiar with the forms of Jewish prayer. At the same time, however, it had a strong desire to separate itself from Judaism. For this it had recourse to Malachi 1:11, a passage often used in the second century to distinguish Christian from Jewish worship. All this indicates a Christian worship tradition sufficiently close to its Jewish roots to provoke an identity crisis, a situation characteristic of the second century. Apart from some minor emendations in the petitions,[58] and possibly the "trinitarian" formula of the first transition,[59] nothing precludes a second-century dating for the prayer in the Strasbourg Papyrus. Indeed, such a dating seems probable.

We have seen that the prayer follows the bipartite structure of Jewish prayer studied by Giraudo, with the two basic elements of praise

[56]"Thanksgiving and Intercession in the Liturgy of St. Mark," 119.

[57]Heinemann, *Prayer in the Talmud*, 18. Texts in Lucien Deiss, *Springtime of the Liturgy* (Collegeville: The Liturgical Press, 1979) 7–14.

[58]For example, the petition for "our orthodox fathers and bishops everywhere" may belong to the fourth century. See Cuming, *The Liturgy of St. Mark*, xxvi.

[59]Although a very similar, possibly related, formula is found in the second-century *Martyrdom of Polycarp*.

and petition. At the same time, however, it is possible to make out the outlines of three distinct units, with two clear, if somewhat awkward, hinges where they are joined: "through whom to you and with him [and] with the Holy Spirit giving thanks we offer . . ." and "over which sacrifice and offering we pray and beseech you: Remember. . . ." There is no necessary contradiction here. Jewish statutory prayer often used blessings in series while retaining the basic ingredients of praise and petition. The chief prayer of the synagogue service, the Eighteen Blessings, for example, was composed of praise and petition, in that order, but each element was distributed over several *berakoth*. The *Birkat ha-mazon* distributes its praise over two sections.[60] The prayer tradition behind the Strasbourg Papyrus apparently did the same. The papyrus, however, shows a marked tendency to smooth out the points of transition. What were once possibly concluding formulas are now formulas which tie the sections of the prayer together. It is this tendency which gives the concluding doxology such an air of finality.

The transition formulas are very important to the structure of the prayer. They give the prayer a narrativity which it may not have originally had. There is a real sense of movement, of descent and ascent, in the prayer. Creation comes down from God and is offered back up to God. The weld between the first two strophes forms the hinge, the defining point in which the movement changes direction: this point is Christ. The second join continues the upward movement initiated in the offering, tying the petitions to the praise. There is a sense in which the petitions are also part of the offering, as we saw in Origen: "To Him to whom we offer . . . we also send up our prayers 'having a great high priest, that is passed into the heavens, Jesus the Son of God.'" (By prayer Origen understands something like petition, as he does in his *On Prayer* (14.2): "Prayer is offered in conjuction with praise of God by one who asks in a more solemn manner for greater things.") The upward movement begun in the offering thus continues through the petitions, culminating in the prayers of the saints in heaven.

The prayer of the Strasbourg Papyrus is cosmological in its focus. The prayer's narrative parallels the cosmological Alexandrian vision of salvation as the return to God through the Savior. In its prayer the community of the papyrus joined, here and now, the cosmic

---

[60]*Springtime of the Liturgy,* 7–14.

thanksgiving to the Creator through the Savior. The community's cosmological vision perhaps included a vital sense of its participation in the "bloodless worship" of the heavenly liturgy of angels and saints. This was not a memorialist tradition. The community did not commemorate or re-experience past events, but rather participated in present realities. It therefore had no need in its eucharistic prayer for an anamnesis or an institution narrative. These elements belong to a different worship tradition, one which was more historical in its focus than cosmological. It was this historicizing tradition which came to predominate in the Christian anaphoras of the fourth century and after.

G. J. Cuming

3. The Anaphora of St. Mark:
A Study of Development

The Anaphora of St. Mark (MARK) is notable for several features
which are peculiar to it among Eastern liturgies, differentiating it
from the Syro-Byzantine type which eventually became universal in
the Orthodox Churches, and is exemplified in the other official Coptic anaphoras, *St. Basil* and *St. Gregory*. These features are not periph-
eral eccentricities such as may be found here and there in the
Ethiopic anaphoras: they are of such importance for the structure of
the prayer as to suggest considerable antiquity, certainly no less and
probably greater than that of the Syro-Byzantine type. Furthermore,
this indication of antiquity is supported by fragments preserved on
papyrus, parchment, earthenware, and even on wood, which make it
possible to reconstruct the text as it was at a far earlier date than that
of the medieval manuscripts which are the main evidence for most of
the great liturgies, and thus to throw light on the development of the
anaphora at a very early stage.

There are four manuscripts of the medieval Greek text: a roll at the
University of Messina (twelfth century, incomplete); Vatican gr 1970
(also twelfth century) and 2281 (A.D. 1207); and a copy of an old manuscript made in 1585–6 known as Pegas, from the patriarch who had it
copied.[1] They present few variants of importance for the present purpose; compared with the early fragments, they show increasingly the
influence of the anaphora of St. James.

The Coptic version is still one of the official anaphoras of the Coptic Church, under the name of St. Cyril, and manuscripts of medieval

---

[1] The first three in C. A. Swainson, *The Greek Liturgies* (Cambridge: Cambridge
University Press, 1884) 25–58; "Pegas," ed. N. Kephalas, in *Theologia* 26 (1955)
23–31.

and later origin abound.[2] The relationship between this version and the Greek is one of considerable complexity. Each contains passages, phrases, and single words which do not appear in the other; and the removal of all such material from either text provides a rough and ready way of restoring it to the state in which it was before the council of Chalcedon. But R.-G. Coquin has pointed out[3] that each version continued to borrow from the other to some extent for many years after the split, so that some of what remains after the process of pruning has been carried out may really fall within the category of later borrowing rather than of original common material. Sometimes also it may be a case of one version retaining what the other has omitted, rather than making an independent addition. Other criteria, such as doctrinal content and affinities with other sources, may need to be applied. In general, it seems safe to say that when the Greek text differs from the Coptic version, the latter is likely to have preserved the earlier reading. The early fragments almost always support the Coptic against the Greek.

The consensus of the medieval Greek and Coptic manuscripts is referred to below as TR *(textus receptus);* where they differ, the Greek text is referred to as TR(G), and the Coptic as TR(C).

The Ethiopic version was clearly made at an advanced stage in the development of MARK, and does not require further comment here.

Of the early fragments, three will be called in evidence below. The earliest is the Strasbourg Papyrus (hereafter S), whose editors cautiously conclude that "there is no apparent reason why PGr 254 should not belong to the fifth century, or even to the fourth." As will appear, the text it contains may well be much older. The other two fragments are the Rylands Library parchment (R) and the wooden tablet in the British Museum published by H. Quecke (Q).[4] The former, written in the sixth century, begins immediately after the *Sanctus*

[2]E. Renaudot, *Liturgiarum Orientalium Collectio* (Frankfurt, 1847) 1:39–48; F. E. Brightman, *Liturgies Eastern and Western* (Oxford: Clarendon, 1896) 164-80; R. G. Coquin, "L'anaphore alexandrine de saint Marc," *Le Muséon* 82 (1969) 307–56. The last-named authoritative article opened a new chapter in the study of MARK. Though I cannot accept all the author's conclusions, I am deeply indebted to his full and lucid presentation of the evidence.

[3]Coquin, "L'anaphore," 311.

[4]M. Andrieu and P. Collomp, "Fragments sur papyrus de l'anaphore de saint Marc," *Revue des sciences religieuses* 8 (1928) 489–515; C. H. Roberts, ed., *Catalogue of the Greek and Latin Papyri in the John Rylands Library* (Manchester: Manchester

and runs to the end of the anaphora; the latter is a Coptic translation, written (or rather, scratched) in the eighth century, which starts at the same point but does not go quite so far. It is, however, better preserved than R; and both give the text in a much earlier form than TR, with small differences which show clearly how an almost continuous process of touching-up must have been going on. Neither includes a lengthy list of attributes of the Holy Spirit found in TR.[5] If this is related to the condemnation of the Pneumatomachi in 381, it would seem likely that the text of Q and R may be dated to the fourth century, Q being perhaps thirty to fifty years earlier than R.

Besides the fragments, there are also various relevant texts more or less closely related to MARK. They raise problems of dating which must be discussed before any use is made of them. They are *The Prayers of Sarapion*, the Deir Balyzeh Papyrus (SB), and the Coptic papyrus fragment (L) which J. Lefort published just before it perished in a fire at Louvain University.[6] When Sarapion's prayers were first published in the 1890s, their authenticity was assumed, which gave a firm dating (by liturgiological standards) of c. 360. This dating was challenged in 1964 by Dom Bernard Botte,[7] who argued that the author of the prayers was an Arian, and therefore could not have been the friend of Athanasius; the collection could by 50 or 100 years later than Sarapion. This argument has been widely accepted, and scholars often now refer to "pseudo-Sarapion." I have ventured elsewhere[8] to suggest that Botte's argument is not entirely convincing, and that a case can still be made out for the authorship of the historical Sarapion. The question of his orthodoxy is important insofar as it bears on the dating of the prayers, which is highly relevant for the dating of the evolution of MARK. Sarapion's anaphora contains passages in common with MARK (*Sanctus* and institution narrative) in a form which is demonstrably earlier than that of TR, or even Q and R. It is not enough to say, as Coquin does,[9] "The liberties which the

University Press, 1938) 3:25–8; H. Quecke, "Ein saïdische Zeuge der Markusliturgie," *OCP* 37 (1971) 40–54.

[5]Brightman, *Liturgies Eastern and Western*, 134, lines 1–8.

[6]These texts are conveniently collected in A. Hänggi and I. Pahl, eds., *Prex Eucharistica*, Specilegium Friburgense 12 (Fribourg, 1968) 116–33; ET in *PEER*, 74–81.

[7]B. Botte, "L'Eucologe de Serapion est-il authentique?" *OC* 48 (1964) 50–7.

[8]G. J. Cuming, "Thmuis Revisited: Another Look at the Prayers of Bishop Sarapion," *TS* 41 (1980) 568–75.

[9]Coquin, "L'anaphore," 326.

author has taken . . . with the Alexandrian tradition are well known": Sarapion is in fact the earliest witness for these parts of MARK.

The date of DB is even less easy to determine. The most recent editors place the writing of the papyrus at the end of the sixth century; but opinions differ widely about the date of the contents. The anaphora shares a common ancestry with MARK, but has developed along different lines. The presence of a prayer from the *Didache* which also appears in Sarapion and in AC suggests a similar date for the papyrus text, i.e. the second half of the fourth century.

The sixth-century Coptic fragment from Louvain is too brief to allow any firm dating on the basis of its content.

To this group of related sources may be added the Jerusalem *Catecheses Mystagogicae*, whether they are by Cyril or John. I have argued elsewhere[10] that they point to a liturgy which is basically Egyptian in structure and content, though already showing signs of strong Syrian influence. To summarize my arguments, Cyril's liturgy has a consecratory epiclesis following immediately after the *Sanctus:* so does MARK. Cyril deals with the preface at length, but makes no mention of any christological passage: the latter is a prominent feature of JAS, but is totally absent from MARK. The same is true of *Benedictus qui venit.* The *Catecheses* have have numerous textual agreements with TR(C), DB, and Sarapion, as against TR(G); and finally, Cyril's baptism service is definitely not Syrian in character. From this it follows that, while there are passages in TR which are undoubtedly taken from JAS at a late date, other passages, in which the verbal coincidence is less than total, may derive from a common ancestor and have been developed in different ways; for example, the second epiclesis (see p. 70). Above all, S or something like it may be an ancestor of JAS.

After this lengthy but essential survey of the material, it is at last possible to begin the consideration of the peculiar features of MARK. They are:

The presence of an offering in the preface.
The position of the intercessions before the *Sanctus.*
The absence of *Benedictus* and of any christological thanksgiving.
The presence of an epiclesis immediately after the *Sanctus,* with "fill" as a link-word rather than "holy."

[10]G. J. Cuming, "Egyptian Elements in the Jerusalem Liturgy," *JTS* 25 (1974) 117–24.

The introduction of the anamnesis by "proclaiming" rather than "remembering."
The inclusion of a second epiclesis.

THE POSITION OF THE INTERCESSIONS
It will be convenient to begin by considering this problem, since
scholars usually assume that the Syrian sequence of preface and
Sanctus is the norm, and that consequently in MARK the intercesions
are an irregular interpolation. Coquin writes: "These formulas bru-
tally interrupt the development of the anaphora."[11] But no scholar
has offered a convincing reason why the intercessions should have
been interpolated *here*. If they had previously taken place before the
anaphora, a reviser would have inserted them after the second epiclesis, just as in Syro-Byzantine anaphoras. The beginning of such an
insertion can actually be seen in Sarapion, where the bulk of the intercessions is contained in prayers said before the anaphora begins,
but the diptychs are read after the second epiclesis, followed by
prayer for the dead and an embryonic intercession. On the other
hand, if the intercessions were already at the end of the anaphora,
there would have been no conceivable reason for moving them to the
beginning. The inference is that they have always been where they
are in S and remain in TR.

It is true that in TR(G) they do not have any close connection with
what precedes and follows them. The preface ends with a quotation
from Malachi (1:11), thus:

"In every place incense is offered to your holy Name and a pure
offering, ἐπιθυσία καὶ προσφορά."[12]

After this, the intercessions begin baldly, "And we pray . . ." The last
three words of the preface are not in the text of Malachi, and add
nothing to the sense. Further, the word ἐπιθυσία is unknown to classical and patristic Greek lexicons. Even the verb ἐπιθύω is very rare.

But in S the intercessions are carefully dovetailed into the preface
and into the doxology with which they end. In the papyrus there is a
colon at the end of the Malachi quotation, ". . . a pure offering"; then

---

[11]Coquin, "L'anaphore," 313; cf. G. Dix, *The Shape of the Liturgy* (London: Dacre,
1945) 218.
[12]Brightman, *Liturgies Eastern and Western*, 126, lines 9–10.

follows εφηθυσια και προσφορα,[13] which is most naturally read as dative, "over which sacrifice and offering," leading straight on to the beginning of the intercessions, "we pray and beseech you . . ." "Ms 1970" has inserted an "And" before "we pray" which is not in S, trying to remedy its mistake in copying by interpolating the text. Confirmation of the reading of S at this point is provided by TR(C):

"And over this sacrifice and offering we pray and beseech you . . ."[14]

and the Jerusalem *Catecheses:*

"Over that sacrifice of propitiation we beseech . . ."[15]

There are two difficulties in the reading ἐφ' ᾗ θυσία . . .: first, the sequence of preposition—relative pronoun—noun is fairly rare (which may be the reason for the scribal alteration); but it is not unknown: 1 Peter has περὶ ἧς σωτ ρίας and Sarapion δι' ὂυ σταυροῦ.[16] The other is the use of the dative after ἐπί to mean "over" (Cyril uses the genitive). But Luke 15:7 has χαρά . . . ἐπὶ ἑνὶ ἁμαρτωλῷ; and in any case such distinctions tend to become blurred in the manuscripts. Significantly, the three main manuscripts of TR(G) (the Messina roll is lacking here) read ἐπὶ θυσία καὶ προσφόρα, even though attaching the word to the previous sentence rather than the succeeding, in which position the dative makes no sense at all. This suggests that the correct reading had not been altogether lost to sight.

Similarly, the doxology with which S concludes grows naturally out of the preceding intercessions:

"Receive (?) . . . their entreaties . . . Grant them (spiritual gifts?) through our Lord, through whom be glory to you to the ages of ages."

Compare the abrupt new start in TR:

"For you are above all rule . . ."

But however early the present position of the intercessions may be, it remains an unusual position: apart from Justin, Hippolytus, and

[13]Andrieu and Collomp, "Fragments," 494, 493; on p. 500 a full-stop is inserted which does not appear on p. 493.

[14]Brightman, *Liturgies Eastern and Western,* 165, line 19.

[15]MC 5.8.

[16]1 Peter 1:10; F. E. Brightman, "The Sacramentary of Serapion of Thmuis," *JTS* 1 (1900) 265 (Prayer 16 = Funk XXV).

Sarapion, who have them outside the anaphora, the normal place in later anaphoras is at the end, "in the presence of the most holy and dread sacrifice."[17] One possible explanation of the Marcan position is that S is in effect a Christian *berakah*, beginning with praise and thanksgiving, passing on to intercession, and ending with a doxology. This possibility is much enhanced if the single leaf which the fragments constitute was complete in itself when new. If there were originally further pages containing the rest of the anaphora as we know it, no fresh light is thrown on the position of the intercessions, and in addition the presence of the doxology has to be explained. But on the supposition that the leaf contained the whole of the prayer, and that the next leaf, if there was one, began with another prayer, then the suggestion of a *berakah* becomes less surprising. Admittedly, it is on a larger scale than the *berakoth* of the Eighteen Benedictions; but so is the *Birkat-ha-mazon,* which Louis Ligier puts forward as a likely source of the Christian eucharistic prayer.[18] This also begins with blessing, continues with intercession, and ends with a brief doxology. The keyword of the Passover embolism in that *berakah* is "remembrance," and the first word of the intercessions in S is μνήσθητι, while over the page comes the phrase τὴν ὑπόμνησιν ποιούμεθα. On the other hand, if S seems too short for a Christian anaphora, it may be pointed out that, if the leaf had survived intact, the prayer would be longer than the anaphora of the *Apostolic Tradition.*

THE PURE SACRIFICE

Into this Jewish framework is inserted the Christian idea of a "pure sacrifice," the exact nature of which will be discussed later. At this stage, the important point is that the offering leads into the intercessions, which begin with prayer for the church (and this is equally true of the Syro-Byzantine type of anaphora). The result is a prayer consisting of thanksgiving for creation, offering, intercession, and doxology. A comparison of S with the earliest forms of prayer and writers about the eucharist reveals a marked similarity of content and, to some extent, structure.

---

[17]MC 5.9.

[18]L. Liger, "De la cène du Seigneur à l'Eucharistie," *Assemblées du Seigneur,* 2nd series, I (1966) 19–57; ET, "From the Last Supper to the Eucharist," in L. C. Sheppard, ed., *The New Liturgy* (London: DLT, 1970) 113–50.

A similar order is evident in the *Didache*, where thanksgiving for creation is followed by prayer for the church and a doxology. The verse from Malachi is also referred to, though not included in the prayers. So too in Justin's *Apology*, "we bless the maker of all things through his Son Jesus Christ and the holy Spirit over all that we receive" (or "offer"), and the president sends up prayers and thanksgiving to which "the people give their assent by saying Amen," which surely implies a doxology; and in his *Dialogue* Justin speaks of giving thanks to God "for creating the world with all things that are in it," and quotes Malachi as foretelling the Christian offering.[19] In Irenaeus the church offers to its maker "a new offering," again as foretold by Malachi; and "there is an altar in heaven, to which our prayers and offerings are directed." He stresses the importance of the doxology,[20] as does Tertullian, who likewise quotes Malachi.[21] The prayer in I Clement 59 passes from an address to the Creator to a series of intercessions which later found their way into TR and DB. Hippolytus's thanksgiving is christocentric, but he does include an offering of the gifts leading into prayer for the church and a doxology.[22]

Thus all the four elements of S are abundantly paralleled in these early sources, and it may well be that the text of S in fact goes back to the second century. The use of Malachi in particular is characteristic of this century. The one element in the sources quoted above which is not found in S is the thanksgiving for Christ's work of redemption, but this remains absent throughout the whole history of MARK. An opportunity to insert it occurred later, but was not taken. At a date which is unlikely to have been earlier than 500, a passage from the postsanctus of JAS dealing with the Fall and its remedy through the Law and the prophets was inserted into the preface of MARK. JAS goes on to the sending of Jesus Christ, and the interpolator of MARK could have done the same. Instead, he breaks off and substitutes a sentence of his own, turning towards the offering.[23] Evidently the lack of any reference to the redeeming work of Christ was recognized, but not regarded as a deficiency. This is in line with the general Alexandrian tendency to play down the incarnate life of Christ.

---

[19]*Apol.* 67.2,5; *Dial.* 41.1; 117.2.
[20]*Adv. Haer.* 4.29,31; 1.1.5.
[21]*De Spect.* 25.5.
[22]AT 4.4–13.
[23]Brightman, *Liturgies Eastern and Western,* 125, lines 25–31; cf. 51, lines 13–17.

The absence of an epiclesis of the holy Spirit is understandable, since consecration was still regarded as effected by thanksgiving.

S, then, is a complete eucharistic prayer. It may seem to lack several essential ingredients, but that is to judge it by fourth-century standards. Again, the intercessions may seem to occupy a disproportionate amount of space, but in relation to the rest of the prayer, they are no longer than the intercessions in TR or JAS.

THE SANCTUS

The next step in the development of the anaphora was most probably the addition of the Sanctus, with its usual introduction (presanctus). The idea of the Sanctus being a very early part of the anaphora probably drew its chief support from an apparent quotation from the liturgy in I Clement. But W. C. van Unnik[24] showed to the satisfaction of the great majority of scholars that the context of Clement's phrase, though undoubtedly liturgical, was not eucharistic. In several early liturgies the presanctus and Sanctus appear to be intrusions; and others, such as the Apostolic Tradition, seem never to have included them at all.[25] And if the presanctus and Sanctus were substituted for the doxology of S, the reason for the unusual position of the intercessions in TR becomes apparent: far from being "interpolated" into a pre-existing unit of preface and Sanctus, they had always been part of the prayer from the start, and it is the Sanctus which is the newcomer.

There seems to be a generally held opinion that the introduction of the Sanctus into the anaphora first took place in Egypt. Whoever first proposed this theory, in England it certainly owes its authority to the writings of Dom Gregory Dix. In The Shape of the Liturgy (1945)[26] he states that Origen provides "the earliest certain evidence of the use of the Sanctus in the liturgy," and refers the reader to an article of 1938. On examination, his case turns out to rest on two references in De Principiis,[27] which both quote the interpretation of the two seraphim of the Sanctus given to Origen by his Hebrew teacher. But the first of these two references does not quote Isaiah's words at all, while the

[24]W. C. van Unnik, "I Clement 34 and the Sanctus," Vigiliae Christianae 5 (1951) 204–48.

[25]Other examples are the fragmentary anaphora of St. Epiphanius of Salamis and the second of the so-called "Mai fragments," in Hänggi and Pahl, Prex Eucharistica, 262–3, 422.

[26]Dix, Shape, 165.

[27]G. Dix, "Primitive Consecration Prayers," Theology 38 (1938) 261–83.

second gives them, not in their liturgical form, "heaven and earth," but in their biblical form, "the whole earth," so that almost certainly Origen had Isaiah in mind, rather than the liturgy. Nor is there anything liturgical in the context. (Dix himself in 1938 had said only: "It begins to look as though . . .").

At Jerusalem, on the other hand, the preface of JAS, instead of thanking God for creation, speaks of creation itself, and especially the heavenly bodies, "hymning" God, which almost demands the immediate introduction of the *Sanctus*. In such anaphoras as *Addai and Mari* and the Egyptian BAS, which have no reference to heavenly bodies, the *Sanctus* has much more the appearance of a later addition. In S the thanksgiving for creation again makes no reference to heavenly bodies, but specifies "seas and rivers," as is natural in Egypt. It then leads rapidly by way of the creation of man to the offering of the "reasonable sacrifice" over which intercession is to be made, and thence to the intercessions themselves. In TR the *Sanctus* has to wait until they are completed, and is then added with only the weakest attempt at a connecting link.

THE FIRST EPICLESIS

After the *Sanctus* JAS turns to thanksgiving for the incarnation, life, and works of Jesus Christ, and, in order to make a smooth transition to this section, appends *Benedictus qui venit* to the *Sanctus*. MARK, as has been said, has no christological thanksgiving, and therefore does not need to introduce the *Benedictus*. Instead, it takes quite a different turn. TR, Sarapion, and DB agree in following the *Sanctus* with an epiclesis linked to the word "full" which begins its last sentence, "Full are heaven and earth of your glory"; and they are supported by Q and R, which begin here, though they do not include the *Sanctus* itself. It may be assumed that the epiclesis was added either simultaneously with the *Sanctus,* or at a later date: it is hard to imagine an existing epiclesis being modified to fit so closely on to the end of the *Sanctus*.

In the epiclesis God is asked to "fill this sacrifice" with his blessing; and the question arises, what is being offered in "this sacrifice"? The first mention of sacrifice is made in the preface:

"You made everything through . . . Jesus Christ, through whom . . . we give thanks to you and offer this reasonable sacrifice and blood-less service, which all the nations offer you . . . In every place incense is offered to your holy Name and a pure sacrifice. Over which sacrifice and offering we pray . . ."

This is the text of S, and TR(C) reproduces it; probably TR(G) did so too originally, though it now omits the word "sacrifice" after "reasonable."

The passage has two scriptural sources, Romans 12:1 and Malachi 1:11. The offering asked for by St. Paul is a self-offering, "a living sacrifice . . . your reasonable (λογικήν) service." In the liturgies the nouns and adjectives are switched round in various ways. The result of comparing the permutations is to suggest that *in this context* θυσία, λάτρεια, and προσφορά are largely interchangeable; but a new term, "bloodless" (ἀναίμακτος), makes its appearance. This adjective, which became a constant feature of liturgical writing, is first found in Athenagoras, c. 177, who speaks of "bloodless sacrifice . . . the reasonable service,"[28] using it to make a simple contrast with the bloody sacrifices of the pagans. But Origen applies it specifically to a *verbal* sacrifice, "continually offering bloodless sacrifices in his prayers to God"[29]; and so does the *Martyrium Apollonii:* "I send up the bloodless and pure sacrifice . . . which is through prayers."[30] The martyrdom took place c. 185, and this sentence at any rate, with its echoes of Justin, is quite congruous with that date. The content of the sacrifice is now seen as prayer rather than self-offering.

A similar ambiguity appears in the interpretation of the verse from Malachi. In the *Didache* this is taken to refer to self-offering,[31] in Tertullian to prayer,[32] and in Irenaeus to the eucharist.[33] Justin also applies it to the eucharist, though he goes on to say, "Prayers and thanksgivings made by worthy men are the only sacrifices that are perfect and well-pleasing to God."[34] The thought has moved on

[28]*Legatio* 13.3.

[29]*Contra Celsum* 8.21; for further details, see C. F. Evans, "Romans 12.1-2: The True Worship," in C. K. Barrett et al., *Dimensions de la vie chrétienne* (Rome: Abbaye de S. Paul, 1979) 7–49; R.P.C. Hanson, *Eucharistic Offering in the Early Church* (Nottingham: Grove Books, 1979), also in *Proceedings of the Royal Irish Academy* 76 (1976) 75–95.

[30]Ch. 8.

[31]14.1–3.

[32]*Adv. Marc.* 3.22.6.

[33]*Adv. Marc.* 4.29.5.

[34]*Dial.* 117.2.

again, now to the gifts, but without abandoning the idea of prayer. But the personal element does not completely disappear: DB reads: "Fill *us* with your *glory*," and L "that glory wherewith you glorified us." And it seems likely that some overtones of the sacrifice of praise and thanksgiving remained.

In any case, the bread and wine were already on the altar when the preface was spoken; and the most likely interpretation of the offering in S is that it covers both thanksgiving and the gifts. Sacrifice here means placing the gifts on the altar and giving thanks over them; and both thanksgiving and gifts are to be filled with blessing.

Sarapion probably has the same conception of sacrifice, although he does not mention the word in his preface; but he does use the Romans phrase in the past tense after the epiclesis, where it gives the grounds for the invocation:

"For we have offered to you this living sacrifice, this bloodless offering."

"We have offered" after the *Sanctus* is equivalent to "we offer" in the preface of S. It seems likely, then, that Q and R also mean "this sacrifice" to refer to the offering in the preface, though they do not make the connection unmistakable.

THE SECOND EPICLESIS

The further question arises, what was to be the result of filling the sacrifice with blessing? As long as the content of the sacrifice was a self-offering or a prayer, the answer is straightforward: the self-offering was to be made effective, the prayer to be heard (cf. Sarapion's "Make us living men"). But when the sacrifice began to be understood as the offering of the gifts, different consequences are expected, and different theologies appear. The new idea of effecting a change in the gifts either takes over the original epiclesis (as in DB and L), or produces a second epiclesis (as in Sarapion and MARK).

For Sarapion, the offering has been made, and the bread and cup are now the likeness of the body and blood of the Only-begotten. In Q and R, and still in TR(G), no consequence is mentioned at this point:

"Fill, O God, this sacrifice also with the blessing from you through your holy Spirit."

But TR(C) continues:

"and in blessing bless, and in sanctifying sanctify,[35] these your precious gifts which have been set before your face, this bread and this cup."

TR(C)'s phrase directs attention to the gifts, and so takes a step towards the unmistakable consecratory epicleses of DB and L:

"Send down your holy Spirit upon these creatures, and make the bread the body of our Lord . . .

"We make the remembrance of his death, offering to you your creatures, this bread and this cup . . . Send out over them your holy Spirit . . . to make (?) the bread the body of Christ . . ."

(It must be remembered that these passages follow immediately after the *Sanctus*.) Here a full conversion theology has been developed.

A parallel development had taken place at Jerusalem, where, in Cyril's time, the *Sanctus* was followed by an epiclesis which asked God to send forth the holy Spirit upon the gifts set before him to make the bread the body of Christ. "The spiritual sacrifice, the bloodless service" was then "perfected," possibly by the recital of the institution narrative.[36]

An epiclesis in similar terms appears in Q, R, and TR, but *after* the institution narrative. This also prays for the conversion of the gifts, but without a fresh offering: the verb is in the aorist, προεθήκαμεν. The relationship between the two epicleses is not clear. The second obviously marks a development in doctrine, but does the first still retain the meaning it had before the addition of the second? Presumably the offering in the preface and the sacrifice of the first epiclesis of MARK can still be thought of as a matter of giving thanks and placing the gifts on the altar, to be filled with the holy Spirit. A. D. Nock put forward a persuasive rationale:

"Πλήρωσον . . . looks forward to the completion of the process of consecration *and makes it clear that something still has to happen:* consecration then follows, at a slower tempo."[37]

---

[35]Coquin, "L'anaphore," 329.

[36]MC 5.8. For "perfecting" (ἀπαρτίζω), see my article (n. 10).

[37]A. D. Nock, "Liturgical Notes: 1. The Anaphora of Serapion," *JTS* 30 (1929) 386; Nock's italics.

But in the case of DB, consecraton follows at once; and in L it is actually embodied in the process of "filling." Nor does Nock explain why two stages were thought necessary or desirable in the first place.

As we have seen, πλήρωσον itself is a second stage, completing the offering made in the preface. MARK thus presents a triple interpretation of the content of the offering as self, thanksgiving, or the gifts. There is a similar development in what happens to the gifts: in S they are simply set on the holy table; then they are to be filled with blessing through the Spirit; and finally they are to be changed into the body and blood of Christ. DB and L certainly present a clearer structure by telescoping the last two stages; but since the preface is lacking from both, it is impossible to say how they regarded the first stage. The one point which is perfectly clear is that in MARK, all through from S to TR, the offering is made in the preface, and thereafter is referred to in the past tense.

At some time after Cyril's episcopate, the epiclesis of JAS was moved from immediately after the *Sanctus* to a place immediately before the intercessions; once again in parallel with developments at Alexandria. As Coquin shows,[38] every word of the brief second epiclesis in Q and R appears in the much longer epiclesis of JAS, of which it is probably the original form.

THE ANAMNESIS

Once the emphasis is placed on the gifts rather than on thanksgiving, the way is clear for the addition of the institution narrative. This is done in Q, R, and TR(G) even more abruptly than that of the *Sanctus:*

"Fill this sacrifice . . . through the descent of your all-holy Spirit. Because our Lord . . ."

TR(C) is much smoother:

"Fill this sacrifice . . . through your holy Spirit, blessing . . . and sanctifying . . . this bread and this cup . . . Because our Lord . . ."

This may well be the original reading, omitted by Q and R after the addition of the second epiclesis, to avoid repetition.

[38]Coquin, "L'anaphore," 352.

A parallel for such an omission occurs in the preface, where TR(C), like S, has "sacrifice" and TR(G) has omitted it, probably for doctrinal reasons.

Sarapion has an equally smooth connection:

"To you have we offered this bread . . . Because the Lord . . ."

There is nothing particularly Egyptian about the institution narrative itself until the end, where all Egyptian sources add 1 Corinthians 11:26:

"For as often as you eat this bread and drink this cup, you proclaim the Lord's death until he comes."

This is put in the first person singular, and treated as part of Jesus's words at the last Supper, "you proclaim *my* death until *I* come." A reference to the resurrection is usually added. In Egypt and Syria, though not further north, the sentence is echoed by a congregational response, "We proclaim . . ." But in Egypt only, the anamnesis is introduced by the word "Proclaiming," whereas elsewhere it is always "Remembering," even though the Pauline comment has intervened since the word "remembrance." The natural inference from this is that the insertion of the verse originated in Egypt, where it is built into the structure of the anaphora, whereas elsewhere it has all the appearance of a late and infelicitous intrusion. Here is yet another instance of material originating in Egypt and migrating elsewhere. It is a clear case of JAS borrowing from MARK.

To sum up:

S is a Christian *berakah*, a complete anaphora, and possibly dates back to the second century.

The intercessions have always been in their present place and are not an interpolation.

The offering was made in the preface and consisted originally of prayer and thanksgiving, but was later applied to the gifts.

The *Sanctus* replaced the original doxology, and the rest of the anaphora was built up gradually by additions after the *Sanctus*.

The intention to "change" the gifts is a later development, producing the second epiclesis.

The use of the Pauline comment to introduce the anamnesis originated in Egypt.

These conclusion have been to some extent anticipated by Lietz-mann[39] and Dix,[40] but their arguments are based solely on Sarapion, and are therefore less soundly based. Lietzmann could not know S, and Dix, though aware of its existence, made very little use of it. What all the conclusions point to is that MARK as found in S is a very early example of an anaphora, certainly as early as *Sharar* or E-BAS, and possibly as early as the *Apostolic Tradition* or even Justin.

Finally, if I am right in regarding S as a complete anaphora and in seeing a close connection between MARK and JAS in their early stages, it becomes possible to make a conjectural reconstruction of the development of *both* anaphoras.

The first stage for both is represented by S.

Then the two prayers begin to diverge with the introduction of the *Sanctus:* at Alexandria it was substituted for the doxology; at Jerusalem it was inserted at the end of the preface.

In both anaphoras, epiclesis and institution narrative were added after the *Sanctus.* This produced at Alexandria the sequence Preface—offering—intercessions—*Sanctus*—epiclesis—institution narrative; at Jerusalem, Preface—*Sanctus*—epiclesis—institution narrative—offering—intercessions. The latter corresponds with the order of events in the *Catecheses Mystagogicae.*

Lastly, at Alexandria a second epiclesis is added after the institution narrative, and the anaphora is rounded off by a prayer for the fruits of communion; at Jerusalem, perhaps under the influence of BAS, the epiclesis is moved to a place between the offering and the intercessions, and its place is taken by a christological thanksgiving. In both anaphoras the institution narrative is linked to what follows by an anamnesis.

Thus the early fragments of MARK throw light not only on the history of that anaphora, but also make it possible to suggest a logical account of the development of JAS.

[39]H. Lietzmann, *Messe und Herrenmahl* (Berlin, 1926) 196; ET, *Mass and Lord's Supper* (Leiden: Brill, 1953–79) 160.
[40]Dix, *Shape,* 221.

Maxwell E. Johnson

4. The Archaic Nature of the Sanctus, Institution Narrative, and Epiclesis of the Logos in the Anaphora Ascribed to Sarapion of Thmuis

There is no current scholarly consensus on the euchologion or collection of thirty prayers ascribed to Sarapion of Thmuis (c. 339–360)[1] in the eleventh-century Athonite manuscript, MS. Lavra 149. While traditional scholarship tended to regard this collection as an early, authentic, and relatively complete euchologion having paramount importance for the history of Christian liturgy in Egypt,[2] more recent

[1]For texts of the prayers see G. Wobbermin, *Altchristliche liturgische Stücke aus der Kirche Aegyptens nebst einem dogmatischen Brief des Bischofs Serapion von Thmuis,* Texte und Untersuchungen 18/3b (Leipzig and Berlin: Hinrichs, 1898); F. E. Brightman, "The Sacramentary of Serapion," *JTS* 1 (1900) 88–113, 247–77; F. X. Funk, *Didascalia et Constitutiones Apostolorum* 2 (Paderborn: Schoeningh, 1905) 158–95; and J. Quasten, *Monumenta eucharistica et liturgica vetustissima,* Florilegium Patristicum 7 (Bonn: Hanstein, 1935) 135–57. The only complete ET of the Greek text is J. Wordsworth, *Bishop Sarapion's Prayer Book: An Egyptian Sacramentary dated probably about A.D. 350–356* (Hamden: Archon, 1964) On Sarapion of Thmuis in general, see J. Quasten, *Patrology III: The Golden Age of Greek Patristic Literature from the Council of Nicea to the Council of Chalcedon* (Utrecht/Antwerp: Spectrum, 1966) 80–85, and D. Dufrasne, "Sérapion de Thmuis," *Dictionnaire de Spiritualité* 14 (Paris: Beauchesne, 1988) 644–52.

[2]As well as Wobbermin, Brightman, and Wordsworth (previous note), see also P. Drews, "Über Wobermins 'Altchristliche liturgische Stücke aus der Kirche Aegyptens,'" *Zeitschrift für Kirchengeschichte* 20 (1900) 291–328, 415–41; A. Baumstark, "Die Anaphora von Thmuis und ihre Überarbeitung durch den h.l. Serapion," *Römische Quartalschrift* 18 (1904) 123–42; A. D. Nock, "Liturgical Notes 1: The Anaphora of Serapion," JTS 30 (1929) 381–90; and P. E. Roudopolos, "Doctrinal Teaching in the 'Sacramentary' of Serapion of Thmuis," *The Greek Orthodox Theological Review* 9 (1963–64) 201–14; and idem, "The Sacramentary of Serapion. From a thesis for the degree of B. Litt. within the University of Oxford," Θεολογία 28 (1957) 252–75, 420–39, 578–91; 29 (1958) 45–54, 208–17.

work, based primarily on studies of the anaphora alone, has suggested other conclusions altogether. Bernard Capelle, for example, argued that Sarapion's text—especially his epiclesis of the λόγος both in the anaphora and prayer over the baptismal waters—reflects a theologically motivated innovation in relation to the Egyptian liturgical tradition.[3] And Bernard Botte suggested, again primarily on the basis of this epiclesis, that the theological orientation of the document (Semi-Arian or Pneumatomachian) is such that it should be dated fifty to one hundred years later than the time of Sarapion of Thmuis. Hence, it was Botte's opinion that authorship should be ascribed to "Pseudo-Sarapion."[4] While Botte's conclusions have been extremely influential in shaping modern approaches to this collection,[5] the preliminary work of Geoffrey Cuming[6] and my own recent doctoral dissertation on the document[7] have attempted to restore both the traditionally accepted mid-fourth-century date as well as the possibility that Sarapion of Thmuis himself functioned as its editor.

Part of the argument for accepting the traditional date of the prayers is the theological orientation expressed by the formulation of the *Sanctus* unit (i.e., the four introductory petitions, the introduction to the *Sanctus*, the *Sanctus* itself, and its concomitant epiclesis), the bipartite structure of the institution narrative, and the second epiclesis (of the λόγος) in the anaphora. These elements, of course, may be later additions to an earlier eucharistic prayer having a tri-partite anaphoral pattern of praise, offering, and supplication/intercession. Indeed, what Geoffrey Cuming has argued concerning the relationship between the Strasbourg Papyrus and the anaphora described in the late-fourth-century *Catecheses mystagogicae* of Cyril of Jerusalem (or his successor, John) is applicable to Sarapion's anaphora as well. Cuming writes:

[3]B. Capelle, "L'Anaphore de Sérapion. Essai d'exégèse," *Travaux liturgiques* 2 (Louvain 1962) 344–58.

[4]B. Botte, "L'Eucologe de Sérapion est-il authentique?" *OC* 48 (1964) 50–6.

[5]Cf. Dufrasne, "Sérapion de Thmuis," 644–52, and E. Mazza, "L'anaphora di Serapione: una ipostesi di interpretazione," *EL* 95 (1981) 510–28.

[6]G. J. Cuming, "Thmuis Revisited: Another Look at the Prayers of Bishop Sarapion," *TS* 41 (1980) 568–75.

[7]M. Johnson, *The Prayers of Sarapion of Thmuis*, OCA 249 (Rome: Pontificium Institutum Orientale, 1995). A summary of this dissertation appears in idem, "A Fresh Look at the Prayers of Sarapion of Thmuis," *SL* 22 (1992) 163–83.

"*St. Mark* and *St. James* probably had a common ancestor. . . . If we had a papyrus fragment of *St. James*, it would probably contain something very like the Strasbourg papyrus of St. Mark. We do not have such a fragment, but we do have Cyril's *Catecheses*. If *Sanctus* and epiclesis are added to the Strasbourg anaphora, not at the end as in *St. Mark*, but between the thanksgiving and the offering, the result is: thanksgiving—*Sanctus*—epiclesis—offering—intercessions; in fact the exact sequence set out by Cyril. When the Jerusalem anaphora was merged with *St. Basil* to produce *St. James*, the first step would be the addition of institution narrative and anamnesis; then a christological section would take the place of the epiclesis, which would be moved to its Basilian position between the offering and the intercessions; the exact sequence of *St. James*."[8]

This is precisely the *structure* we have in Sarapion's prayer. In the same location that JAS adds the institution narrative and anamnesis Sarapion mixes his bi-partite institution narrative with offering language and includes no formal anamnesis. And between the thanksgiving and offering sections of a Strasbourg-type prayer Sarapion, like Cyril, inserts his *Sanctus* unit with its concomitant epiclesis. Then he ultimately adds a second epiclesis (of the λόγος) between the institution narrative and the intercessions and thus produces the final shape of this prayer. Nevertheless, as will be demonstrated in what follows, these additions are consistent with earlier theological interpretations and eucharistic euchological formulations noted elsewhere within the Egyptian Christian liturgical and theological tradition. On the basis of the structure and theological orientation of these additions a date for this anaphora no later than the mid-fourth century is strongly suggested.

A. THE *SANCTUS*

δεόμεθα ποίησον ἡμᾶς ζῶντας ἀνθρώπους· δός ἡμῖν πνεῦμα φωτός, ἵνα γνῶμεν σὲ τὸν ἀληθινὸν καὶ ὅν ἀπέστειλας Ἰησοῦν Χριστὸν· δὸς ἡυῖν πνεῦμα ἅγιον, ἵνα δυνηθῶμεν ἐξειπεῖν καὶ διηγήσασθαι τὰ

We pray, make us living people. Give us spirit of light, in order that we may know you the true (God) and Jesus Christ whom you sent. Give us holy Spirit, in order that we may be able to proclaim and describe

[8]G. J. Cuming, "The Shape of the Anaphora," *SP* 20 (1989) 341.

ἄρρητά σου μυστήρια. λαλησάτω ἐν ἡμῖν ὁ κύριος Ἰησοῦς καὶ ἅγιον πνεῦμα καὶ ὑμνησάτω σὲ δι᾽ ὑμῶν.

your inexpressible mysteries. Let the Lord Jesus and holy Spirit speak in us and hymn you through us.

Σὺ γὰρ ὁ ὑπεράνω πάσης ἀρχῆς καὶ ἐξουσίας καὶ δυνάμεως καὶ κυριότητος καὶ πάντος ὀνόματος ὀνομαζομένου οὐ μόνον ἐν τῷ αἰῶνι τούτῳ ἀλλὰ καὶ ἐν τῷ μέλλοντι· σοὶ παραστήκουσι χίλιαι χιλιάδες καὶ μύριαι μυριάδες ἀγγέλων ἀρχαγγέλων θρόνων κυριοτήτων ἀρχῶν ἐξουσιῶν· σοὶ παραστήκουσιν τὰ δύο τιμιώτατα σεραφεὶμ ἐξαπτέρυγα, δύσιν μὲν πτέρυξιν καλύπτοντα τὸ πρόσωπον, δύσι δὲ τοὺς πόδας, δύσι δὲ πετόμενα, καὶ ἁγιάζοντα· μεθ᾽ ὧν δέξαι καὶ τὸν ἡμέτερον ἁγιασμὸν λεγόντων Ἅγιος ἅγιος ἅγιος κύριος σαβαώθ πλήρης ὁ οὐρανὸς καὶ ἡ γῆ τῆς δόξης σου.

For you are above all rule and authority and power and dominion and every name which is named, not only in this age but also in the coming one. Beside you stand a thousand thousands and a myriad myriads of angels, archangels, thrones, dominions, principalities and powers. Beside you stand the two most-honored six-winged seraphim. With two wings they cover the face, and with two the feet, and with two they fly, sanctifying. With them receive also our sanctification as we say: Holy, holy, holy Lord of Sabaoth; heaven and earth are full of your glory.

In his 1938 essay, "Primitive Consecration Prayers,"[9] Gregory Dix argued that both Thmuis and Alexandria used variants of the same Egyptian liturgical tradition, which could be dated back to the first half of the third century. In doing so, he called attention to the distinction between the *Sanctus* units of Sarapion and MARK in the use of the singular noun προσωπον. While Sarapion refers to the two "most honored (τιμιώτατα) seraphim" who cover the "face," MARK instead refers to the two "most honored living creatures" (τιμιώτατα ζῶα) before describing the cherubim and seraphim, who with two wings cover the "faces."[10] For an early equation of the two ζῶα with

[9]*Theology* 37 (1938) 261–83.
[10]G. J. Cuming, *The Liturgy of St. Mark*, OCA 234 (Rome: Pontificium Institutum Orientale, 1990) 37–9.

both the seraphim and with the Son and Holy Spirit, Dix cited two passages in the *De principiis* of Origen (written sometime after 217):

"For all knowledge of the Father, when the Son reveals him is made known to us through the Holy Spirit. So that both of these, who in the words of the prophet [Habbakuk 3:2] are called 'animals' or 'living beings' [ζῶα], are the cause of our knowledge of God the Father. For as it is said of the Son that 'no one knoweth the Father but the Son, and he to whom the Son willeth to reveal Him' [Matt 11:27], so in the same way does the apostle speak of the Holy Spirit; 'God hath revealed them unto us by his Spirit: for the Spirit searcheth all things, even the deep things of God'" (*De principiis* I. 3, 4).[11]

"My Hebrew teacher also used to teach as follows, that since the beginning or the end of all things could not be comprehended by any except our Lord Jesus Christ and the Holy Spirit, this was the reason why Isaiah spoke of there being in the vision that appeared to him two seraphim only, who with two wings cover the face of God, with two cover his feet, and with two fly, crying one to another and saying 'Holy, holy, holy is the Lord of hosts; the whole earth is full of thy glory' [Isa 6:2-3]. For because the two seraphim alone have their wings over the face of God and over his feet, we may venture to declare that neither the armies of the holy angels nor the holy thrones, nor the dominions, nor principalities, nor powers can wholly know the beginnings of all things and the ends of the universe" (*De principiis* IV. 3, 14).[12]

According to Dix, then, while some anti-Arian editing is probably present in the final shape of Sarapion's text, the parallels with Origen—e.g., the revelatory activity of the Father and the Son, the common use of Matthew 11:27, and the idea of the telling forth of God's "inexpressible mysteries" by the power of the Holy Spirit—demonstrate that the introduction to the *Sanctus* is "a traditional Egyptian arrangement."[13] Furthermore, including Origen's reference to Colossians 1:16 in close relationship to the *Sanctus*, he concluded that:

[11]Origène, *Traité des principes*, ed. H. Crouzel, M. Simonetti, SC 252 (Paris: Cerf, 1978) 148–50; ET from G. W. Butterworth, *Origen on First Principles* (London: SPCK, 1936) 32.

[12]Origène, *Traité des principes*, ed. H. Crouzel, M. Simonetti, SC 268 (Paris: Cerf, 1980) 394; ET Butterworth, *Origen on First Principles*, 311.

[13]Dix, "Primitive Consecration Prayers" (n. 9 above) 274.

"We can now see that *Sarapion's* Preface still faithfully reflects the old idea that the wings of the Seraphim veil *'The* Face' (i.e., of God), while *St. Mark* was adapted to the later notion of *'their* faces.' And *Sarapion's* . . . reference to 'the Lord Jesus speaking in us and the Holy Spirit hymning Thee through us' (i.e., in the *Sanctus*), still carries on the old idea of that hymn as sung to the glory of the Father primarily *by the Son and the Holy Ghost themselves.*"[14]

This portion of Sarapion's anaphora, therefore, according to Dix, stood, in substance at least, in the third-century rite of Alexandria, and traces of this older tradition remained not only in the overall structure of the Egyptian anaphora but especially in the reference to the τιμιώτατα ζῷα "even after they had been degraded into angels" in the interests of trinitarian orthodoxy.[15]

This conclusion was presupposed in Dix's classic study, *The Shape of the Liturgy*, first published in 1945. Here he claimed further that the *Sanctus* and its introduction were interpolated into the local liturgy of Thmuis from Alexandria where they were already used within the eucharistic liturgy in the first half of the third century. From Alexandria then their use spread to the rest of Egypt, "and ultimately all over christendom."[16] It was thus Dix's opinion that the universal anaphoral use of the *Sanctus* had an Alexandrian origin.

This conclusion, however, is far from certain. It is clear that parallels between Sarapion and MARK and parallels between Sarapion and the Deir-Balyzeh Papyrus[17] against MARK do suggest that Sarapion represents an earlier form of MARK. And, it seems clear that there is some kind of common theological thread running between Sarapion and the *De principiis* of Origen in this context. But it can by no means be considered a proven fact that Origen knew an anaphoral *Sanctus* in the first half of the third century or that the anaphoral *Sanctus* itself had its origins in the Alexandrian liturgical tradition. Cuming rightly noted that the references to the *Sanctus* in Origen's *De principiis* I and IV are references to the biblical *Sanctus* of Isaiah 6:2-3 (i.e., "the whole earth is full of his glory") and not to the liturgical text (i.e., "heaven and earth . . ."), "so that almost certainly Origen had

---

[14]Ibid., 275.

[15]Ibid., 276.

[16]Dix, *The Shape of the Liturgy* (London: Dacre, 1945) 165.

[17]For the text of the Deir-Balizeh Papyrus see A. Hänggi and I. Pahl, eds., *Prex Eucharistica*, Specilegium Friburgense 12 (Fribourg, 1968) 124–7.

Isaiah in mind, rather than the liturgy."[18] Along similar lines Georg Kretschmar claims that Origen does not refer to an anaphoral *Sanctus,* but that Origen's theology strongly influenced its particular shape and interpretation when it finally came to be added to the Alexandrian anaphoral structure. According to him, the relationship between the Egyptian *Sanctus* and Origen's theology is so strong that only a bishop influenced by his theology could have introduced it into the anaphora. This, he concludes, must have happened in the second half of the third century, and so is probably the work of Dionysius the Great, who was bishop of Alexandria from 247–64.[19]

Recent scholarship on the origins of the *Sanctus* in Christian eucharistic liturgy has challenged further Dix's influential assumption that Alexandria was the place where the *Sanctus* began to be used and from where it passed into universal Christian anaphoral use. In 1980, Bryan Spinks reopened the question of the possible influence of Jewish synagogue morning prayer upon the developing Christian anaphoral structure—most notably the *Yotzer Or* benediction with its accompanying *Qedushah*—and suggested third-century Aramaic speaking East Syrian Christianity, as represented by (W. Macomber's reconstructed text of) the anaphora of *Addai and Mari,* to be the place of origin.[20] But the first indisputed references to the use of the *Sanctus* in the eucharistic liturgy—as well as in a non-eucharistic setting— have been discovered by H.-J. auf der Maur in the paschal vigil homilies (c. 337) of Asterios Sophistes of Cappadocia (in the region of Antioch).[21] Noting this important discovery Thomas Talley concludes:

". . . that the Christian synagogue had adopted forms including *Sanctus* for morning prayer, such forms as we find in *Ap. Const.* 7:35 and *Te Deum,* and that it was from such Christian usage rather than

---

[18]G. J. Cuming, "The Anaphora of St. Mark: A Study in Development," *Le Muséon* 95 (1982) 123 [above, 66].

[19]G. Kretschmar, *Studien zum frühchristlichen Trinitätstheologie* (Tübingen: Mohr, 1956) 164.

[20]B. Spinks, "The Jewish Liturgical Sources for the *Sanctus,*" *The Heythrop Journal* 21 (1980) 178–9. See also idem, "The Original Form of the Anaphora of the Apostles: A Suggestion in the Light of Maronite Sharar," *EL* 91 (1977) 146–61.

[21]H.-J. auf der Maur, *Die Osterhomilien des Asterios Sophistes als Quelle für die Geschichte der Osterfeier* (Trier: Paulinus-Verlag, 1967) 74–94. For a summary of this important study see R. Taft, "The Interpolation of the *Sanctus* into the Anaphora: When and Where? A Review of the Dossier," *OCP* 58 (1992) 96–104.

directly from the synagogue in Judaism that such a praise of the Creator ending in *Sanctus* entered the anaphoral tradition."[22]

Against Dix, therefore, current scholarship has been converging towards viewing the anaphoral *Sanctus* as having its origins in Syria (Cappadocia). Nevertheless, the fact of the matter remains that the form of the *Sanctus* unit in the pertinent Egyptian sources is not Syrian at all but obviously and uniquely Egyptian. If the origins of the anaphoral use of the *Sanctus* are Syrian, then, as Robert Taft notes, one cannot rule out the possibility "that the Egyptians reworked this Syrian *Sanctus* on the basis of their native Origenist exegesis of Is 6:2-3, and only later referred to the Trinity the *Sanctus* and *Sancta sanctis* response."[23] But the differences between the Egyptian and Syrian uses of the *Sanctus* may also suggest that either: (1) the Egyptian and non-Egyptian anaphoral structures represent two independent liturgical traditions; or (2) the anaphoral *Sanctus* is of Egyptian origin and at least the idea of its anaphoral use was borrowed and adapted by the Syrians.[24]

Bryan Spinks had previously noted that "the textual evidence suggests that the *Sanctus*-epiklesis unit of the Egyptian tradition was firmly established by the time Sarapion composed his anaphora, and that it was independent of the Antiochene use of the *Sanctus*."[25] But in his recent book on the *Sanctus* he argues, against both Dix and Kretschmar, that there is "little justification for seeing the theology of Origen" behind Sarapion's text at all.[26] According to Spinks, Sarapion's reference to the δύο τιμιώτατα σεραφεὶμ ἐξαπρέρυγα merely reflects an Alexandrian identification of the two living creatures in the LXX version of Habakkuk 3:2 (ἐν μέσῳ δύο ζῴων) with the seraphim of Isaiah 6:3, an identification known by both Clement of Alexandria (*Stromateis* 7:12)[27] and Athanasius (*In illud omnia mihi tradita sunt* 6).[28] Consequently:

[22]T. Talley, "The Literary Structure of the Eucharistic Prayer," *Worship* 58 (1984) 414.

[23]Taft, "The Interpolation of the *Sanctus*," 116.

[24]See ibid., 117–8.

[25]B. Spinks, "A Complete Anaphora? A Note on Strasbourg Gr. 254," *The Heythrop Journal* 25 (1984) 52.

[26]B. Spinks, *The Sanctus in the Eucharistic Prayer* (Cambridge: Cambridge University Press, 1991) 87.

[27]Clemens Alexandrinus, *Stromata Buch VII und VIII*, ed. O. Stählin, GCS 17 (Berlin: Akademie-Verlag, 1970) 57; ET from *ANF* 2:546.

[28]PG 25:220; ET from *NPNF*, ser. 2, IV:90.

"This link, together with the strange petition which introduces the pericope, might suggest to the speculative mind Origen's theology equating seraphim with the Son and Spirit. However, the text does not actually make this equation and is perfectly consistent with the understanding found in Clement and Athanasius that the two living creatures were the seraphim. The thought of the Thmuis eucharistic prayer seems to be: Christ and the Holy Spirit speak in us, so that we, like the living creatures [seraphim] who stand beside you, may praise you with the Holy, holy, holy."[29]

Spinks continues with a discussion of the postsanctus epiclesis and claims that there is a parallel function to be noted here with Jewish and Gnostic invocations both within the Egyptian Greek magical papyri and in documents from Nag Hammadi. These texts demonstrate, in his opinion, an emphasis upon "power" and a use of the name "Sabaoth" for God in ways that suggest the Egyptian eucharistic prayer.[30] He writes that

"in the Egyptian anaphora the *Sanctus*—the name of the Lord *Sabaoth* —is recited, and then he is asked to fill the bread and wine with power (Serapion) or his blessing (St. Mark). All that can be concluded is that whereas in the Syro-Byzantine and East Syrian traditions the *Sanctus* is used in a manner akin to that of the Jewish *qeduššah de Yoser*, praise of God's majesty, in the Egyptian anaphora it has similarities with the ideas regarding the divine Name which were current in Jewish and Gnostic groups in the second to the fourth centuries. It was regarded as an acclamation which could be used for petition, and its function in Egypt as represented by Serapion and St. Mark is quite unlike that of Syria or, for that matter, its use in the West."[31]

Spinks may be correct in drawing attention to a parallel function between the *Sanctus* unit in Egypt with various invocations in Jewish and Gnostic texts from the second to the fourth centuries. Indeed, given both the probable Jewish character of the origins of Christianity in Egypt[32] and what C. W. Griggs calls the early "undifferentiated

---

[29]Spinks, *The Sanctus in the Eucharistic Prayer,* 89.
[30]For texts see ibid., 90–2.
[31]Ibid., 93.
[32]See C. H. Roberts, *Manuscript, Society, and Belief in Early Christian Egypt* (London: Oxford University Press, 1979) 49–73, and B. Pearson, "Earliest Christianity

Christianity" of Egypt influenced by the Gnosticism of Basilides and Valentinus until sharper distinctions were later made between "orthodoxy" and "heresy,"[33] the presence of such parallels would not be surprising at all.

But should Origen's particular theological interpretation be glossed over or dismissed so easily from consideration, and is it true that Sarapion's text "is perfectly consistent with the understanding found in Clement and Athanasius that the two living creatures were the seraphim"? The answer to both questions is in the negative. *Pace* Spinks, Sarapion's anaphora does not say that the Son and Holy Spirit are praised by the *Sanctus* of both the seraphim and the community. What it does say is that the Son and Holy Spirit themselves are to "speak in" the community and "hymn" *God* through the *Sanctus*. And this is "perfectly consistent" not with Clement and Athanasius but with Origen, who also knows the traditional equation of the ζῷα of Habbakuk 3:2 with the two seraphim of Isaiah 6, but nevertheless associates them with the Son and the Holy Spirit.

Furthermore, Spinks' passing reference to Athanasius (*In illud. omnia mihi tradita sunt* 6) is not all that convincing. While it is true that Athanasius does reflect the same association of the ζῷα with Isaiah 6, it is clear he is referring here not to the seraphim alone but to both the seraphim and the cherubim. Moreover, he uses the word "faces"—not "face"—in this text, and indicates that the context of his remarks is decidedly anti-Arian in a defense of an orthodox trinitarian interpretation of the *Sanctus*. This Athanasian text, then, would tend to support the theses of both Dix and Kretschmar that an earlier theological interpretation (covering the "face" of God) consistent with what is seen in both Origen and Sarapion is being changed in the interests of trinitarian orthodoxy (covering the "faces"). Taft, therefore, is more convincing in his conclusion when he says:

"That the *Sanctus* in Egypt, when it does appear, shows the characteristics Dix and Kretschmar note in Origen, is clear. It is also evident that the *Sanctus* is central to the flow of the reworked Egyptian anaphoral structure, and not just a crude interpolation. Kretschmar is

---

in Egypt: Some Observations," in B. Pearson and J. Goehring, eds., *The Roots of Egyptian Christianity* (Philadelphia: Fortress, 1986) 132–59.

[33]C. W. Griggs, *Early Egyptian Christianity: From its Origins to 451 C.E.* (Leiden: Brill, 1990) 45–78. See also Pearson, "Earliest Christianity in Egypt," 72–3.

certainly right, too, in viewing this Egyptian liturgical setting of the *Sanctus* as the result of the Judeo-Christian, Alexandrian exegesis of Isa 6 adopted and developed by Origen, and in concluding that this influenced the Egyptian anaphoral tradition, and that decisively. But when? That this *Sanctus* is already in place ca. 350 in Sarapion is also clear, though Cuming holds it to be an earlier interpolation there, albeit 'at an earlier date than in any other source.' So just when, in the years between 250–350, the *Sanctus* was actually introduced into the Egyptian anaphoral structure is by no means clear. . . . Kretschmar believes already in the third century, and though I am unable to confirm this dating, I also see no reason to challenge it."[34]

Indeed, Sarapion's *Sanctus*-unit appears to be nothing other than the theological interpretation of Origen expressed in a liturgical form. And in this connection, it may be significant that, according to Severus of Al-Asmunein (*History* IV), Origen himself once functioned as a presbyter in Thmuis under Bishop Ammonius until he was banished by Demetrius.[35]

B. THE BI-PARTITE INSTITUTION NARRATIVE

. . . ὅτι ὁ κύριος Ἰησοῦς Χριστός ἐν ᾗ νυκτὶ παρεδίδοτο ἔλαβεν ἄρτον καὶ ἔκλασεν καὶ ἐδίδου τοῖς μαθηταῖς ἑαυτοῦ λέγων· λάβετε καὶ φάγετε, τουτό ἐστιν το αῶμα μου τὸ ὑπὲρ ὑμῶν κλώμενον εἰς ἄφεσιν ἁμαρτιῶν.

. . . for the Lord Jesus Christ, in the night when he was handed over, took bread, broke it, and gave it to his disciples, saying: take and eat, this is my body which is broken for you for the forgiveness of sins.

. . . καὶ ὥσπερ ὁ ἄρτος οὗτος ἐσκορπισμένος ἦν ἐπάνω τῶν ὀρέων καὶ συναχθεὶς ἐγένετο εἰς ἕν, οὕτω καὶ τὴν ἁγίαν σου ἐκκλησίαν σύναξον ἐκ παντὸς

. . . and as this bread was scattered over the mountains and, when it was gathered together, became one, so also gather your holy church out of every

---

[34]Taft, "The Interpolation of the *Sanctus*," 94–5.

[35]Severus, *History of the Patriarchs of the Coptic Church*, ed. B. Evetts, PO 1 (Paris: Firmin-Didot, 1948) 170–1. For a listing of the known bishops of Thmuis beginning with Phileas (+ 306) see G. Fedalto, ed., *Hierarchia Ecclesiastica Orientalis*, II: *Patriarchus Alexandrinus, Antiochenus, Hierosolymitanus* (Padua: Edizioni Messaggero, 1987) 611. If Severus is correct, however, the name of Ammonius, the immediate predecessor of Phileas, should be added to Fedalto's list.

ἔθνους καὶ πάσης χώρας καὶ
πάσης πόλεως καὶ οἴκου καὶ
ποίησον μίαν ζῶσαν καθολικήν
ἐκκλησίαν.

nation and every region and
every city and village and
house, and make one living
catholic church.

. . . ὅτι κύριος Ἰησοῦς Χριστός
λαβὼν ποτήριον μετὰ τὸ
δειπνῆσαι ἔλεγεν τοῖς ἑαυτοῦ
μαθηταῖς· λάβετε πίετε τοῦτο
ἐστιν ἡ καινὴ διαθήκη, ὅ ἐστιν
τὸ αἷμα μου τὸ ὑπὲρ ὑμῶν
ἐκχυνόμενον εἰς ἄφεσιν
ἁμαρτημάτων.

. . . for the Lord Jesus Christ,
taking a cup after supper, said
to his disciples: Take, drink,
this is the new covenant, which
is my blood poured out for you
for the forgiveness of sins.

Like almost everything else in Sarapion's anaphora, the unique structure of the institution narrative—divided by the citation of *Didache* 9.4[36]—has also been the subject of scholarly debate. A simple comparison of this narrative with the other pertinent Egyptian anaphoral sources demonstrates that it lacks formal anamnesis, the citation of 1 Corinthians 11:26, and the characteristically later "addition of verbs and honorific adjectives."[37] While it undoubtedly reflects an earlier level of the Egyptian tradition than these sources, scholarship has focused on the questions of its unique two-part structure and of its presence in or absence from the earliest version of the text.

Traditional scholarship is particularly divided on the presence and meaning of *Didache* 9.4 in this text. Opinions have ranged from George Wobbermin and John Wordsworth, who have seen it as support for the document's Egyptian character or for the historical accuracy of its ascription to Sarapion of Thmuis (since *Didache* 9.4 also appears in the *De virginitate* 13 of [Pseudo-] Athanasius);[38] to Paul Drews, who suggested that its function of dividing the institution narrative was a traditional element;[39] to Klaus Gamber[40] and Edward

[36]For the relevant eucharistic texts of the *Didache,* see Hänggi and Pahl, *Prex Eucharistica,* 66–8.

[37]Cuming, *The Liturgy of St. Mark,* 123. See R.-G. Coquin, "L'Anaphora alexandrine de saint Marc," *Le Muséon* 82 (1969) 335.

[38]Wobbermin, *Altchristliche liturgische Stücke,* 26, and Wordsworth, *Bishop Sarapion's Prayer Book,* 30–1.

[39]Drews, "Über Wobermins," 305–28.

[40]K. Gamber, "Die Serapion-Anaphora ihrem ältesten Bestand nach untersucht," *OS* 16 (1967) 33–42.

Kilmartin, who claimed that behind this formulation could be discerned "a former practice in Egypt of introducing the meal between the Eucharistic rites";[41] all the way to Dix, who argued that it could be omitted as "a rather unimaginative literary quotation" making no sense in the context of the Nile delta.[42] And, while Capelle saw it as part of Sarapion's innovative theological approach (i.e., a change from an eschatological focus to an ecclesiological one now related to the return of heretics (Arians) to the "one, living, catholic church"),[43] it was Louis Bouyer, who suggested that this structure of bread words/*Didache* 9.4/cup words, along with the fact that the same quotation is present in the Deir-Balyzeh Papyrus, "leads one to think that it resulted from remodeling found in the 7th book of the *Apostolic Constitutions*."[44] Contrary to most scholarship, therefore, Bouyer did not see *Didache* 9.4 as an unrelated interpolation into the text. Rather, he suggested a possible source which not only provides a similar bread/*Didache* 9.4/cup context but, in fact, also parallels the conclusions of Gamber and Kilmartin on the earlier structure of the eucharistic meal supposedly behind Sarapion's text.

That Bouyer's suggestion has merit is supported further by the independent work of Enrico Mazza.[45] Like Bouyer, Mazza also points to what he considers to be the parallel structure in the *Eucharistia Mystica* of AC VII:25, where the two thanksgiving prayers over cup and bread and the petition for the church from *Didache* 9 have been revised and expanded by the addition of explicit references to Christ's incarnation, death, resurrection, ascension, and last supper (i.e., references to body and blood and the command to proclaim his death but without an institution narrative), and rearranged, with the bread prayer now placed before that of the cup. Unlike Bouyer's implicit suggestion, however, Mazza does not claim that AC VII:25 is itself a source for Sarapion's text. According to him both Sarapion and AC VII:25 are dependent here upon a common "paleoanaphoric" source. This source, he argues, may also have a structural relationship with the description of the bi-partite eucharistic celebration in the third-century *Didascalia*

[41]E. Kilmartin, "Sacrificium Laudis: Content and Function of Early Eucharistic Prayers," *TS* 35 (1974) 284.

[42]Dix, *The Shape of the Liturgy,* 167.

[43]Capelle, "L'Anaphore de Sérapion," 353–4.

[44]L. Bouyer, *Eucharist: Theology and Spirituality of the Eucharistic Prayer* (Notre Dame: Notre Dame Press, 1968) 208.

[45]Mazza, "L'anaphora di Serapione," 512–8.

Apostolorum 58.3.[46] Consequently, while Sarapion's institution narrative itself may be an addition to the anaphora, *Didache* 9.4 is not an independent interpolation. Rather, the entire unit of bread words/ *Didache* 9.4/cup words has "the character of a truly unique and exceptional witness to an archaic and pre-anaphoric structure of eucharistic celebration."[47]

Far from being an enigma in Sarapion's text, therefore, the citation of *Didache* 9.4 between the bread and cup words of the institution narrative may be an important clue as to how the institution narrative itself came to be added to his anaphora. If the conclusions of Bouyer and Mazza are correct, *Didache* 9.4 is not only an integral part of this narrative, but with AC VII:25 it is based upon a common anaphoral source. Consequently, *Didache* 9.4 provides the structural remnant of an earlier tradition of eucharistic celebration still reflected in Sarapion's prayer.

C. THE EPICLESIS OF THE LOGOS
The Anaphora (Prayer 1)

Ἐπιδημησάτω θεὲ τῆς ἀληθείας ὁ ἅγιός σου λόγος ἐπὶ τὸν ἄρτον τοῦτον, ἵνα γένηται ὁ ἄρτος σῶμα τοῦ λόγου, καὶ ἐπὶ τὸ ποτήριον τοῦτο, ἵνα γένηται τὸ ποτήριον αἷμα τῆς ἀληθείας.

God of truth, let your holy Word come upon this bread, in order that the bread may become body of the Word, and upon this cup, in order that the cup may become blood of truth.

Sanctification of the Waters (Prayer 7)

Καὶ ὡς κατελθὼν ὁ μονογενής σου λόγος ἐπὶ τὰ ὕδατα τοῦ Ἰορδάνου ἅγια ἀπέδειξεν, οὕτω καὶ νῦν ἐν τούτοις κατερχέσθω καὶ ἅγια καὶ πνευματικὰ ποινσάτω

And as your only-begotten Word, when he descended upon the waters of the Jordan, made them holy, so also let him descend into these. Let him

---

[46]Ibid., 516. In addressing the local bishop on the proper liturgical role for a visiting bishop, the text of *Didascalia* 58.3 reads: "And when you offer the oblation, let him [i.e., the visiting bishop] speak the words; but if he is wise and gives the honour to you, and is unwilling to offer, at least let him speak the words over the cup" (A. Vööbus, ed., *The Didascalia Apostolorum in Syriac*, CSCO 402 [Louvain, 1979] 147; ET from S. Brock and M. Vasey, eds., *The Liturgical Portions of the Didascalia*, Grove Liturgical Study 29 [Nottingham: Grove Books, 1982] 16).

[47]Mazza, "L'anaphora di Serapione," 518–9.

πρὸς τὸ μηκέτι σάρκα καὶ αἷμα   make them holy and spiritual
εἶναι βαπτιζομένους . . .   in order that those who are
                                      baptized may no longer be
                                      flesh and blood . . .

1. The Orthodoxy of the Epiclesis

The most controversial element of Sarapion's prayers has been the inclusion of an epiclesis of the λόγος instead of an epiclesis of the Holy Spirit in both the anaphora and in the prayer for the sanctification of the baptismal waters. Traditional scholarship has tended to agree that at least the anaphoral epiclesis witnesses to an early and traditional form of eucharistic invocation found also in Clement of Alexandria, Origen, and Athansius. The following statement of Wordsworth may be taken as representative of this earlier consensus:

"It appears . . . that in various parts of Christendom, up to the fourth century, a Prayer for the advent [ἐπιδημία or *adventus*] of the Second Person of the Trinity upon the Eucharistic oblation took the place afterwards usually assigned to the invocation of the Third Person. How the change took place, and why it is has left so little mark on history, we have as yet insufficient means of judging; but it may be certainly concluded that it was connected with the development of the doctrine of the holy Spirit which was forced upon the Church by Macedonian error."[48]

Even Hans Lietzmann, who argued most strongly that this anaphoral epiclesis was an interpolation due to Syro-Byzantine influence, thought that the use of the λόγος and the description of communion as φάρμακον ζωῆς reflected a more ancient form of this type of prayer.[49] Similarly, Johannes Quasten not only argued that the λόγος epiclesis over the baptismal waters in Prayer 7 "is the oldest formula of this kind that we possess" but that Cyril of Jerusalem reflects the same school of thought in his reference to "Christ-bearing (Χριστο-φόρων) waters" in *Procatechesis* 15.[50]

This early consensus, however, was challenged significantly by the work of both Bernard Capelle and Bernard Botte. Against Lietzmann,

[48]Wordsworth, *Bishop Sarapion's Prayer Book*, 47–8.
[49]H. Lietzmann, *Mass and Lord's Supper* (Leiden: Brill, 1979) 63.
[50]J. Quasten, "The Blessing of the Font in the Syriac Rite of the Fourth Century," *TS* 7 (1946) 309–10.

on the basis of verbal parallels with other prayers in the text as well as the vocabulary of Syrian anaphoras (e.g., Cyril of Jerusalem and JAS), Capelle argued that the epiclesis was not an interpolation into Sarapion's text from elsewhere. From the writings of those who refer to the descent of the Holy Spirit on the baptismal waters (i.e., Tertullian, Basil, Gregory of Nyssa, and Ambrose—none of which, it should be noted, are Egyptian), he claimed further that there is no evidence for an epiclesis of the λόγος in the Alexandrian liturgical tradition prior to Sarapion in c. 350, and that later Egyptian sources (e.g., Peter II of Alexandria and Theophilus of Alexandria) assume that the epiclesis of the Holy Spirit is a traditional element both in the anaphora and in the consecration of the baptismal waters. Sarapion's "suspect tendency of attributing to the Logos the role others assigned to the Holy Spirit" suggested to Capelle that the epiclesis of the λόγος, while in "perfect harmony" with the economic theology of Athanasius, was Sarapion's own innovation, a deliberate substitution of λόγος for the Spirit. According to Capelle, therefore, "an epiclesis of the Logos at Alexandria before 350 is a phantom" and its presence at Thmuis was the result of "the . . . innovative genius of bishop Sarapion."[51]

Capelle never offered any reasons why a fourth-century Egyptian bishop might take this particular innovative theological approach in distinction to what was the "received tradition." It was Botte's influential opinion, however, that this document should not be viewed as the work of Sarapion of Thmuis at all, but rather as a deliberate Arianizing or Pneumatomachian redaction dating from a half to a whole century later.[52] According to him, this conclusion is suggested by the "astonishing frequency" of the word ἀγένητος applied to the Father in opposition both to creation (ὑπόστασις instead of φύσις) and to the Son (called μονογενής or μονογενής υἱός), the lack of allusion either to the Son's divinity or to his equality with the Father, an impersonal understanding of the Holy Spirit (a term which "always occurs" without the definite article), the absence of the Spirit from the blessing of oils, the consistent use of the uncoordinate form of the doxology, and the epiclesis of the λόγος instead of the Spirit in the anaphora and Prayer 7. Sarapion of Thmuis was neither an innovator nor one who faithfully reflected an archaic theology of the Holy

[51]Capelle, "L'Anaphora de Sérapion," 355–8.
[52]Botte, "L'Eucologe de Sérapion," 50–7.

Spirit. According to Botte, "Pseudo-Serapion" was thus a Pneumatomachian heretic who deliberately attempted "to put the Holy Spirit in the shade."[53] Botte's interpretation has been more recently accepted and defended by Dieudonné Dufrasne.[54]

In spite of his own conclusions regarding earlier sources used and reflected in Sarapion's text, Enrico Mazza accepts Botte's thesis as a presupposition for his own work. According to him, "Pseudo-Sarapion" was not only a Pneumatomachian but an archaizer, who displayed stubborn fidelity to the Alexandrian liturgical tradition in the first half of his anaphora and to the Antiochene in the second half. However, Mazza offers no evidence in further support of Botte's interpretation and, in fact, claims that the epiclesis of the λόγος was the result of a binitarian theological orientation in the hypothetical source behind both AC VII and Sarapion.[55] Given the lack of such a "source," however, this should be dismissed as pure conjecture. Even if this "source" were to be discovered, it would suggest only that Sarapion was following one tradition, not that he was not orthodox.

Against both Capelle and Botte, Geoffrey Cuming appealed to Athanasius' *Epistulae IV ad Serapionem episcopum Thmuitanum* (c. 359–360),[56] a text to which both of them referred in passing, and correctly noted that following instances where Athanasius closely links together the λόγος and the Spirit:

Ep. III, 6: The Spirit is in the Logos.

Ep. I, 23: The Spirit is the anointing and seal with which the Logos anoints and marks everything.

Ep. I, 31: There is nothing which does not happen and operate itself by the Logos in the Spirit.

Ep. I, 31: When the Logos descended on the holy virgin Mary, the Spirit came with Him.

Ep. III, 5: The Father creates all things by the Logos in the Spirit, because where the Logos is, there the Spirit is also; and the things created by the medium of the Logos receive the power of existing from the Spirit by the Logos.[57]

[53]Ibid., 55.
[54]Dufrasne, "Sérapion de Thmuis."
[55]Mazza, "L'anaphora de Serapione," 520–3.
[56]PG 26:529–676.
[57]ET as provided by Cuming, "Thmuis Revisited," 573.

Cuming, therefore, concluded that:

"For Athanasius an epiclesis of the Logos necessarily involves the Spirit also. The first half of the fourth century did not make the sharp distinction between Logos and Pneuma which we take for granted. On this count, at any rate, Sarapion can claim to be complete orthodox."[58]

Againt Botte's charge of the subordination of the Son on the basis of the supposed Arian contrast between the Father as ἀγένητος and the Son as μονογενής, Cuming argued further that: (1) ἀγένητος is often confused with ἀγέννητος in manuscripts and the loss of a ν easily could be an error on the part of the eleventh-century copyist; (2) the appropriate Arian distinction is between ἀγένητος and γένητος (not μονογενής), a distinction that the text of Sarapion does not make; and (3) the description of the Father as γέννητωρ τοῦ μονογενοῦς in Prayer 20 offers possible support for ἀγέννητος as the original reading elsewhere in the document.[59]

That Cuming was correct in pointing to the close relationship between the λόγος and Holy Spirit in Athanasius is confirmed by the work of Charles Kannengiesser on Athansius' theology of the Spirit between the Councils of Nicea and Constantinople. Kannengiesser points to the works of Athansius prior to his *Epistulae ad Serapionem* and notes that in *Orationes contra Arianos* I–II (339–340) the Spirit is regarded as the perfect gift of the Son who sanctifies, the "power" (δύναμις) of the Son in whom and through whom the Son acts, and as the one who acts and dwells in us.

"The Spirit which dwells among us becomes our relative, he is *participated in* by 'us' *(meteschomen . . .)* by the same title and by the same grace as the Incarnate Logos is . . . . Working salvation in us, the Spirit *speaks to us,* as once to the prophets, but he never speaks of himself: it is the Word who gives to the Spirit to speak, who makes the 'seal' eloquent, the 'gift' intelligible."[60]

Such an Athanasian understanding not only lends credibility to Cuming's defense of Sarapion's orthodoxy—and hence to a traditional dating for the text—but it may also render intelligible Sarapion's re-

[58]Ibid., 573.
[59]Ibid., 574.
[60]C. Kannengiesser, "Athanasius of Alexandria and the Holy Spirit between Nicea 1 and Constantinople 1," *Irish Theological Quarterly* 48 (1981) 176.

quest for the filling of the sacrifice with God's δυναμέως and μεταλ-ήψεως in the first epiclesis as an implicit petition for the Holy Spirit.

It was the thesis of Anton Baumstark that the anaphoral invocation of the λόγος was originally attached to this postsanctus petition for the "filling" of the sacrifice, thus originally forming a single prayer for the transformation of the eucharistic gifts. In support of this, he pointed not only to Athanasius for the introduction of invoking the λόγος but to the parallel postsanctus passage in MARK (πλήρωσον ὁ θεὸς καὶ ταύτην τὴν θυσίαν τῆς παρὰ σοῦ εὐλογίας διὰ τῆς ἐπιφοιτήσεως τοῦ παναγίου σοῦ πνεύματος).[61] According to him, διὰ τῆς ἐπιφοιτήσεως τοῦ παναγίου σοῦ πνεύματος was the substitution made at some point between the time of Athanasius and Dioscurus of Alexandria for the earlier invocation for the descent (ἐπιδημησάτω) of the λόγος which would have appeared here prior to Sarapion's revision.[62]

Given the Athanasian relationship between λόγος and Spirit, Baumstark's thesis may well be correct. If so, then the prayer for the sanctification of the baptismal waters (7), where the Spirit is to "fill" them but the λόγος (who is without a doubt the principal actor) is to "change" them, is a close parallel to the epiclectic portions of the anaphora. Regarding this baptismal epiclesis, there is a curious thematic and theological parallel, which other scholars have not observed, in John Chrysostom's explanation of the use of the passive voice in the Syrian baptismal formula. In *Cat.* III, 3, one of his baptismal catecheses given at Antioch in 388, Chrysostom refers to the activity of the λόγος in the Jordan, saying:

". . . what happened in the case of our Master's body also happens in the case of your own. Although John appeared to be holding his body by the head, it was the divine Word (Θεὸς Λόγος) which led his body down into the streams of Jordan and baptized him. The Master's body was baptized by the Word, and by the voice of his Father from heaven which said: This is my beloved Son, and by the manifestation of the Holy Spirit which descended upon him. This also happens in the case of your body. The baptism is given in the name of the Father and of the Son and of the Holy Spirit. Therefore, John the Baptist told us for our instruction, that man does not baptize us, but God."[63]

[61] F. E. Brightman, *Liturgies Eastern and Western* (Oxford: Clarendon, 1896) 132.
[62] Baumstark, "Die Anaphora von Thmuis," 134–5.
[63] Jean Chrysostome, *Trois Catéchèses Baptismales,* ed. A. Piédagnel, SC 336 (Paris: Cerf, 1990) 222; ET from E. C. Whitaker, *Documents of the Baptismal Liturgy* (London: SPCK, 1970) 36.

While there is no evidence for a formal epiclesis of the λόγος in Chrysostom's baptismal rites, a similar theological interpretation of the active role of the λόγος in the Jordan and, consequently, in the rite of baptism appears to be implied.

Futhermore, in both Prayers 8 and 10 of Sarapion it is the λόγος himself who is to guide the newly baptized in worship and observance (Prayer 8) and, ultimately, to the baptismal washing (λουτρόν) much as, for Chrysostom, it was the Θεὸς Λόγος who led the body of Jesus to the Jordan. Against both Capelle and Botte, therefore, Sarapion's so-called "innovative" or "heretical" theological approach to the tradition seems to be neither all that innovative nor heretical.

There is more, however, that can be said in response to Botte's thesis. Cuming referred in his *Liturgy of St. Mark*,[64] but not in "Thmuis Revisited," to the statement against Botte by Louis Bouyer that, given the four references to the Holy Spirit in Sarapion's preface, "we cannot understand how a *pneumatomachos* could . . . have introduced the Spirit in a number of places where he does not figure in any other eucharistic liturgy."[65] But even beyond this, a number of other points must be noted.

While Botte pointed to the presence of ὑπόστασις, rather than φύσις or κτίσις, in juxtaposition to ἀγένητος in the preface, he failed to notice that in the very next phrase φύσις does appear. And, more importantly, a simple word count reveals that the "astonishing frequency" of ἀγένητος is actually nine occurences in the entire document, three of which appear in the anaphora, with the other six appearing only in Prayers 5, 7, 13, 26, 27, and 28.[66] Even this infrequent occurence of the word, however, might be enough to imply a theological orientation.

It is true that in c. 350–351 Athanasius argues strongly against the use of ἀγένητος θεός in his disputes with the Arians and suggests that "Father" is a more appropriate term (*De decretis* 7, 31).[67] But earlier in this same treatise he says:

". . . let a man call God unoriginated (τὸν θεόν ἀγένητον), if it so please him; not however as if the Word were of originated, but

[64]Cuming, *The Liturgy of St. Mark*, xxxvii.

[65]Bouyer, *Eucharist*, 207, n. 20.

[66]I have argued elsewhere that these prayers are part of one early literary stratum of the document. See Johnson, "A Fresh Look," 169–73.

[67]H.-G. Opitz, ed., *Athanasius Werke* II (Berlin: de Gruyter, 1940) 27.

through His proper Word is He the maker of things which are so" (*De decretis* 7, 30).[68]

And, as late as c. 359–361, he still suggests that ἀγένητος as a description of God is correct and appropriate, if not taken in an Arian sense (*De synodis* III: 47).[69]

In Sarapion's prayers three of the nine appearances of ἀγένητος are liked to θεός: two in the anaphora and one in Prayer 13. These might be taken in support of Botte's interpretation. But apart from these, ἀγένητος always appears with "Father" in the texts of the prayers and, significantly, Father also occurs in the opening addresses of both the anaphora and Prayer 13. In other words, ἀγένητος θεός never appears in the document outside of references to God as "Father." And, as Catherine Mowry LaCugna notes in her recent work on trinitarian theology, the mere juxtaposition of "Father" with "only-begotten" in this context is itself an indication of an anti-Arian orientation. She writes:

"In the *Euchologion* of Serapion, a mid-fourth-century Egyptian liturgy, the God addressed in prayer is now often named 'Father of the Only-Begotten Son' . . . The substitution of 'Son' for 'Christ' highlights the divinity of Christ, and conveys that the mediation of our prayer takes place through Christ in both his humanity *and* divinity. . . . With . . . the increasingly common reference to Christ as the only-begotten, the name of God as Father also takes on a more pronounced intratrinitarian meaning. This is in keeping with concurrent doctrinal developments. . . . Prior to the fourth century, in the Bible and early creeds and in Greek theology, Father was a synonym for God and did not denote God's special eternal relationship as Begetter of the Son."[70]

Botte's suggestion, therefore, that the use of ἀγένητος is a sign of an Arian or semi-Arian theological orientation is not supported by the document. With the frequent use of "Father" and "only-begotten" there is nothing in Sarapion's text to suggest that he understands the Son as "originated" or "made," or in any way different than what is suggested by Athanasius above.

---

[68]Ibid., 27; ET from *NPNF* 4:171.
[69]Ibid., 271–2.
[70]C. M. LaCugna, *God For Us: The Trinity and Christian Life* (San Francisco: Harper, 1991) 116.

Botte's further conclusion that Holy Spirit "always" occurs without the definite article except for what he calls the "formula for confirmation" in Prayer 16 was also incorrect. In Prayers 8 and 10 "Holy Spirit" does appear with the definite article; in Prayer 13, even if "holy" is not present, it is "*the* Spirit of the only-begotten" who is invoked upon the candidates for the presbyteral office; and in Prayer 15, the prayer for the prebaptismal oil, the baptismal candidate is to be "molded again through this oil and purified through the bath and renewed in *the* Spirit."

Finally, Botte asked whether the uncoordinate form of the doxology could still be considered "orthodox" in 350–360. Not only is it significant that the definite article does appear with Holy Spirit in one of Sarapion's doxologies (Prayer 8), but, based on the following doxological citations in contemporary writings of Athanasius, the answer to Botte's question is, obviously, in the affirmative:

Ad episcopos Aegypti 23 (356): "*through* whom *to* the Father be glory and dominion *in* the Holy Spirit, both now and for ever, world without end. Amen."[71]

Apologia de fuga 27 (357): "in Christ Jesus our Lord, *through* whom *to* the Father *in* the Holy Spirit be glory and power for ever and ever. Amen."[72]

Similarly, as Shapland notes in his English edition of the *Letters to Serapion*, "the alternative forms of the doxology were, of course, the immediate cause of the writing of the *de Spiritu Sancto* of Basil."[73] But even for Basil—writing *de Spiritu Sancto* in defense of the coordinate form of the doxology against his Pneumatomachian critics in 375—the uncoordinate form was still considered to be "orthodox":

De Spiritu Sancto 1, 3: "Lately while I pray with the people, we sometimes finish the doxology to God the Father with the form 'Glory to the Father *with* the Son, *together with* the Holy Spirit,' and at other times we use 'Glory to the Father *through* the Son *in* the Holy Spirit.'"[74]

---

[71]PG 25:593; ET from *NPNF*, ser. 2, IV:235 [emphasis added].

[72]Opitz, *Athanasius Werke* II:86; ET from *NPNF*, ser. 2, IV:265 [emphasis added].

[73]C.R.B. Shapland, *The Letters of Saint Athanasius Concerning the Holy Spirit* (London: Epworth, 1952) 189, n. 3.

[74]Basil de Césarée, *Sur le saint Esprit*, ed. B. Pruche, SC 17 (Paris: Cerf, 1968) 256–8; ET from D. Anderson, ed., *St. Basil the Great on the Holy Spirit* (Crestwood: St. Vladimir's Seminary Press, 1980) 17.

De Spiritu Sancto 25, 59: "Both doxologies are used by the faithful, and so we use both; we believe that either one ascribes perfect glory to the Spirit."[75]

De Spiritu Sancto 26, 63: "If we say, 'Glory to the Father through the Son *in* the Holy Spirit,' we are not describing the Spirit's rank, but confessing our own weakness, since we show that we are not capable of glorifying God on our own; only *in* the Spirit is this made possible."[76]

In all cases, therefore, Botte's thesis that the anaphora of Sarapion represents a conscious heretical theological orientation stemming from a time later than the middle of the fourth century may be rejected as lacking any foundation. It is refuted, in fact, by such "orthodox" theologians as Athansius of Alexandria, Basil of Caesarea, and John Chrysostom themselves. Nevertheless, all that this suggests is that the theology of Sarapion, including his epiclesis of the λόγος, may be orthodox. It does not address Capelle's claim that his epiclesis is a liturgical innovation in the Egyptian anaphoral tradition, "a reality at Thmuis" due only to Sarapion's creative genius.

2. Is the Epiclesis of the Λογος Sarapion's Liturgical Innovation?
In 1938, Walter Frere[77] called attention to the two following excerpts from a sermon to the newly baptized attributed to Athanasius and cited by Eutychius of Constantinople in the sixth century:

Ὄψει τοὺς λευΐτας φέροντας ἄρτους καὶ ποτήριον οἴνου, καὶ τιθέντας ἐπὶ τὴν τράπεζαν. Καὶ ὅσον οὔπω ἱκεσίαι καὶ δεήσεις γίνονται, ψιλός ἐστιν ὁ ἄρτος καὶ τὸ ποτήριον ἐπ᾽ ἃ δὲ ἐπιτελέσθωσιν αἱ μεγάλαι καὶ θαυμασταὶ εὐχαί, τότε γίνεται ὁ ἄρτος σῶμα καὶ τὸ ποτήριον αἷμα, τοῦ Κυρίου ἡμῶν Ἰσοῦ Χριστοῦ.

Ἐλθῶμεν ἐπὶ τὴν τελείωσιν τῶν μυστηρίων. Οὗτος ὁ ἄρτος καὶ τοῦτο τὸ ποτήριον, ὅσον οὔπω εὐχαὶ καὶ ἱκεσίαι γεγόνασι ψιλά ἐστιν· ἐπὰν δὲ αἱ μεγάλαι εὐχαὶ καὶ αἱ ἅγιαι ἱκεσίαι ἀναπεμφθῶσι, καταβαίνει ὁ λόγος εἰς τὸν ἄρτον καὶ τὸ ποτήριον, καὶ γίνεται αὐτοῦ σῶμα.[78]

According to Frere, these two citations not only demonstrate a continuation of the tradition that "prayers and supplications" are considered

[75]Pruche (previous note), 458; ET from Anderson (previous note) 90.
[76]Pruche (note 74 above), 474; ET from Anderson (note 74 above) 96.
[77]W. H. Frere, *The Anaphora or Great Eucharistic Prayer* (London: SPCK, 1938) 82.
[78]PG 26:1325; or 86:2401 [emphasis added].

to be consecratory in the eucharist, but "that the mode in which they find their climax is an invocation and descent of the Word."[79] Yet, according to Capelle, following E. Atchley,[80] Athanasius is not referring here to an explicit epiclesis of the λόγος but only to the *content* of the eucharist. For Capelle, then, an epiclesis of the Spirit is not necessarily excluded from these "prayers and supplications" which consecrate the bread and cup as Christ's body and blood.

In further support of this interpreation, as noted above, Capelle pointed to two of Athanasius' successors in the patriarchate of Alexandria, Peter II (373–380) and Theophilus (382–413), both of whom witness to an invocation of the Spirit in the Alexandrian eucharistic liturgy. According to Theodoret, Peter notes in a letter describing a riot that took place after his ascendancy that a young boy dressed in women's clothes danced "on the holy altar itself where we call on (ἐπικαλούμεθα) the coming of the Holy Ghost" (HE 4:19, c. 449–450).[81] And, preserved only in Jerome's Latin translation, is the Second Paschal Letter of Theophilus (c. 402) in which he attacks Origen for denying the work of the Holy Spirit upon inanimate things including the baptismal waters and the bread and wine of the eucharist:

"Dicit enim Spiritum Sanctum non operari ea quae inanima sunt, nec ad irrationabilia pervenire. Quod asserens, non recogitat aquas in baptismate mysticas adventu Sancti Spiritus consecrari, panemque dominicum . . . et sacram calicem, quae in mensa Ecclesiae collocantur et utique inanima sunt, per invocationem Sancti Spiritus sanctificari."[82]

For Capelle, both of these citations demonstrated that an epiclesis of the Holy Spirit was not a recent development in the Alexandrian liturgy but part of the inherited tradition. "Why blame Origen for not having paid attention in the third century to an epiclesis which did not exist then," he asked, "if it had only been introduced at Alexandria a few years before Theophilus?"[83]

[79]Frere, *The Anaphora*, 82.

[80]E.G.C.F. Atchley, *On the Epiclesis of the Eucharistic Liturgy and in the Consecration of the Font* (London: Oxford University Press, 1935) 91–2.

[81]Theodoret, *Kirchengeschichte*, ed. L. Parmentier, GCS 19 (Berlin: Akademie-Verlag, 1954); ET from *NPNF*, ser. 2, III: 122.

[82]PL 22:801.

[83]Capelle, "L'Anaphore de Sérapion," 358.

Capelle's conclusion is by no means certain. The fact remains that Peter's reference to an invocation of the Holy Spirit in the eucharist is the first such explicit reference to be found anywhere in the Egyptian tradition. Furthermore, since the only place where this reference is found is in Theodoret, this makes it a mid-fifth—not fourth-century—reference in a source characterized by Johannes Quasten as having "a strong anti-heretical and apologetic tendency . . . [whose] . . . purpose is to show the victory of the Church over the Arians."[84] Similarly, that Theophilus would criticize Origen for any reason should come as no surprise. Again, as Quasten has noted about Theophilus' career:

"For reasons that were not all metaphysical, Theophilus changed sides in the quarrel about Origen. An ardent admirer of his until 399 and a friend of his adherents like John of Jerusalem, he later condemned him. It seems that Theophilus in one of his Paschal Letters had expressed himself in favor of God's incorporeity. Thereupon some monks conceived grave doubts regarding his orthodoxy and sent a commission to examine him. To forestall a riot by these anthropomorphists and, at the same time, anxious for political reasons to come to terms with them, he condemned Origenism at a Synod of Alexandria in 401."[85]

In such an ecclesiastical and political context, therefore, Theophilus' critique could be telling us more about the *absence* of a Spirit epiclesis from the Alexandrian tradition than about its so-called traditional presence. In other words, *pace* Capelle, it is just as likely, that Theophilus, by specifically focusing on the liturgical invocation of the Holy Spirit in the baptismal and eucharistic rites, is drawing attention to and underscoring something which is, in fact, a relatively recent liturgical development, a development first witnessed to by Peter II of Alexandria, the immediate successor of Athanasius himself.

Furthermore, the work of Ezra Gebremedhin on the eucharistic theology of Cyril of Alexandria (+ 444) suggests that even when an epiclesis of the Holy Spirit was clearly a part of the Alexandrian anaphora, Cyril still understood the λόγος to be the principal agent and δύναμις of consecration. Cyril writes:

[84]Quasten, *Patrology* III:551.
[85]Ibid., 100–1.

"That we may not be stupified by seeing flesh and blood lying on the holy tables of the churches, God, condescending to our infirmities, sends the power of life into the gifts that are set forth and changes them into the energy of His own flesh (ἐνίησι τοῖς προκειμένοις δύναμιν ζωῆς καὶ μεθίστησιν αὐτὰ πρὸς ἐνεργείαν τῆς ἑαυτοῦ σαρκός) that we may have them for life-giving participation, and that the body of Life may be found in us as a life-giving seed" (*Comm. in Lucam* 22:19-20, c. 430).[86]

Because Cyril refers in an epicletic manner to the "power of life" and not explicitly to the Holy Spirit in this comment on the eucharistic liturgy, Gebremedhin states:

"We have several reasons to doubt that the use of [this] phrase . . . referred to the Holy Spirit. In the first place, judging from the texts that are available to us, Cyril does not state *expressly* that it is the Spirit who brings about the consecration and change of the elements. He can speak quite unequivocally about the interaction between the Logos or Christ and the elements of bread and wine . . . In his *Letter to Tiberius the Deacon* Cyril writes, 'But we believe that the bringing of gifts celebrated in the churches are hallowed, blessed and perfected by Christ.' About the interaction between the Spirit and the elements, Cyril does not say much. We realize that this cannot imply that Cyril did not accept the theological implications of the invocation of the Spirit . . . But it does seem to indicate an understanding of the con-secration which is more in line with the views of Athansius and Sera-pion."[87]

And, because "the description of the Logos as life (ζωή), life by nature (ζωή κατὰ φύσιν) and the power of life (δύναμις ζωῆς) occurs frequently in Cyril's theology of the Incarnation and the Eucharist,"[88] Gebremedhin concludes that

". . . for Cyril and Logos and the Incarnation stand at the very centre of that divine counsel with which God saw fit to meet the plight of Fallen Man. The eucharistic liturgy as a cultic prolongation of the In-

[86]PG 72:912; ET from E. Gebremedhin, *Life-Giving Blessing: An Inquiry into the Eucharistic Doctrine of Cyril of Alexandria* (Uppsala, 1977) 63.
[87]Gebremedhin, *Life-Giving Blessing*, 64.
[88]Ibid., 64.

carnation of the Logos also stands at the very centre of Cyril's understanding of the remedy provided by God, for the restoration of Fallen Man. This emphasis is evident in Cyril's interpretation of the epiclesis, in which Christ is given a prominent place. It is this theme of the centrality of the Word made flesh as vivifier of man through the Eucharist which Cyril elaborates in his understanding of the nature of the consecrated elements and his view of what the eating of these elements implies."[89]

If Gebremedhin is correct in his interpretation of Cyril, not only is the focus on δύναμις and the λόγος in Sarapion's anaphora "orthodox," but a eucharistic theology which ascribed a consecratory role to the λόγος may have been more influential within the Egyptian liturgical tradition than has often been assumed. With regard to this, R.-G. Coquin has noted that among Eastern anaphoras the postsanctus epiclesis of MARK is unique in focusing on the mediatorial role of Christ in relationship to the eucharistic sacrifice (διὰ τῆς ἐπιφανείας τοῦ κυρίου καὶ θεοῦ καὶ σωτῆρος ἡμῶν Ἰησοῦ Χριστοῦ).[90] More significantly, however, some versions of the prothesis rite of MARK (i.e., Coptic MARK and a twelfth-century Greek manuscript, *Vat. MS gr. 2281*), have a prayer addressed directly to Christ the λόγος—δέσποτα Ἰησοῦ Χριστέ κυριέ ὁ συνάναρχος λόγος τοῦ ἀνάρχου Πατρὸς—who is asked to shine his face (ἐπίφανον τὸ πρόσωπόν) upon the eucharistic bread and cup.[91] And, in both Coptic MARK and the *textus receptus* of MARK this prayer specifically asks Christ to change (εἰς μεταποίησιν) the bread and cup into his "pure body" and "precious blood."[92] Since this is a prothesis prayer, its use as evidence for an anaphoral λόγος

[89]Ibid., 70.

[90]R.-G. Coquin, "L'anaphore Alexandrine," 328. For the text of MARK see Brightman, *Liturgies Eastern and Western*, 132.

[91]For Coptic MARK see Brightman, *Liturgies Eastern and Western*, 148. For the reading of *Vat. MS gr. 2281* see C. A. Swainson, *The Greek Liturgies* (Cambridge: Cambridge University Press, 1884) 2–3.

[92]For Coptic MARK, see Brightman, *Liturgies Eastern and Western*, 148. For the *textus receptus* of MARK see Cuming, *The Liturgy of St. Mark,* 4. It should be noted that in the *textus receptus* of this prothesis prayer in MARK the word υἱός rather than λόγος appears. Nevertheless, in a thirteenth-century manuscript of MARK *(Vat. MS gr. 1970)* a less consecratory variant of this prayer, addressed to the λόγος, also occurs in the Great Entrance rite. See Brightman, *Liturgies Eastern and Western,* 124–5.

epiclesis in Egypt is extremely limited.[93] But along with Cyril's eucharistic theology, which appears to underscore the consecratory role of the λόγος, it is intriguing that Coptic MARK, presumably in c. 451, has a consecratory prayer addressed to Christ the λόγος. If this is not an explicit anaphoral parallel to Sarapion's epiclesis, it is, nevertheless, a theological one.

Is Capelle correct, therefore, in claiming that Sarapion was the first to have an anaphoral epiclesis of the λόγος and that this was an intentional substitution for a Spirit epiclesis? It was also Bouyer's opinion that Sarapion's prayer was the first to have a λόγος epiclesis but, according to him, this was no substitution for an earlier invocation of the Spirit. Instead, argued Bouyer, Egyptian epicleses originally contained no reference whatsoever to any divine person, and the origins of invoking the λόγος were to be found in the reference to the angel in the post-anamnesis *Supplices te regamus* of the Roman *canon missae*, who descends to carry the eucharistic gifts to the altar in heaven. But, while in his opinion, the Roman *canon missae* preserved the ancient tradition more clearly, this angelic focus became problematic in the mid-fourth century. Consequently, he claimed that:

". . . in the apparent confusion between the Angels and their ministry, Christ or the Spirit and their respective missions, we can discern here an ambiguity that ran the risk of being useful to the heretics. It is at this time, during the first phase of the Arian conflict, as we see with Serapion, that the Logos must have been introduced

[93]It was Hieronymus Engberding's opinion, however, that this prayer, occuring with variations also in the prothesis of CHR, E-BAS, and in an eleventh-century Coptic anaphoral fragment, had its origins as the anaphoral epiclesis of MARK and was later revised to become the prothesis prayer in CHR and MARK (see H. Engberding, "Neues Licht über die Geschichte des Textes der ägyptischen Markusliturgie," OC 40 [1956] 51–68). But this hypothesis, according to Cuming, is "extremely doubtful" and "there is nothing particularly Egyptian about the prayer" (Cuming, *The Liturgy of St. Mark*, 128–9; see also ibid., 79–82). Cuming, however, has ignored the witness of Coptic MARK entirely in this context and does not address the fact that λόγος does appear even in some Greek manuscripts. Finally, while R.-G. Coquin ("L'anaphore alexandrine de saint Marc," in B. Botte, ed., *Eucharisties d'Orient et d'Occident* II [Paris: Cerf, 1970] 79) has stated that this prayer does have "a singular flavor of antiquity," he has also noted, given the considerable number of variant readings and locations within different liturgical documents (i.e., prothesis or Great Entrance) that neither its original text nor its original location can be known with certainty.

into the epiclesis, as the only one in whom the earthly sacrifice can become one with the heavenly sacrifice. When the controversy turned from him and focused on the divinity of the Spirit, they came to pray that the Spirit be sent upon the elements . . . so that these elements might 'manifest' . . . the presence of the very body and blood of the redeeming Logos."[94]

Against both Capelle and Bouyer, however, a case can be made for a theological parallel between Sarapion's epiclesis of the λόγος and eucharistic theology prior to the middle of the fourth century. Whether an explicit liturgical invocation of the λόγος is intended or not, the following early texts might lead one to the conclusion that Sarapion is not innovating here but preserving an earlier tradition of eucharistic theology:

Justin Martyr, *Apology* I, 66, 2: "Just as, through the word of God, our Savior Jesus Christ became Incarnate and took upon Himself flesh and blood for our salvation, so, we have been taught, the food which has been made the Eucharist by the prayer of His word (δι εὐχῆς λόγου τοῦ παρ᾽ αὐτοῦ), and which nourishes our flesh and blood by assimilation, is both the flesh and blood of that Jesus who was made flesh."[95]

Irenaeus, *Adversus Haereses*, IV 18, 5: "When, therefore, the mingled cup and the manufactured bread receives the Word of God (ἐπιδέχεται τὸν λόγον τοῦ θεοῦ) . . . the Eucharist becomes the body and

---

[94]Bouyer, *Eucharist*, 224–5.

[95]Hänggi and Pahl, *Prex Eucharistica*, 70; ET from *ANF* 1:185. On the difficulty in translating and interpreting δι᾽ εὐχῆς λόγου see G. Cuming, "ΔΙ᾽ ΕΥΧΗΣ ΛΟΓΟΥ," *JTS* 31 (1980) 80–2; A. Gelston, "ΔΙ᾽ ΕΥΧΗΣ ΛΟΓΟΥ," *JTS* 33 (1982) 172–5; and A. Agrelo, "El 'Logos,' potencia divina que hace la eucaristia. Testimonio de san Justino," *Antonianum* 60 (1985) 601–63. While Cuming argued that this phrase refers to a formula or "form of words" through Jesus (i.e., the institution narrative), Gelston claims that the best interpretation is that Justin's words refer to the whole eucharistic prayer itself. In other words, it is not a prayer formula ("form of words") but a "word of prayer" that Justin intends by this phrase. Agrelo's interpretation is close to that of Gelston when he argues that just as Justin understands the λόγος to be the agent of his own incarnation, so also is the λόγος to be understood as the one who makes the eucharist. In both cases it is the reality of the flesh and blood of Christ which is the end result of the activity of the λόγος. Consequently, it is the prayer of the presider which is the "prayer of the λόγος" and the λόγος "has as its main objective the reality of the body and blood of Christ" (Agrelo, "El Logos," 662–3).

blood of Christ. . . . For as bread from the earth, receiving the invocation of God (προσλαβόμενος τὴν ἐπίκλησιν τοῦ θεοῦ) is no longer common bread but a Eucharist composed of two things, both an earthly and a heavenly one, so also our bodies, partaking of the Eucharist, are no longer corruptible, having the hope of eternal resurrection."[96]

Clement of Alexandria, *Paedagogus* 1, 6, 43, 2: "The flesh figuratively represents to us the Holy Spirit; for the flesh was created by Him. The blood points out to us the Word, for as rich blood the Word has been infused into life; and the union of both is the Lord, the food of babes—the Lord who is Spirit and Word."[97]

Clement of Alexandria, *Paedagogus* 2, 2, 19, 4–20, 1: "The blood of the Lord is twofold. For there is the blood of His flesh, by which we are redeemed from corruption; and the spiritual, that by which we are anointed. And to drink the blood of Jesus, is to become partaker of the Lord's immortality; the Spirit being the energetic principle of the Word, as the blood is of the flesh. . . . Accordingly, as wine is blended with water, so is the Spirit with man. And the one, the mixture of wine and water, nourishes to faith; while the other, the Spirit, conducts to immortality. . . . And the mixture of both—of the drink and of the Word—is called Eucharist, renowned and glorious grace; and they who by faith partake of it are sanctified both in body and soul."[98]

---

[96]Irénée de Lyon, *Contre les hérésies,* livre IV, ed. A. Rousseau, B. Hemmerdinger, SC 100, t. 2 (Paris: Cerf, 1965) 610–2; ET from *ANF* 1:486. Again, as in Justin, there is no clear indication that "the invocation of God" or "Word of God" refer either to an institution narrative or to an explicit anaphoral epiclesis of the λόγος. Rather, what appears to be established is a parallel between the prayer of the church (the invocation or epiclesis of God) and the bread and cup's reception of the Word of God. As A. Agrelo, "Epíclesis y eucharistia en S. Ireneo," *Ecclesia Orans* 3 (1986) 26–7, writes: "The presence of the Lord's body and blood in the eucharist . . . is not independent of the elements of bread and wine, from which they have been formed; the operative presence of the Word of God in the celebration cannot be considered as independent of the word of the church which seeks it." Accordingly, the λόγος is the operative agent who, in response to the Church's invocation, "consecrates" the eucharist as the body and blood of Christ. A similar parallel is made by Irenaeus in *Adversus Haereses* 5.2.3.

[97]Clément d'Alexandrie, *Le Pédagogue,* livre I, ed. H.-I. Marrou, SC 70 (Paris: Cerf, 1960) 188; ET from *ANF* 2:220.

[98]Clément d'Alexandrie, *Le Pédagogue,* livre II, ed. H.-I. Marrou, SC 108 (Paris: Cerf, 1965) 46–8; ET from *ANF* 2:242–3.

Origen, *Com. in Matt.* 11:14: "And in the case of the bread of the Lord, accordingly, there is advantage to him who uses it, when with undefiled mind and pure conscience he partakes of the bread. And so neither by not eating, I mean by the very fact that we do not eat of the bread which has been sanctified by the word of God and prayer (τοῦ ἁγιασθέντος λόγῳ θεοῦ καὶ ἐντεύξει), are we deprived of any good thing; . . . but in respect of the prayer which comes upon it, according to the proportion of the faith, becomes a benefit and is a means of clear vision to the mind which looks to that which is beneficial, and it is not the material of the bread but the word which is said over it is of advantage to him who eats it not unworthily of the Lord."[99]

Origen, *Contra Celsum*, 8, 33: "We give thanks to the Creator of all, and, along with thanksgiving and prayer (μετ᾽ εὐχαριστίας καὶ εὐχῆς) for the blessings we have received, we also eat the bread presented to us; and this bread becomes by prayer a sacred body, which sanctifies those who sincerely partake of it."[100]

Origen, *In Matth. ser.* 85: "The bread which God the Logos says is his body is the Logos himself as food of souls, the Logos who proceeds from God. Such is the bread that has come down from the heavenly bread and is placed on the table . . . And this drink that God the Logos says is his blood is the mighty Logos himself who fills the hearts that drink him with intoxication . . . For it was not the visible bread he held in his hands that God the Logos pronounced to be his body. He spoke rather of the word, in the mystery of which this drink was to be poured out. What else can the body or the blood of God the Logos be but the word which nourishes and the word which gives joy to the heart?"[101]

That an explicit epiclesis of the λόγος was known in the eucharistic liturgies of these various ante-Nicene theologians remains to be proven. Edward Kilmartin notes, however, that prior to the middle of the fourth century:

[99]Origène, *Commentaire sur l'évangile selon Matthieu*, t. 1, livres X et XI, ed. R. Girod, SC 162 (Paris: Cerf, 1970) 344–6; ET from *ANF* 10:443.

[100]Origène, *Contre Celse*, IV, ed. M. Borret, SC 150 (Paris: Cerf, 1969) 246; ET from *ANF* 4:651–2.

[101]E. Klostermann, ed. *Origenes Werke*, XI, GCS 71 (Berlin: Akademie-Verlag, 1976) 196–7; ET from P. Jacquemont, "Origen," in W. Rordorf and others, *The Eucharist of the Early Christians* (New York: Pueblo, 1978) 187–8.

". . . the uniqueness of Jesus is explained by a Logos Christology or a Spirit Christology. But the limits of the latter christology, at an earlier date, must be recognized. Justin Martyr speaks of the Logos effecting his own incarnation, identifying the Spirit of Luke 1:35 with the Logos. From the middle of the second to the middle of the fourth century, the Logos is frequently described as providing the essential anointing of his humanity by the assumption itself. But in the latter part of the fourth century, in the wake of the controversies over the divinity of the Holy Spirit, more attention is paid to the role of the Spirit in the conception of Jesus. . . . Up to the middle of the fourth century the Logos, generally viewed as accomplishing his own incarnation, was also understood as the one who effects the change of bread and wine into his body and blood. Afterwards, the Holy Spirit is assigned both the role of effecting the incarnation and the transformation of the Eucharistic gifts in Greek theology."[102]

And, on the basis of some of the patristic sources cited above, Johannes Betz similarly concluded that:

"the special *Logos-epiclesis* is already well attested for Egypt in Clement, Origen, Athanasius. It must therefore be treated in Sarapion as a primitive formula, not as a correction. If the Prayers of Sarapion do not yet have a fully developed doctrinal precision regarding Logos and Pneuma, that is no valid argument against their authenticity."[103]

While these conclusions regarding the early existence of the epiclesis are stronger than the evidence permits, there can be no doubt but that the theology of Sarapion's epiclesis is indeed consistent with these earlier sources. Even in Origen's use of "body or blood of God the Logos" (*In Matt. ser.* 85) is there a parallel with Sarapion's phrase requesting that the bread might become the σῶμα τοῦ λόγου.[104] And,

[102]E. Kilmartin, *Christian Liturgy 1. Theology* (Kansas City: Sheed & Ward, 1988) 165–6.

[103]J. Betz, *Eucharistie in der Schrift und Patristik, Handbuch der Dogmengeschichte* IV, fasc. 4a (Basel and Vienna: Herder, 1979) 65, n. 8; ET from Cuming, *Liturgy of St. Mark,* xxxvii.

[104]I am unable to find any parallel passages to Sarapion's reference to the "blood of truth" as a description of the contents of the eucharistic cup. Some Gnostic influence may have suggested this. In the late-third-century *Gospel of Philip,* for example a parallel seems to be drawn between the life-giving proper-

in this same context, Sarapion's use of φάρμακον ζωῆς certainly points to a primitive conception of the eucharist, an understanding as old as Ignatius of Antioch's φάρμακον ἀθανασίας, "an antidote against death but life in Jesus Christ forever" (*Ad Eph.* 20:1-2).[105]

Is Sarapion's epiclesis of the λόγος, then, either an innovation within the Alexandrian liturgical tradition (Capelle) or a conscious and deliberate attempt to down play the role of the Holy Spirit (Botte)? Neither of these alternatives is convincing. While we lack early liturgical texts which would either confirm or deny an anaphoral epiclesis of the λόγος within the Egyptian tradition, we also lack early texts from that tradition which might support an epiclesis of the Holy Spirit. And with this observation, Capelle's charge of innovation appears as being too speculative to be given any credence. If Botte's hypothesis on the date of the document and the heretical orientation of the epiclesis is accepted, however, the second alternative is possible. But Botte's overall thesis, as we have demonstrated, is easily refuted both by a careful reading of the text and by other fourth-century patristic sources (e.g., Athanasius and Basil). Is Bouyer correct, then, in conjecturing that Sarapion's anaphora represents a first attempt to introduce any divine person into the epiclesis? This, too, is possible, but again, given the same lack of earlier Egyptian liturgical sources, there is no foundation upon which this assumption might be based.

What we do have, however, is an early theological tradition which understands the λόγος as both the agent of his own incarnation and of the content of the eucharist itself. There is absolutely no reason to interpret Sarapion's epiclesis in a manner different from this. What Sarapion expresses in a liturgical form is consistent with an archaic christological understanding, a theology of the λόγος as old as Justin Martyr and still operative to some extent in Athanasius. This, of course, does not prove the existence of a λόγος epiclesis prior to Sarapion's prayers. But, given both the content and theology of his *Sanctus* unit and the possible archaic shape of the eucharist reflected in

---

ties of Christ's flesh and blood and truth: "no one nourished by [truth] will die. It was from this place that Jesus came and brought food. To those who so desired he gave [life, that] they might not die" (*Gospel of Philip* 73.20-25; cf. 57.1–10). See J. M. Robinson, *The Nag Hammadi Library in English* (San Francisco: Harper & Son, 1988) 153 and 144. But nothing certain can be concluded from this.

[105]Ignace d'Antioche, *Lettres,* ed. T. Camelot, SC 10 (Paris: Cerf, 1958) 90.

his bi-partite institution narrative, the most logical conclusion is this epiclesis also represents the preservation, or at least the remnant, of an earlier euchological form. That this would change in further liturgical development when doctrinal controversies focused greater attention on the role of the Holy Spirit in relation to the incarnation, baptism, and the eucharist, is exactly what one would expect to happen in the later Egyptian tradition. *Pace* Botte and Capelle, therefore, the epiclesis of the λόγος should not be viewed either as an innovative shift in euchology or as reflecting a deliberate heretical theological orientation. Such an invocation is doctrinally orthodox and has at least a theological—if not a clear liturgical—precedent within the pre-Nicene Eastern Christian tradition. Without Botte's improbable thesis on the authorship and date of Sarapion's prayers, uncritically accepted by others, there would be no reason whatsoever to assume that the epiclesis of the λόγος is anything other than one early Egyptian Christian euchological formulation.

CONCLUSION

There is no reason to doubt the traditional scholarly view of Sarapion's anaphora as an Egyptian eucharistic prayer of the mid-fourth century. If, as I have argued, the epiclesis of the λόγος represents an early Egyptian euchological and theological tradition, then, along with the particular Origenist theological orientation of the *Sanctus* unit still reflected in the prayer, the bi-partite structure of the institution narrative separated by *Didache* 9.4, and the parallels with a Strasbourg-type anaphora, a date even earlier than the middle of the fourth century might be indicated. Indeed, if the Antiochene or West Syrian type anaphora commonly called Egyptian Basil could have attained its form by the beginning of the fourth century, then certainly a date no later than the middle of the fourth century is appropriate for Sarapion's text.

The conclusions of Botte, therefore, do not hold up in the light of either textual or contextual evidence. And, based on the presupposition that Botte's interpretation was correct, Mazza's conclusion, that "Pseudo-Sarapion" the Pneumatomachian was an "archaizer" who merely reflected earlier liturgical traditions, must also be dismissed. In fact, without Botte's thesis there would be no reason at all to suggest deliberate archaism on "Pseudo-Sarapion's" part. Sarapion's use of earlier traditions is thus neither deliberate "archaism" (Mazza) nor theologically motivated "innovation" (Capelle). While the *Sanctus* unit, institution narrative, and λόγος epiclesis may all be additions to an earlier anaphoral text, they also appear to reflect the "preservation" of relatively early euchological forms or archaic theological orientations. And, since this is so, there is every reason to consider the possibility that Sarapion of Thmuis himself was the collector and at least one of the editors of this mid-fourth century Egyptian liturgical document which bears his name.

D. Richard Stuckwisch

5. The Basilian Anaphoras

INTRODUCTION

In many ways, the Anaphora of St. Basil the Great [BAS] is a key to some of the many anaphoral changes and developments that took place among Christians in the fourth century. While it could not be called an "archetypical" example of early Christian liturgy in all places (since the uniformity implied by such an identification did not exist), BAS is paradigmatic of the liturgies that eventually did gain exclusive prominence among the Eastern Orthodox churches. Indeed, a developed form of BAS remains one of the two liturgies commonly used by those churches to this day (the other and more prominent one being the Liturgy of John Chrysostom). Furthermore, among the more liturgical churches of the West, BAS has been one of the most influential models for modern developments in eucharistic prayers.

Actually, when dealing with BAS, it is more appropriate to speak of several anaphoras, since there are at least two clear groupings of the liturgy, obviously related to each other in some way and yet substantially different. Identifying the similarities and differences between these different versions of BAS, and investigating the nature and significance of their relationship, is one of the ways in which BAS can serve as a key to fourth-century anaphoral development.

One of the most appealing aspects in the study of BAS is the relative certainty with which it can actually be identified with Basil the Great himself. For example, John Fenwick points to several pieces of early historical evidence that link this Cappadocian Father to a liturgy bearing his name:[1]

(1) Leontius of Byzantium (c. 540–545) indicates that the church of Constantinople was using the "Liturgy of St. Basil" at the time of Theodore of Mopsuestia (c. 425–430).

[1] John R. K. Fenwick, *The Anaphoras of St. Basil and St. James*, OCA 240 (Rome: Pontificium Institutum Orientale, 1992) 22–3.

(2) A letter attributed to Peter the Deacon (c. 520) includes a quotation from a liturgy bearing the name of St. Basil. Although the quotation is not found in all of the various forms of BAS, it does indicate an early association of the saint with a widely-used liturgy.

(3) Reference is made to the Liturgy of St. Basil also in the canons of the Constantinopolitan Council of 692 ("in Trullo"). Having appealed to the Liturgy of John Chrysostom to support a point, the Council continues with appeals to St. James "and Basil the archbishop of Caesarea," who "in handing on in writing to us the sacramental form, in the divine liturgy. . . ."

(4) Finally, in the oldest extant text of Byzantine BAS, the name of Basil is ascribed before the prayer of the Proskomide in the liturgy now attributed entirely to him.

For these and other reasons (many of which will surface in the course of this essay), most scholars readily accept some connection between BAS and the fourth-century bishop of Caesarea. That will be the operative assumption of our discussion here as well.

TEXTUAL EVIDENCE FOR THE BASILIAN ANAPHORAS
The Basilian anaphoras are well-represented by ample textual evidence, which may be grouped precisely into four geographical regions: Egypt, Syria, Armenia, and (most prominently) "Byzantium."

(1) *Byzantine Basil (Byz-BAS)*. A rather large number of textual witnesses exist for this: over two hundred Greek manuscripts, along with approximately one hundred and fifty manuscripts in Slavonic, Syriac, Arabic, Georgian, and Armenian. Remarkably, a detailed comparison of these numerous manuscripts reveals only minor variations in the text.[2] The Slavonic, Syriac, Arabic, and Georgian faithfully follow the Greek, while the Armenian differs primarily by way of added material. This high level of consistency across so many different manuscripts allows a fair degree of confidence in the text of Byz-BAS, in spite of the absence of any critical edition. Most scholars have relied on the oldest textual source of the Byzantine rescension, the eighth-century Codex Barberini 336.

(2) *Armenian Basil (Arm-BAS)*. It is not surprising that BAS should also be found in a distinctively Armenian recension, since the Armenian church had significant contacts with Cappadocia in the third and fourth centuries. The liturgy in this case is actually preserved under

---

[2]Ibid., 55–6. ET of Byz-BAS in *PEER*, 116–23.

the name of Gregory the Illuminator, the "founder" and patron saint of the church in Armenia, who was himself consecrated as bishop by Bishop Leontius of Caesarea. But the anaphora "of St. Gregory the Illuminator" is obviously a distinctive, older, form of BAS.[3] This survives in three manuscripts and is attested by a fifth-century reference in the writings of Faustus of Byzantium (discussing events of the early fourth century).

(3) *Syriac Basil (Syr-BAS)*. This is preserved in four manuscript sources, only two of which have been published; and also in three further collections of liturgical texts. In general, it tends to include numerous (and sometimes extensive) interpolations, as compared to Byz-BAS.[4]

(4) *Egyptian Basil (E-BAS)*. In contrast to all three of the textual traditions already mentioned, E-BAS represents a substantially shorter version of the Basilian anaphoras. Although possessing some "Egyptian" characteristics (even in the earliest available text), it presumably brings us closer to "Ur-BAS," that is, to a common denominator underlying all the forms of BAS. It exists in three linguistic forms:

a. The Sahidic version (ES-BAS). This is the most important witness to E-BAS, and is preserved on four small sheets of parchment.[5] A combination of palaeographical and internal evidence has supported a late-seventh-century date for this manuscript, making it the earliest extant witness to a substantial portion of BAS. Unfortunately, this very early text does not begin until the end of the postsanctus, thus providing only about two-thirds of the entire anaphora.[6] In spite of this drawback, however, the portion of the text that does survive is remarkably complete. And, thankfully, small extant fragments of ES-BAS in other sources are helpful in supporting the integrity of the entire anaphora.[7] These clues suggest a high degree of continuity be-

[3]Various Armenian manuscripts do include a liturgy under St. Basil's name, which is simply a form of Byz-BAS.

[4]Fenwick, *The Anaphoras of St. Basil and St. James,* 54.

[5]Critical edition: Jean Doresse and Emmanuel Lanne, *Un témoin archaïque de la liturgie copte de S. Basile,* Bibliothèque du Muséon 47 (Louvain, 1960). ET in *PEER,* 70–2.

[6]It should also be noted that the words with which the extant text begins, ". . . by His blood," have no precise parallel in any other version of BAS. We would like to suggest it parallels the phrase, "He sanctified us *by the Holy Spirit*," in later redactions of the anaphora.

[7]Fenwick, *The Anaphoras of St. Basil and St. James,* 49–50.

111

tween ES-BAS and the other versions of E-BAS. Even so, ES-BAS is especially important precisely because it does *not* include material found in both the Bohairic and Greek versions of E-BAS, and thus (evidently) preserves an earlier recension of the original text. For example, it contains no specific request for the elements to be transformed into the Body and Blood of Christ, nor does it commemorate any saint other than Mary.[8]

b. The Bohairic version (EB-BAS). This survives in a rather large number of manuscripts, along with four published editions.[9]

c. The Greek version (EG-BAS). Unlike the Bohairic, this survives in only a handful of (relatively late) manuscripts, even though Greek is supposed to be the original language of the liturgy.[10]

Whereas E-BAS clearly represents an earlier (and simpler) version of the Basilian anaphoras (relatively close in proximity to Ur-BAS), Syr-BAS, Arm-BAS, and Byz-BAS seem to represent alternative developments from another (later) redaction of that original text. In his careful analysis and detailed comparison of BAS and JAS, Fenwick reconstructed a hypothetical text of this common redaction (Ω-BAS). Broadly speaking, then, for the sake of our present discussion, the various texts of the Basilian anaphoras can most simply be divided into two categories, E-BAS and Ω-BAS.

A COMPARISON OF E-BAS AND Ω-BAS

The basic structure of BAS in all its forms is essentially the same, representing in each case the paradigmatic "standard shape of the anaphora," as identified by Jasper and Cuming in their collection of eucharistic texts:[11]

1. *Sursum corda* ("Lift up your hearts. . . .")
   (opening dialogue, common to all known anaphoras)
2. Preface (adoration of the Immanent Trinity)
3. Presanctus (references to angelic worship, culminating in *Sanctus*)
4. *Sanctus* ("Holy, Holy, Holy. . . .")

[8]Ibid., 53.

[9]Ibid., 50.

[10]The most accessible text is that in A. Hänggi and I. Pahl, eds., *Prex Eucharistica*, Specilegium Friburgense 12 (Fribourg, 1968) 348–57.

[11]*PEER*, 6.

5. Postsanctus (confession of the Economic Trinity, one of the most distinctive features of BAS)
6. Institution narrative
7. Anamnesis (remembrance of Christ, with many parallels to the second article of the Creed)
8. Offering of the eucharistic sacrifice
9. Epiclesis (invocation of the Holy Spirit, for "consecration" of both the people and the offering)
10. Intercessions for the church and the world (flowing out of the epiclesis)
11. Doxology of the Father, Son, & Holy Spirit.

Actually, to make any statements about BAS and the "standard shape of the anaphora" could easily be misleading. For one thing, several of these "standard" portions of the eucharistic prayer differ significantly from one liturgy to the next; their commonality, in other words, is somewhat arbitrary. Furthermore, we should like to suggest that the full eleven-point "shape" (which excludes the Alexandrian anaphoras in any case) really arises with BAS in the first place—and afterwards only in those liturgies influenced by BAS. Which is to say, rather redundantly, that BAS is "paradigmatic" for its own liturgical family and *not* for any "universal" anaphora. And that being the case, the familial relationship that certainly does exist between E-BAS and Ω-BAS (and even Ur-BAS) begs for some identification and explanation.

Within their common structure, E-BAS and Ω-BAS exhibit many similarities in language and imagery. Indeed, it is quite clear that some sort of interdependence exists between them; the question really has never been whether or not the anaphoras are related to each other, but only what is the nature and direction of their relationship. In comparing the two, Ω-BAS differs from E-BAS in two fundamental ways: (1) a considerable expansion of the text, especially by way of scriptural language and allusions; and (2) a theological sharpening of the text, most noticeable in the clearly-defined trinitarian character of Ω-BAS.[12]

[12]"Both in form and content the difference between [E-BAS] and [Ω-BAS] is rather like that between the old form of the apostles creed and the creed drawn up at Nicaea (325) and Constantinople (381)": Albert Houssiau, "The Alexandrine Anaphora of St. Basil," in L. C. Sheppard, ed., *The New Liturgy* (London: DLT, 1970) 229.

Regrettably, for many years the study of BAS was misled by the pseudo-tradition of "Proclus." A work that was attributed to the fifth-century Proclus of Constantinople names Basil (among others) as a compiler of the liturgy; more to the point, it asserts that Christian liturgies had been much longer at one time, but that the waning piety of the people required condensed versions—which is to say, that the shorter version of BAS (E-BAS) was a later redaction of the longer "original" (Byz-BAS). Because this testimony came (ostensibly) from shortly after the death of Basil himself, it was simply assumed as a given. However, as demonstrated by F. J. Leroy in 1962, the "tradition of Proclus" was in fact a sixteenth-century forgery.[13]

Even prior to Leroy's exposure of the Proclus fraud, a major turning point in Basilian scholarship had come already in 1931. In that year, Dom Hieronymus Engberding published the conclusions of an exhaustive study, in which he had identified and compared over four hundred manuscripts of BAS.[14] On the basis of his analysis, he identified the four geographical families that we have already discussed; likewise, as indicated above, he traced Byz-BAS, Arm-BAS, and Syr-BAS to a common source (which we have followed Fenwick in calling Ω-BAS). For Engberding, Ω-BAS represents the work of Basil the Great, an expansion of the original prayer that we have called Ur-BAS; whereas E-BAS is a separate (Egyptian) redaction of Ur-BAS, with no discernible connection to the work of Basil himself.

The single most important development in the study of BAS was the publication of ES-BAS in 1960, edited by Doresse and Lanne, along with an essay by Bernard Capelle. We have already suggested the significance of this Sahidic text. The appended essay is also quite important, as it examines verbal similarities between the Basilian anaphoras and the writings of Basil the Great.[15] Setting forth a number of phrases from the works of the Cappadocian Father with parallels in Byz-BAS, Capelle argued that Basil himself was the redactor of

---

[13]F. J. Leroy, "Proclus, 'De Traditione Divinae Missae': un faux de C. Paleocappa," *OCP* 28 (1962) 288–99.

[14]H. Engberding, *Das eucharistisches Hochgebet der Basileiosliturgie. Textgeschichtliche Untersuchungen und kritische Ausgabe,* Theologie der christlichen Ostens 1 (Münster: Aschendorff, 1931).

[15]Bernard Capelle, "Les liturgies 'basiliennes' et saint Basile," in Doresse & Lanne, *Un témoin archaïque,* 45–74.

the liturgy now bearing his name. He was apparently prepared to regard ES-BAS as (more or less) the text that Basil used as the foundation for his redaction, thus suggesting a connection between the saint and E-BAS that Engberding did not envisage.

Another scholar, J. M. Hanssens, turned the switch even further. In contrast to Engberding, he argued that Basil himself was responsible only for E-BAS, and that one of his episcopal successors produced the longer Byz-BAS.[16] Although not altogether satisfactory, this view does provide an explanation for the attachment of the saint's name to the Egyptian version of BAS. A third (mediating) alternative was offered by Louis Bouyer, who suggested (like Hanssens) that E-BAS was the work of the saint, but then also (like Capelle) that Byz-BAS was a subsequent reworking by the same. Bouyer further suggested that it was Basil himself who introduced E-BAS to the Egyptians, thus providing two reasons for the naming of Egyptian "Basil."[17]

Unfortunately, Capelle's examination stopped short of the institution narrative, and thus includes only the first half of the anaphora. But this shortcoming was corrected to some extent by Boris Bobrinskoy.[18] Extending the comparison from the institution narrative through the epiclesis to some of the intercessions—and considering theological ideas and images in addition to verbal phraseology—Bobrinskoy further substantiates the relationship between BAS and its namesake.

Shortly after the publication of ES-BAS by Doresse and Lanne, the text was reviewed by Alphonse Raes.[19] Apparently, the availability of this very early document caused him to reassess his interpretation of the Basilian anaphoras and their relationship. Two years previously, he had concluded that Basil the Great was the author of both E-BAS and Byz-BAS.[20] However, in his review of ES-BAS, Raes takes a new (and fairly unique) position, now regarding as most decisive the Egyptian features of E-BAS. The existence of the early Sahidic text

[16]J. M. Hanssens, *Institutiones Liturgicae de Ritibus Orientalibus* 3 (Rome: Gregorianum, 1932) 574ff.

[17]L. Bouyer, *Eucharist* (Notre Dame: Notre Dame Press, 1968) 290ff.

[18]B. Bobrinskoy, "Liturgie et ecclésiologie trinitaire de Saint Basile," *Verbum Caro* 23 (1969) 1–32.

[19]A. Raes, "Un nouveau document de la liturgie de S. Basile," *OCP* 26 (1960) 401–11.

[20]A. Raes, "L'authenticité de la liturgie byzantine de Saint Basile," *Revue des Études Byzantines* 16 (1958) 158–61.

compelled him to reject the existence of an original Greek version (and so also, the legitimacy of a hypothetical Greek retroversion, like the one that Doresse and Lanne created and published along with ES-BAS). For Raes, ES-BAS really is "Egyptian" (but not "Basilian"); that is, a liturgy originating in Egypt (from which Egyptian elements were later removed), and not a Greek original with Egyptian additions. On this view, Byz-BAS would be the redaction of an Egyptian base.

Although published in 1961, an article on the origins of BAS by W. E. Pitt is, in a sense, a step backwards in our survey of Basilian scholarship.[21] Understandably, he has no reference to the freshly-published text of ES-BAS; nor does he use Engberding's work, which (as he indicates in a footnote) was unavailable to him. Furthermore, he gives no attention to the relationship between Byz-BAS and E-BAS. Consequently, his conclusions are less than satisfying, despite some worthwhile observations. Pitt begins with the argument of G. A. Michell, that the anaphora used at Caesarea in the third century consisted of an invocation of the Trinity ending in the *Sanctus,* and that this early form of eucharistic prayer survives in the first part of BAS. He notes that the Grotta Ferrata MS of the ninth or tenth century includes the heading, Εὐχη ("Prayer"), between the epiclesis proper and a prayer for the fruits of communion, and comments that "it is difficult not to think that this heading indicates that what follows it was once a separate prayer, added to, but not part of, the Eucharistic Prayer itself." The question is then posed, whether the remainder of BAS is "an original composition, or whether it is borrowed from another church." In answer to that question, Pitt draws two major conclusions: First, BAS includes much that was developed from the same Antiochene anaphoral tradition as that reflected in the East Syrian liturgy of Addai and Mari (and in the catecheses of Theodore of Mopsuestia). Second, BAS also includes material borrowed directly from JAS—specifically, the institution narrative, anamnesis, and epiclesis; and it was the introduction of these elements that resulted in the differences between BAS and Antioch.

A contribution from Albert Houssiau deals quite specifically with E-BAS. He concludes that E-BAS stems from a time before Basil himself (and also prior to the major theological controversies of the

[21]W. E. Pitt, "The Origin of the Anaphora of the Liturgy of St. Basil," *JEH* 12 (1961) 1–13.

fourth century), probably originating in Cappadocia or northern Syria; it understands the celebration of the sacrament as a means of sanctification, in which the holiness of God is bestowed upon communicants by the agency of the Holy Spirit.[22]

Previous references to the work of John Fenwick have already implied the importance of his contribution to Basilian scholarship. In fact, his doctoral dissertation on BAS and JAS is without a doubt the most significant investigation of these anaphoras to date.[23] Certainly, Fenwick has not resolved all the problems, nor answered all the questions, in a definitive way; but he has demonstrated, to the satisfaction of many scholars, that Ur-BAS (most closely preserved in ES-BAS) provided the liturgical foundation for *both* the Ω-BAS group (Byz-BAS, Syr-BAS, and Arm-BAS) *and* JAS.

Citing omissions and deficencies in Engberding's work, Fenwick sets out to follow his lead but to broaden the scope and go further along the path of investigation. For one thing, working fifty years after the publication of Engberding's seminal study, Fenwick is able to make use of additional critical texts, including especially ES-BAS. Methodologically, Fenwick focuses on the structure of the anaphoras, in addition to the sort of verbal analysis that Engberding emphasized. Furthermore, Fenwick extends his investigation to the entire anaphora, including those portions that Engberding did not consider: the institution narrative, anamnesis, and epiclesis. Of particular note, also, is Fenwick's examination of the intercessions, which provide an important key to the relationship between Byz-BAS, Syr-BAS, and Arm-BAS. He concludes that Syr-BAS reflects the initial ordering of Ω-BAS, which maintained the sequence of Ur-BAS; Arm-BAS and Byz-BAS, in turn, stem from subsequent redactions of Ω-BAS.[24] And of course, all of this work on BAS is done in conjunction with a study of JAS and the relationship between these anaphoras.

Fenwick attempts to demonstrate conclusively that JAS is essentially a combination of Ur-BAS and the anaphora described in the *Mystagogical Catecheses* of Cyril of Jerusalem. Thus, where previous scholarship guessed (and debated) about whether Byz-BAS had

[22]Houssiau, "The Alexandrine Anaphora of St. Basil," 228–43.

[23]Fenwick, *The Anaphoras of St. Basil and St. James.*

[24]In addition to the dissertation, see also John Fenwick, "The Significance of Similarities in the Anaphoral Intercession Sequence in the Coptic Anaphora of St. Basil and Other Ancient Liturgies," *Studia Patristica* 18/2 (1989) 355–62.

borrowed from JAS or vice versa, Fenwick traces their parallels to a common reliance on Ur-BAS. For all practical intents and purposes, this hypothetical text is substantially represented by ES-BAS; whereas Byz-BAS, etc., stem from a redaction of this Ur-text by Basil himself (his redaction being the hypothetical Ω-BAS).

Fenwick also raises the possibility that Basil was responsible (in some way) for all four geographical versions of BAS (including E-BAS), and actually makes a fairly compelling case for this hypothesis. He argues that St. Basil had sufficient influence—even before he became bishop of Caesarea—to make an impact upon the Cappadocian liturgy, thus resulting in the shorter form of BAS (as preserved in E-BAS). Then, in the early years of his episcopate, St. Basil inserted additional material into the same liturgical structure, producing an early form of Ω-BAS (preserved in Syr-BAS). Subsequent redactions by the Cappadocian Father produced additional forms (preserved in Arm-BAS and Byz-BAS, respectively).[25]

In a very recent contribution to the field of Basilian scholarship, Todd Johnson endeavors to question and reassess certain presuppositions, which have otherwise ruled out *a priori* what might be legitimate possibilities and solutions.[26] Perhaps playing "devil's advocate" to a certain extent in order to demonstrate a methodological point, Johnson earnestly defends the position of Raes and argues heartily in favor of an Egyptian provenance for E-BAS, as opposed to an Antiochene-Cappadocian origin.

Johnson cites three *a priori* assumptions, in particular, that have influenced the approach of scholars to the Basilian anaphoras: (1) That Basil himself is in some way connected, not only to Byz-BAS, but also to E-BAS, even though, in Johnson's opinion, there is no historical evidence linking the Bishop of Caesarea to the Egyptian version of the anaphora; (2) That BAS originated as a single anaphora, which was at some point imported to Egypt and afterwards modified with various Egyptian elements, whereas Johnson believes it is best to assume that the core of ES-BAS is a collection of Egyptian prayers; (3) More generally, that all early anaphoras were more or less homogeneous. By way of an example, Johnson notes that Doresse and Lanne used other prayers (such as the anaphora of the *Apostolic Tradition*) to shape their

[25]Fenwick, *The Anaphoras of St. Basil and St. James,* 299–301.

[26]Todd Johnson, "Recovering Ägyptisches Heimatgut: An Exercise in Liturgical Methodology," *Questions Liturgiques* (1995) 182–98.

Greek retroversion of E-BAS. In striking contrast, recent scholarship has tended to emphasize the diversity of early liturgies, and the way in which "bits and pieces" of eucharistic prayer could be moved about independently and manipulated from one liturgy to another.

Setting aside these presuppositions in his own analysis of ES-BAS, Johnson concludes (not unlike Engberding) that "an indigenous Egyptian prayer was combined with a 'second prayer' to form Egyptian Basil." He further suggests that this "second prayer" might also have been Egyptian. In any case, it was after this Egyptian anaphora came together (our E-BAS) that Basil himself expanded it further (into Ω-BAS).

QUESTIONS TO BE ANSWERED REGARDING THE BASILIAN ANAPHORAS

In any consideration of BAS, certain questions necessarily assume a central position. Some of these have already been answered with a relative degree of certainty by Engberding, Fenwick, and others, while some of the other questions remain elusive. The four questions that follow—all of them inter-related—are by no means exhaustive, but they do represent the basic foundation of any scholarship in the Basilian anaphoras.

Todd Johnson has, in effect, already spelled out for us the first important (and to some extent, *the* most fundamental) question:

(1) *Where did E-BAS originate, and where did it go from there?*
This question is answered with the greatest degree of ambiguity and uncertainty by those who have investigated BAS. Johnson has pointed out some of the misleading presuppositions that have been assumed in the past, but his own approach is in many ways even less compelling. There are too many factors for which the necessary evidence does not exist, and in the end we must rely on conjecture. Important clues are perhaps to be gathered from other quarters, if one only knew where (and how) to look for them.

(2) *In what sense, if any, is E-BAS Egyptian? And in what sense, if any, is it Basilian?*
Obviously, these questions are simply the continuation of the first, and they touch upon the heart of Johnson's critique. In any case, no matter where and when it was that E-BAS originated, a question remains as to why it is preserved in Egypt under the name of "Basil."

On the one hand, if it did originate in Egypt, as Raes and Johnson argue, then how did it come to be associated with St. Basil? And if not, then whence, when and how did it come to Egypt?

(3) *What is the relationship or connection between E-BAS and Byz-BAS?* Brushing aside the details, this question is fairly elementary and probably the most obvious. In considering the two anaphoras side-by-side, it seems clear that Byz-BAS is the result of developments upon the same foundation and structure that support E-BAS. As for the existence and role of those texts that we have referred to as Ur-BAS and Ω-BAS, which no doubt fill in the cracks and complete the syntax between E-BAS and Byz-BAS, we shall have to be content with hypothetical reconstructions—at least until the discovery of additional texts.

(4) *What is the connection between the Basilian anaphoras and Basil himself?*
Here, too, as in the previous question, there does appear to be a scholarly consensus of sorts. "Where" and "When" the great Cappadocian is brought into the development of BAS remains up for grabs, but the presence of his hand at some point is recognized.

TAKING AN HISTORICAL APPROACH TO BAS
We would like to suggest that one of the most effective ways to approach these questions is by taking an explicitly historical (and theological) approach to the study of BAS. The student of the anaphoras has a special opportunity in this respect, because of the reasonably-certain connection between Basil the Great himself and (at least) Ω-BAS. If one begins with this assumption as a starting point, an investigation of the historical circumstances surrounding the Bishop of Caesarea—and the theological battles that demanded his episcopal time and attention in that volatile fourth century—might very well unlock the answers still needed. As far as our own considerations will go in the remainder of this essay, we will endeavor to provide a foundation for this tactic.

Origen and Gregory Thaumaturgus
In order to understand Basil the Great, one must place him—along with his fellow "Cappadocian Fathers" (his brother, Gregory of Nyssa, and his friend, Gregory of Nazianzus)—in a line beginning

with the (in-)famous Origen, and passing through the less-famous Gregory Thaumaturgus of Pontus. There is an important connection here that remains largely untapped; nor can we explore it fully here. It should simply be recognized that Basil lived and worked very much within the heritage of Origen, and that he was likewise greatly influenced by the legacy of Gregory Thaumaturgus. With that in mind, we note the following.

In the first place, we call attention to Origen's *Treatise on Prayer* (c. 232), an important discussion of Christian prayer (including an interpretation of the Our Father). This treatise on prayer is revealing on a number of points, not the least of which is the fact that it does not deal with the sacramental eucharist at all, but rather with the theology and practice of daily prayer (both at home and in the assembly of the congregation). Yet, the "shape" of this daily prayer is clearly "eucharistic":[27]

(1) It ought to begin with "something having the force of praise," offered to "God through Christ, who is praised with Him, and by the Holy Spirit, who is hymned with Him" *[Preface]*.

(2) Next should come a general thanksgiving for all the benefits that God has given to many people, including of course those benefits given to the one who is praying *[Postsanctus]*.

(3) Then should follow a confession of sins, and petitions, "first, for healing that [the one praying] may be delivered from the habit that brings him to sin and, second, for forgiveness of the sins that have been committed" *[Pre-communion (Epiclesis)]*.

(4) Then, "the request for great and heavenly things, both private and general," including intercession for the household and dearest of the one who is praying *[Intercessions]*.

(5) Just as it began, "the prayer should be concluded with a doxology of God through Christ in the Holy Spirit" *[Doxology]*.

Adding to this "eucharistic" character of Origen's description of Christian prayer is the suggestion that one should not only set aside a special place for prayer in the home but also attend "the spot where believers assemble together." For "when a great number of people

---

[27]Origen, *On Prayer* 33.1. All citations from this treatise are taken from the ET by Rowan A. Greer, *Origen: Exhortation to Martyrdom . . .* (New York: Paulist Press, 1979).

are assembled genuinely for the glory of Christ, each one's angel, who is around each of us who fear Him, encamps with that man whom he is believed to guard and order," and thus, "there is a double Church, one of men and the other of angels."[28] There is clearly a foundation here for a liturgical use of the *Sanctus*.

Origen spent five years (c. 233–238) in Caesarea (Palestine) catechizing Gregory Thaumaturgus, who would become the first bishop of Neo-Caesarea (Pontus) and who would be regarded in the fourth century (by the Cappadocian Fathers) as the "apostle and founder" of the church in Cappadocia. Basil reports that, when Gregory arrived, there were only seventeen Christians in Pontus; by the time he died, there were only seventeen pagans! His trinitarian confession of the faith is preserved by Gregory of Nyssa and is cited by Basil and by Gregory of Nazianzus. Basil includes Gregory Thaumaturgus (along with Origen and others) as an authority for a "new" way of praying the doxology. In particular, Basil emphasizes that the church in Pontus still used the liturgy of Gregory without any changes or additions; in fact, it is so primitive that many might think that something is missing.[29]

We take note of these things for the sake of two points: (1) Gregory Thaumaturgus is without a doubt an influential hero for the Cappadocians and their church. (2) The liturgy that Gregory would have known, and thus the one that he would have brought with him to Pontus (and from there, by way of influence, to nearby Cappadocia), would have been the *Palestinian* liturgy that he must have learned during his catechesis under the *Alexandrian* Origen. This liturgy, we would like to suggest, provided a foundation for much of E-BAS—from the preface through the *Sanctus*, and from the epiclesis through the doxology (what would have looked rather similar to the Palestinian anaphora witnessed by Cyril of Jerusalem, or the Alexandrian prayer of the Strasbourg Papyrus).

The Pneumatomachian Controversy
The defining issue of the church in Basil's lifetime was the Pneumatomachian controversy, which concerned the nature of the Holy Spirit and the Spirit's relationship to the Father (and the Son). This

[28]Ibid., 31.5.
[29]Basil, *On the Holy Spirit* 29 (§ 74); all citations from this treatise are taken from the ET by David Anderson, *St. Basil the Great: On the Holy Spirit* (Crestwood, N.Y.: St. Vladimir's Seminary Press, 1980).

fact invites a consideration of the Basilian anaphoras in the light of pneumatology; and by the same token, a consideration of Basil's important treatise, *On the Holy Spirit*, with an eye toward liturgical questions and considerations.

This treatise was written in response to a liturgical question, and so it stands to reason that it would have a great deal to offer any study of the fourth-century liturgy. In fact, we shall barely scratch the surface in our comments here—perhaps enough to raise a few good points and give some indication of the work's significance.

It emerged after Basil had been attacked for using the doxological form, "Glory to the Father *with* (μετά) the Son *together with* (σύν) the Holy Spirit," in his prayers, instead of the traditional doxology of the Greek-speaking churches: "Glory to the Father *through* (διά) the Son *in* (ἐν) the Holy Spirit." The Cappadocian bishop actually used (and defended the use of) both doxologies, depending on the liturgical context; he considered the first ("with"–"with") as more appropriate for adoration offered to the Godhead (the Immanent Trinity), and the second ("through"–"in") as more appropriate for confessing the salvific acts of God in history (the Economic Trinity). But there were those who accused Basil of novelty (not a compliment in those days), and of "using strange and mutually contradictory terms."[30]

The way in which Basil describes the difference between the two types of doxology (which may be designated, for the sake of discussion, as "Doxology" and "Thanksgiving") is quite important in our understanding of the anaphora. He might just as well be describing the difference between the preface and the postsanctus when he writes: "Whenever we reflect on the majesty of the nature of the Only-Begotten, we ascribe glory to Him *with* the Father. On the other hand, when we consider the abundant blessings He has given us, and how He has admitted us as co-heirs into God's household, we acknowledge that this grace works for us *through* Him and *in* Him."[31] Significantly, the Bishop of Caesarea writes, with respect to the second manner of glorification, that "when we remember His mighty works, we find the proper means of praise." "Therefore," he concludes, "we use both phrases, expressing His unique dignity by one, and His grace to us by the other."[32]

[30] Ibid., 1 (§ 3).
[31] Ibid., 7 (§ 16); emphasis is translator's.
[32] Ibid., 8 (§ 17).

Another passage, which reads like a description of the preface and presanctus, describes the sequence of glorification. Here Basil moves from God as the Creator of all things—from the Father, as the First Cause of everything that exists; and the Son, Who is the Creator; and the Holy Spirit, as the Perfector—to a discussion of the angels (as an example of creation at its best). These "ministering spirits," he writes, "exist by the will of the Father, are brought into being by the work of the Son, and are perfected by the presence of the Spirit, since angels are perfected by perseverance in holiness." Parallels to the structure of the Basilian anaphora continue when he continues shortly thereafter: "How can the Seraphim sing, 'Holy, holy, holy,' without the Spirit teaching them to constantly raise their voices in praise? If all God's angels praise him, and all his host, they do so by cooperating with the Spirit. Do a thousand thousands of angels serve him? Do ten thousand times ten thousand stand before him? They accomplish their proper work by the Spirit's power."[33]

Thus, we would argue, one of the most important clues to be gathered from the treatise *On the Holy Spirit* is an indication that (at some point) some manner of "epiclesis" was understood as a prayer for the sanctification of the *Sanctus* (as the church's sacrifice of praise and thanksgiving). For example, in describing the spiritual blessings received by Christians from the Holy Spirit, Basil includes "a place in the choir of angels."[34] Furthermore, just as the angels are holy and serve God only by the grace of the Holy Spirit, so must Christians worship "in" the Spirit, in order to offer rightly their sacrifice: "We are not capable of glorifying God on our own; only in the Spirit is this made possible. In him we are able to thank God for the blessings we have received. To the extent that we are purified from evil, each receives a smaller or larger portion of the Spirit's help, that each may offer the sacrifice of praise to God."[35]

Following his discussion of God as Creator (and of the angels as creation), Basil moves on to a treatment of the Economic Trinity, in this case with a passage that reads like a brief description of the postsanctus:

"When we speak of the plan of salvation for men, accomplished in God's goodness by our great God and Savior Jesus Christ, who

[33]Ibid., 16 (§ 38).
[34]Ibid., 9 (§ 23).
[35]Ibid., 26 (§ 63).

would deny that it was all made possible through the grace of the Spirit? Whether you wish to examine the Old Testament—the blessings of the patriarchs, the help given through the law, the types, the prophecies, the victories in battle, the miracles performed through righteous men—or everything that happened since the Lord's coming in the flesh, it all comes to pass through the Spirit."[36]

Thus, we have seen in the course of the treatise a movement that runs parallel to the first part of the anaphora: Doxological praise of the Immanent Trinity, culminating in the angelic *Sanctus*, followed by a Thanksgiving confession of the Economic Trinity.

In chapter 27 of Basil's treatise, he discusses "the unwritten laws of the Church," in which he includes "the words to be used in the invocation over the eucharistic bread and the cup of blessing." In this context, he then goes on to say, that "we are not content in the liturgy simply to recite the words recorded by St. Paul or the Gospels [i.e., the institution narrative], but we add other words both before and after, words of great importance for this mystery." These are words received "from unwritten teaching."[37] Whatever they were, it seems likely that Basil would have used these words of tradition in some way when he worked on his anaphora.

One way in which the connection between tradition and liturgy is made quite explicit is found in Basil's insistence that the church should pray as she confesses; that is to say, she prays and praises with the language of the Creed received at baptism.

"Through this confession I was made a child of God, I, who was His enemy for so long because of my sins. May I pass from this life to the Lord with this confession on my lips. I exhort them to keep the faith inviolate until the day of Christ's coming: they must not divide the Spirit from the Father and the Son, but must preserve in the profession of faith and in the doxology the teaching they received at their baptism."[38]

In fact, Basil writes, that "we treat the profession of faith as the origin and mother of the doxology."[39]

[36]Ibid., 16 (§ 39).
[37]Ibid., 27 (§ 66).
[38]Ibid., 10 (§ 26).
[39]Ibid., 27 (§ 68).

Returning now to the specific controversy addressed by the treatise *On the Holy Spirit:* Basil clearly prefers the use of "with" in the doxology, because it guards especially well against both the Sabellians (who confuse the divine Persons) and those who divide the divine Persons.[40] However, for the sake of peace and compromise, he suggests the possibility of using "and" instead, thereby avoiding completely the question of prepositions. Thus, "if someone wishes to join the names in the doxology with the word *and* (as the Gospel does and as we do in Baptism: Father *and* Son *and* Holy Spirit), let him do it; no one will object. If you wish, these could be the terms of the treaty."[41]

In the preface of Ω-BAS, we find a fully-developed confession of the Trinity, with explicit roles attributed to each of the three Persons in order. This highly-credal portion of the preface also provides a description, "based on a theology of revelation, of the relation of the Son to the Father and of the Holy Spirit to the Son, as well as of the Spirit as the source of sanctification and vitality for every spiritual creature."[42] The Father is addressed as the "Master of all, Lord of heaven and earth and all Creation, what is seen and what is not seen." He sits on the throne of glory and beholds the depths, without beginning and invisible. Going on to address the Father as "the Father of our Lord Jesus Christ," Ω-BAS moves to a confession of the Son. He is described as "the great God and Savior of our Hope, Who is the Image of Your goodness, the identical Seal, manifesting You the Father in Himself, living Word, true God, before all ages Wisdom, Life, Sanctification, Power, the true Light. . . ." And at this point, the anaphora moves to a confession of the Holy Spirit, who is revealed by the Son. This reference to the revelation of the Spirit by the Son picks up the idea of a gradual revelation of the Trinity, which Gregory of Nazianzus used to defend the gradual development of pneumatology in the fourth century.

The confession of the Third Person is every bit as full and developed in Ω-BAS as are those of the Father and the Son. He is amply described as "the Spirit of Truth, the Spirit of sonship, the Pledge of the inheritance to come, the First Fruits of eternal good things." Then, hinting at the role of the Holy Spirit in the Mysteries (baptism and

[40]Ibid., 25 (§ 59).
[41]Ibid., 25 (§ 60).
[42]Hans-Joachim Schulz, *The Byzantine Liturgy* (New York: Pueblo, 1986) 146.

eucharist), the preface goes on to describe the Spirit as "Lifegiving Power, the Fountain of sanctification, by Whose enabling the whole rational and spiritual Creation is enabled to hymn You [the Father], and to send up to You the eternal doxology." Both on the basis of the anaphora itself, and on the basis of Basil's treatise *On the Holy Spirit,* we would like to suggest that this "hymn" and the "eternal doxology" are quite specific references to the *Sanctus* (which soon follows); and also, that we have here the remnant of an earlier intention for the epiclesis, namely, the sanctification of the church's *Sanctus* as her own proper sacrifice of praise and thanksgiving.

Boris Bobrinskoy points out that, for Basil, there is a reciprocal relationship between the revelation of God (as a *descending* movement) and the worship of the church (as an *ascending* movement). That is to say, the Father is revealed *through* the Son *in* the Spirit *to* the church, whereas the church offers her worship *in* the Spirit *through* the Son *to* the Father.[43] Perhaps this reciprocal relationship best explains the use of the same word, "show," both in the institution narrative (ἀναδείξας) and in the epiclesis (ἀναδεῖξαι) of Ω-BAS. In the first case, when Jesus is said to "show" the bread to the Father, the anaphora surely reflects the liturgical action of the priest at that point in the eucharist. As such, ἀναδείξας describes an act of worship offered to God by the church (the ascending movement). In the second case, when the Holy Spirit is requested to "show" the bread and wine as the body and blood of Christ, ἀναδεῖξαι describes an act of revelation from the Holy Triune God to the church (the descending movement).

In comparing the epiclesis of Ω-BAS with that of ES-BAS, we find significant points of both continuity and development. Both anaphoras use the same key terms, namely, ἐλθεῖν ("to come") and ἀναδεῖξαι ("to show"). Bryan Spinks demonstrates that ἐλθεῖν reflects the earliest *(Maranatha)* forms of "epiclesis," as found for example in the New Testament, the *Didache,* and the Apocryphal *Acts of Thomas.*[44] The other term, ἀναδεῖξαι, often translated "to make," is best understood as a revelatory word, that is, "to show." This usage fits the understanding of St. Basil (as discussed above), that the Father is *revealed* through the Son in the Holy Spirit. Thus, here in the epiclesis, the

[43]B. Bobrinskoy, "The Indwelling of the Spirit in Christ: 'Pneumatic Christology' in the Cappadocian Fathers," *St. Vladimir's Theological Quarterly* 28 (1984) 55.

[44]B. Spinks, "The Consecratory Epiklesis in the Anaphora of St. James," *SL* 11 (1976) 25ff.

Spirit comes to reveal the Son. Another similarity between the Egyptian and "Ω" epicleses, is that the Spirit is requested to come "upon us" *and* "upon these gifts," a duality that is missing in the *Mystagogical Catecheses* of Cyril of Jerusalem, but which has been incorporated into JAS. The prayer for the Holy Spirit to come "upon us" reflects the role of the Spirit as the agent of deification (as also in an earlier reference in the postsanctus to the sanctification of the Spirit in the waters of baptism). Thus, when the epicleses go on to request that the Spirit "sanctify," the object of sanctification is as much the church as it is the elements of bread and wine; it should come as no surprise, then, that both epicleses continue with a prayer for the communicants.

As far as significant differences go between the epicleses of Egyptian and Ω-BAS, the most obvious is the expansion of the "Holy of Holies" (ES-BAS) into a long and explicit description of the bread as the body of Christ and the cup as the blood of Christ. Because the operative word is still ἀναδεῖξαι, the development is not so much toward any language of "change" (much less a "moment of consecration"), but rather a more explicit description of the Holy Spirit as the one who reveals the Son to the church. In this way, the epiclesis becomes a coherent desciption of the Trinity in action (the "Economic Trinity"), since it is addressed to the *Father* as the one whose *Holy Spirit* comes to reveal his *Son*.

Another difference between the two epicleses is in the prayer for communicants, which has been completely reworked in Ω-BAS. Whereas the Egyptian anaphora prays that "all of us" would be made worthy "to partake of Your holy things," the text of Ω-BAS leaves open the possibility that not everyone will commune, since the prayer is for "all of us *who partake*." Also, in ES-BAS the fruits of communion are "sanctification of *soul and body*, that we may become *one body and one spirit*." But in Ω-BAS, the prayer is that all who partake "of the one bread and the cup" might be united "into fellowship with *the one Holy Spirit*." Thus, all references to "body" are gone, and there has been a development from a common "spirit" to a fellowship in *the* "Holy Spirit." Surely, this reflects an emphasis on the identity of the Spirit as a distinct Hypostasis.

Finally, in comparing the doxologies of ES-BAS and Ω-BAS, we note first of all that both include the Spirit *with* the Father and the Son— just as Basil prefers and defends in his treatise *On the Holy Spirit*. However, Ω-BAS includes some further development. First of all, the language of glorification has been added (i.e., "with one mouth and one heart to glorify"). And the object of this glory is "Your magnificent *Name*," recalling the baptismal invocation that was so important to Basil's pneumatology. In Byz-BAS, the three persons of the Trinity are given equal footing with the phrase "the Father *and* the Son *and* the Holy Spirit," which avoids the use of prepositions (both *in* and *with*) altogether. This last change concurs with the treatise *On the Holy Spirit*, in which Basil argues for "Scripture's identical use of the conjunction *and* and the preposition *with*"; and in which he also proposed the use of "and" as a "term of compromise."[45] We should also mention that the unique doxological ending of ES-BAS, (i.e., "the Father in the Son, the Son in the Father") is reminiscent of another passage in the treatise: "The Son is in the Father and the Father in the Son."[46]

CONCLUSION

What was it, then, that Basil contributed to the development of eucharistic prayers? Briefly stated, the contribution of E-BAS is primarily "liturgical," whereas that of Ω-BAS is primarily "theological" (in the typical sense of the word). E-BAS represents an expansion of the "Thanksgiving" (as opposed to "Doxology") to include a confession of the Economic Trinity (which is what we have in the postsanctus). Furthermore, the christological remembrance (including the narrative) has been moved (or added) to the "soft spot" between the *eucharistia* (preface, presanctus and *Sanctus*) and the precommunion prayer (epiclesis), thus associating and identifying the sacrament itself with the eucharistic sacrifice, and (theoretically) allowing the whole church once again to participate in the remembrance of Christ (as opposed to only the few individual communicants). In 357, Basil embarked on a "whirlwind tour" that included Egypt, Palestine, Syria, and Mesopatamia. In the course of these travels, specifically in Egypt, the future bishop of Caesarea would have encountered anaphoras such as those of Bishop Sarapion and MARK that represent some early attempts to incorporate both sacrificial thanksgiving and narrative/anamnesis together in a "single" eucharistic prayer. These prayers would have been a catalyst for the alternative approach taken in the Basilian anaphoras.

[45]Basil, *On the Holy Spirit* 25 (§ 59–60).
[46]Ibid., 18 (§ 45).

Finally, the precommunion (epiclesis) has been expanded to include a fuller "litany" of intercessions, thus integrating the traditional prayers of the faithful into the celebration of the sacrament. We are not suggesting that Basil was the first to introduce such intercessions into the eucharistic prayer; clearly, he was not. But perhaps it is not too much to suggest that Basil normalized and expanded a practice that began rather naturally in the epiclesis as a precommunion consecration of the people.

Ω-BAS does provide some fine-tuning of the same liturgical structure—and certainly a reinforcement of it. But more significantly, it represents the clear articulation of a more developed and precise trinitarian theology (especially with respect to pneumatology). From this perspective, the contributions of the two Basilian anaphoras are quite distinct. Whereas E-BAS has left an indelible mark on the shape of the eucharistic prayer for a vast number of Christians around the world and over the years, the various forms of Ω-BAS have preserved a living Cappadocian legacy of theological confession at its poetic best.

Kent J. Burreson

6. The Anaphora of the Mystagogical Catecheses of Cyril of Jerusalem

The *Mystagogical Catecheses* of Cyril of Jerusalem (hereafter MC)[1] are the turning point in the fourth century between the anaphoral structures and theologies of the first half of the century and those of the latter half of the century. Cyril, probably born to Christian parents in Caesarea (Palestine) around 315, was shaped in many ways by the theological outlook of the pre-Constantinian church while yet deeply engaged in the theological and ecclesiastical debates of the tumultuous fourth century. MC, post-Easter instruction of the newly baptized regarding the sacramental rites they experienced on Holy Saturday, witness to Jerusalem, with Cyril as its bishop (351–86), as one of the crossroads of fourth-century ecclesiastical trends. The eucharistic prayer, to which Cyril testifies in MC, reflects the ecclesiastical conservatism of its bishop, while also displaying the influence of the ecclesiastical centers of Alexandria, Antioch, and Caesarea (Cappadocia). It is a crucial indicator of fourth-century anaphoral developments and of the role of Cyril at the center of those developments.

THE DEBATE ABOUT AUTHORSHIP

There has been some debate as to whether MC is truly the work of Cyril or of his successor, John (bishop 387–417). The case for John's authorship is based primarily upon the manuscript attribution. None of the manuscripts attribute MC to Cyril alone, while one manuscript attributes them to John alone and four manuscripts to both bishops.[2]

---

[1] The definitive critical edition is Auguste Piédagnel, ed., *Catéchèses Mystagogiques*, SC 126 (Paris: Cerf, 1966).

[2] The definitive article which challenged Cyril's authorship is W. J. Swaans, "À Propos des *Catéchèses Mystagogiques* Attribuées à s. Cyrille de Jérusalem," *Le Muséon* 55 (1942) 1–43. See also Frances M. Young, *From Nicaea to Chalcedon: A*

Edward Yarnold, in two articles in the mid-1970s,[3] attempted to uphold the attribution of MC to Cyril. He argued that Ambrose's *De Sacramentis* and *De Mysteriis* demonstrate that Ambrose was familiar with Cyril's lectures and that MC must therefore be dated prior to Ambrose's two works in 390–391. He noted the striking differences between the *Lenten Catecheses* of Cyril and MC: the lack of verbal echoes, the concept of faith in the Lenten lectures which is missing from MC, and the author's indication in *Lenten Catechesis* 18.33 that the post-baptismal catechesis will entail six or seven lectures, the final lecture concerning "how you must behave in word and deed." However, he argued that, along with the striking dissimilarities, there are striking similarities in style, in spirituality, and in theology. Furthermore, the theology does not reflect the Origenistic interests of John of Jerusalem. Thus, he contended that MC were originally Cyril's work and were later utilized and expanded by John.[4]

The arguments against Cyriline authorship in general, and also against an early date for MC within Cyril's episcopate, depend upon the assumption that the liturgical aspects of MC are too developed to have appeared so early. However, in an era of theological ferment and rapid theological development, the possibility of MC's developed liturgical features being present in Jerusalem by the 360s is not beyond question. The liturgical tradition of Jerusalem and West Syria evolved rapidly throughout the fourth century. There is no reason to suppose that this evolution was any less rapid immediately after the

---

Guide to the Literature and its Background (London: SCM Press, 1983) 128–30; Anthony A. Stephenson, "Introduction," in *The Works of Saint Cyril of Jerusalem 2*, The Fathers of the Church 64 (Washington, D.C.: Catholic University of America Press, 1970) 143–9.

[3] E. J. Yarnold, "Did St. Ambrose Know the Mystagogic Catecheses of St. Cyril of Jerusalem?" *SP* 12 (1975) 184–9; "The Authorship of the Mystagogic Catecheses Attributed to Cyril of Jerusalem," *Heythrop Journal* 19 (1978) 143–61.

[4] Similar conclusions are reached by Johannes Quasten, *Patrology* 3 (Utrecht: Spectrum, 1966) 366; F. L. Cross, ed., *St. Cyril of Jerusalem's Lectures on the Christian Sacraments* (Crestwood, N.Y.: St. Vladimir's Seminary Press, 1995) xxxix; and Stephenson, *The Works of Saint Cyril of Jerusalem* 2:147–8. As Frances Young, *From Nicaea to Chalcedon*, 128, notes, although these conclusions may be correct, the fact that the extant text possesses many circumstantial details points to a specific occasion for its delivery. Likewise, it must be kept in mind that the extant text appears to be notes prepared for the occasion of delivery and not a full-fledged manuscript.

Council of Nicea than it appears to have been at the end of the fourth century.

Much like Athanasius, Cyril's life revolves around three exiles from office as the bishop of Jerusalem, the first taking place in 357. He occupied his bishopric again from 362 until 367. If MC are his, then he must have composed and delivered them either during this period or after 378, following his third exile. The differences in theological emphasis between MC and his *Lenten Catecheses* preclude dating them to the same period, around 348–351. The arguments for the period from 362 to 367 for MC are persuasive, albeit in no way unassailable. C. L. Beukers argued for the period from 383 to 386 as the most likely date for the delivery of MC. On the basis of MC 5.8, where Cyril indicates that "we beseech God . . . for emperors, armies and auxiliaries," Beukers contended that the plural "emperors" refers specifically to a period when the empire was led by two emperors, either 364–367 or 378–386. "Auxiliaries," he believed, was a technical term for those autonomous bodies united by a treaty of friendship and military aid with Rome. He concluded that these allies were the Goths with whom Emperor Theodosius had registered a treaty in 382.[5] Others, including Edward Yarnold, have disputed Beukers' primary claim regarding the plural of the term "emperors," indicating that it is rather a stock reference to 1 Timothy 2:2.[6]

MC WITHIN CYRIL'S THEOLOGICAL PERSPECTIVE

In the first two centuries of the common era, Alexandrian Christianity appears to have been heavily dependent upon Hagiopolite Christianity. After Rome's destruction of Jerusalem in 115, the situation was reversed. Thereafter, Jerusalem owed its theological heritage to the Christian traditions of Alexandria, particularly those descended from Origen.[7] Cyril was certainly influenced by the Alexandrian theological tradition in his educational training, presumably in

[5]C. L. Beukers, "'For Our Emperors, Soldiers and Allies': An Attempt at Dating the Twenty-third Catechesis by Cyrillus of Jerusalem," *Vigiliae Christianae* 15 (1961) 177–84.

[6]See Yarnold, "The Authorship of the Mystagogic Catecheses," 143; and idem, *The Awe-Inspiring Rites of Initiation: Baptismal Homilies of the Fourth Century* (Slough: St. Paul Publications, 1971) 46.

[7]For a sketch of Alexandria's influence upon Jerusalem see Anthony A. Stephenson, "St. Cyril of Jerusalem and the Christian Gnosis," *SP* 1 (1957) 143; "St. Cyril of Jerusalem and the Alexandrian Heritage," *TS* 15 (1954) 573.

Caesarea (Palestine) and Jerusalem. Leonel L. Mitchell contends that the instruction embodied in the *Lenten Catecheses* and MC received its shape from Alexandrian catechesis. Catechetical instruction was the "organizing principle" of Origen's academy in Caesarea (Palestine). He argues that Cyril derived the outline of his Lenten catechetical lectures four through eighteen from the arrangement of Origen's *Peri Archon*.[8]

Anthony Stephenson maintains, by comparing sections of the *Lenten Catecheses* and MC with Cyril's *Sermon on the Paralytic*, that his theology is influenced by the type of Alexandrian Christian gnosis introduced by Clement of Alexandria and popularized by Origen. Like the Alexandrians, Cyril's sermon and catechetical lectures embody *theoria*, the search for the knowledge of God, divine gnosis. The primary content of the gnosis for Cyril, as with the Alexandrians, is the revelation contained in Scripture.[9] Although the Alexandrians based their *theoria* upon Scripture, they felt obligated to provide philosophical demonstration of the faith. This is something for which Cyril never opts, although his search for *theoria* in the heart of Scripture does reflect the background of philosophical reasoning and terminology. Cyril consistently uses scriptural terms and language to explain the doctrines enunciated in the baptismal creed.[10] The creed provides the systematic basis for constructing a comprehensive synthesis, a Christian gnosis in the Alexandrian tradition.[11] The dependency of Jerusalem and Cyril upon the theological and catechetical heritage of Alexandria may also point to dependencies in other areas, including liturgical dependence, especially with regard to the shape and theology of the anaphora.

Cyril depended upon Alexandria as well for his defense of a proper christology. Although Cyril was not an adherent of the *homoousios* until late in his life, it would be incorrect to assume he took no interest in christology. His entire MC focus around the incorporation of

---

[8]Leonel L. Mitchell, "The Development of Catechesis in the Third and Fourth Centuries: From Hippolytus to Augustine," in John H. Westerhoff III and O. C. Edwards, Jr., eds., *A Faithful Church: Issues in the History of Catechesis* (Wilton, Conn.: Morehouse-Barlow, 1981) 54; see also Stephenson, "St. Cyril of Jerusalem and the Christian Gnosis," 149.

[9]Stephenson, "St. Cyril of Jerusalem and the Christian Gnosis," 150.

[10]See Harry A. Wolfson, "The Theology of Cyril of Jerusalem," *Dumbarton Oaks Papers* 11 (1957) 3–19.

[11]Stephenson, "St. Cyril of Jerusalem and the Alexandrian Heritage," 583.

the believer into Christ, the divine Son of God. MC 4 specifically focuses on incorporation into the body and blood of the Lord encompassed in the bread and wine of the eucharist. Christology was central to Cyril's entire theological enterprise. As at Alexandria, at the heart of Cyril's christology would be the scriptural witness to Christ, the study of the incarnate Word. As a result, Cyril limited his christology to scriptural statements and terms, the foundation of *theoria*. Thus, one might call Cyril a traditionalist, committed to the traditional theological heritage as embodied in Alexandria without the philosophical excesses of Origen. As a consequence Cyril would frame his responses to doctrinal errors, such as those of the Manichees[12] and the Arians, within the framework of his scipturally based *theoria*. Only gradually does Cyril take an interest in opposing Arian christology and even then, such as in MC 4, he does not directly address Arian errors. Yet, because of this interest in a proper christology, Cyril had doctrinal concerns that were similar to those of Nicea throughout his entire career. Cyril defended the fleshly incarnation of the only-begotten Son. For Cyril, Christ became incarnate so that humanity might be able to receive him. Similarly, in MC 4.7 the Holy Spirit makes Christ's body and blood present in the eucharist so that humanity might become "the sanctuary of God." Defense of Christ's incarnation, a proper christology, and the reality of Christ's bodily presence in the eucharist cannot be divided from one another. Defending Christ's presence in the eucharist entails defending the incarnation of the only-begotten Son of God.

Cyril inherited such an incarnational, sacramental approach to christology and the doctrine of redemption from Alexandria. As Anthony Stephenson indicates, "In Alexandrian theology the apprehension of the Logos through teaching and contemplation was not unrelated to sacramental communion, but provided its wider context."[13] As a result, christology and the sacraments were of a piece in Cyril's theology. For Cyril, Christ came that he might make humanity one with God through physical means which provide access to Christ and to God through Christ. The believer is assimilated into Christ

---

[12]The Manichees, Cyril's chief opponents, denied fundamental aspects of the incarnation. See *Lenten Catechesis* 4.4; 10.4; 11.21; 15.3; 13.14,37; 14.21, where Cyril opposes christological errors, although he does not always identify these errors with the Manichees.

[13]Stephenson, *The Works of Saint Cyril of Jerusalem* 2:183, n. 9.

through the sacraments as means of salvation. Frances Young refers to this transformation as "Christification."[14]

It appears that the Arians did not emphasize this sacramental union of the believer with Christ in the eucharist. Rather, for the Arians the central experience of Christ was spiritual union with him for the sake of perfecting a greater imitation of Christ's life in the believer. This advancement in the believer's life mirrored, for the Arians, earthly advancement toward divinity in the life of Christ. In the *Lenten Cate-cheses,* according to Robert Gregg, Cyril's primary opposition to the Arians[15] revolves around this christological teaching of advancement, or *prokope,* in which the Son of God earns or matures into his divinity through his life on earth. Clearly such a doctrine of the Son's advancement into divine sonship dissolves distinctions between divine and human life and obviates the unique reality of the incarnation.[16] Cyril appears to be dependent upon a common tradition which he shared with Eusebius of Caesarea for this focal point in his defense against Arianism.[17] For Eusebius such advancement into the godhead was clearly impossible for Christ and evoked a heretical christology. Such advancement was only possible for human beings.[18]

Yet, the nature of salvation for Eusebius, as for the Arians, was just that: advancement. Christ provided the possibility for advancement

[14]Frances Young, *From Nicaea to Chalcedon,* 131.

[15]Arians were opponents whose errors Cyril regularly had to refute in Jerusalem. Yet, as Rebecca Lyman notes in "A Topography of Heresy: Mapping the Rhetorical Creation of Arianism," in Michael R. Barnes and Daniel H. Williams, eds., *Arianism after Arius: Essays on the Development of the Fourth-Century Trinitarian Conflicts* (Edinburgh: T. & T. Clark, 1993) 51, at least at the time of the *Lenten Catecheses* Cyril drew a distinction between "overt heretical teachings" and "varied theological errors in reflection." Cyril classified Manicheeism in the former category and Arianism in the latter. Over the course of his episcopate Cyril's convictions concerning the seriousness of the Arian threat to Nicene, orthodox views of christology apparently solidified. After his third exile and by the time of the Council of Constantinople he was considered to be an anti-Arian hero.

[16]Robert C. Gregg, "Cyril of Jerusalem and the Arians," in Robert C. Gregg, ed., *Arianism: Historical and Theological Reassessments,* Patristic Monograph Series 11 (Philadelphia: Philadelphia Patristic Foundation, 1985) 91–2.

[17]See Leo D. Davis, *The First Seven Ecumenical Councils (325–787): Their History and Theology,* Theology and Life Series 21 (Collegeville: The Liturgical Press, 1990) 72–3. This is also a consistent part of Athanasius' polemic against Arianism. Cyril might have acquired such a viewpoint from Athanasius, but this is purely hypothetical. See Gregg, "Cyril of Jerusalem and the Arians," 93.

[18]Gregg, "Cyril of Jerusalem and the Arians," 96.

into salvation in him. This makes Cyril's christology radically different from the decidedly subordinationist view of Eusebius. P.W.L. Walker notes that Eusebius had little interest in the incarnation and redemption. For him, the very essence of Christianity was spiritual.[19] In this regard Cyril seeks to stress the physical reality of the incarnation for the sake of humanity's redemption. Christ became incarnate physically so that enfleshed humanity might be able to experience God's salvation in the flesh. The sacramental reality of salvation depended upon the incarnation. For Eusebius, on the other hand, the incarnation's intention was not sacramentally oriented, but to enable humanity to engage in reflection upon the Logos in his pure, heavenly reality.[20] He focused upon the spiritual union of the believer with Christ and God, an important aspect of Alexandrian teaching, while ignoring the sacramental union of the believer, the other aspect of Alexandrian teaching, as indicated above.[21]

Thus, I would contend it is not only the Manichees that Cyril opposes throughout his Lenten lectures and MC with his emphasis upon the believer's union by means of the sacraments with the only-begotten yet incarnate Son of God. He emphasizes this union particularly in MC 4, his discussion of the words of institution outside the context of the eucharistic prayer discussed in MC 5, in order to counteract the Arian and Eusebian overemphasis upon spiritual union with Christ apart from a sacramental union.[22] As will be shown later, Cyril's understanding of redemption revolves around the experience of "Christification" conveyed to the believer in and by the sacraments. Christ became incarnate in order to enable humanity's union with God both physically and spiritually. In the light of Arian denials of such a sacramental union with the incarnate divinity, Cyril emphasizes this fundamental reality of christology and the doctrine of

[19]P. W. L. Walker, "Gospel Sites and 'Holy Places': The Contrasting Attitudes of Eusebius and Cyril," *Tyndale Bulletin* 41 (1990) 106, n. 49; see also 96–7.

[20]Ibid., 106.

[21]See also Ze'ev Rubin, "The Church of the Holy Sepulchre and the Conflict Between the Sees of Caesarea and Jerusalem," in Lee I. Levine, ed., *The Jerusalem Cathedra* (Detroit: Wayne State University Press, 1981) 79–105, for a thorough discussion of the differences between Eusebius and Cyril over the importance of physical means—both sacraments and the holy sites in Jerusalem—for apprehending Christ and rising to unity with him.

[22]Athanasius also emphasized sacramental and physical union with God in Christ in opposition to Arian negligence of such a union. See Archibald Robertson, *St. Athanasius: Select Works and Letters,* in *NPNF* 4:lxxix, & 578–9.

redemption in MC, especially in the fourth lecture on Christ's institution of the eucharist.

THE STRUCTURE AND THEMES OF THE ANAPHORA

Both structurally and with regard to content, the anaphora in MC opens the window on anaphoral development in the mid-fourth century. It witnesses to what may have been the structure of the eucharistic prayer throughout Christendom by the early fourth century, a structure to which other prayers also bear witness. This structure may be outlined as follows: Introductory thanksgiving → Offering → Supplication. Yet, the Cyriline anaphora also demonstrates the influence of various forces, in opposition to heretical movements and tendencies like Manicheeism and Arianism, that shaped and augmented the anaphoral structure with such elements as the *Sanctus*, epiclesis, anamnesis, and institution narrative. These elements altered the content of the eucharistic prayer in such a way that it emphasized christocentric, anamnetic, and sacramental elements. The Cyriline anaphora witnesses to the presence of at least two of these additional elements: the *Sanctus*, which expands the understanding of the eucharist as image of the heavenly liturgy, and an epiclesis, which accentuates the christological/anamnetic element. As a result, the anaphora takes this shape in MC 5:[23]

Hand washing[24] (2)
Holy kiss[25] (3)
Sursum Corda[26] (4)

[23]The numbers in parentheses refer to the paragraph numbers in the edited texts.

[24]John Baldovin, *Liturgy in Ancient Jerusalem*, Alcuin/GROW Liturgical Study 9 (Nottingham: Grove Books, 1989), 24, notes that even though Cyril fails to mention it, the hand-wahing may have occurred before the clergy entered the sanctuary from the nave after preparing the gifts. Cyril's mention of the ceremony hints at the developing piety of awe and trembling in the sacrament. Interestingly, JAS does not mention the handwashing.

[25]The kiss prepares for the eucharistic prayer and communion, emphasizing the symbolism of forgiveness and reconciliation. See Baldovin, *Liturgy in Ancient Jerusalem*, 25.

[26]The introductory dialogue appears to be missing its first couplet, "The Lord be with you—and with your spirit." Jasper & Cuming, *PEER*, 82–3, suggest that, like the Egyptian anaphoras, "The Lord be with you" was replaced by "The grace . . ." (2 Cor 13:13). This is what occurred in JAS. However, why would Cyril

Habemus ad Dominum (5)
Preface (6)
Presanctus (6)
Sanctus (6)
Epiclesis (7)
Supplications for the living (8)
Supplications for the dead (9)
Lord's Prayer (11–18)
Communion invitation: Holy things for the holy ones (19)
Communion psalm: Psalm 34:9 (20)
Communion (21–22)
Blessing (23)

Cyril does not quote the anaphora verbatim, but rather seems to provide its outline, selected quotes from it, and his own theological commentary. Discerning between these elements can be a tricky affair, especially since the transitions between sections have led many scholars to conclude that Cyril omitted some elements, such as the institution narrative, which were actually part of the anaphora upon which he was commenting. Nevertheless, Cyril does appear to comment upon each element in succession within the anaphora he has received.[27]

As has already been shown, Cyril was a cosmopolitan bishop and Jerusalem a cosmopolitan city in the fourth century. Given Cyril's numerous exiles and probable visits to other sees, including those of Antioch, Alexandria, and Caesarea (Cappadocia), not to mention the heavy influx of Christian pilgrims which Jerusalem attracted after the Peace of Constantine, he and Jerusalem undoubtedly were influenced by the theological and liturgical practices of other sees, especially that of Alexandria. Yet, the development of the anaphora in Jerusalem

---

leave out comment on "The grace . . ." in that case? Perhaps there is nothing missing at this point.

[27]Cyril almost consistently uses *eita*, "next," and *meta tauta*, "after this," to denote his movement from one part of the anaphora to the next. Gregory Dix was the first to note this. See Dix, *The Shape of the Liturgy* (London: Dacre, 1945) 197–8. John R. K. Fenwick, *The Anaphoras of St. Basil and St. James*, OCA 240 (Rome: Pontificium Institutum Orientale, 1992) 38, notes that Cyril is not totally consistent in his usage of these terms, yet he concedes that Cyril's terminology seems to indicate that he is commenting upon all the sections of the anaphora and not omitting any.

cannot be linked solely to the influence of one see, nor identified with one specific type of anaphora (i.e., West Syrian [Antiochene] or Alexandrian).[28] It most certainly attests to a variety of influences from numerous areas, as well as its own peculiarities, and can only represent how those influences were assimilated within Jerusalem's unique environment.

Cyril's anaphora does seem to bear witness to an anaphoral structure which the various sees, including Antioch, Alexandria, Edessa (East Syria), and Jerusalem, may have shared early in the fourth century. If the *Sanctus,* epiclesis, and Lord's Prayer are removed, what remains is structurally very similar to two other early prayers: the prayer to which Eusebius of Caesarea refers in his sermon at the dedication of the Tyre basilica and the prayer of the Strasbourg Papyrus.

MC	EUSEBIUS	STRASBOURG PAPYRUS
	Prayers of Faithful	
Sursum Corda		
Habemus ad Dominum		
Preface	Preface	Preface
(Presanctus)		
(Sanctus)	*(Sanctus)*	
	Postsanctus:	
	Oblation w. prayer	Offering
	for forgiveness	
(Epiclesis)		
Supplications/Living		Supplications/Living
Supplications/Dead		Supplications/Dead
		Doxology

Massey Shepherd has compared the language and composition of Eusebius' sermon (which was delivered sometime between 314 and 319) to the anaphoras of MC and JAS, particularly the preface and

---

[28]As Fenwick notes, it is "precisely the fact that it is not West Syrian in form which has proved so problematic" and led scholars to try to identify the location in MC's anaphora of various Antiochene features *(The Anaphoras of St. Basil and St. James,* 36, n. 32). Part of the problem with identifying MC's anaphora as Antiochene is that, if it is dated to the mid-fourth century, we possess no peculiarly Antiochene anaphora with which to compare it. The truly Antiochene anaphoras—CHR and AC 8—come from the late fourth century. We simply have no idea what the Antiochene anaphora looked like before this period.

anamnesis sections of the latter.[29] Although Eusebius does not quote the *Sanctus,* he does make allusions to it. The sermon witnesses to an anaphoral structure which would include praise of God by the entire creation, especially the heavenly choirs composed of saints and angels, concluding with the "bloodless and immaterial sacrifices of prayers." Thus, Cyril's anaphora parallels that of Eusebius not only structurally, but also in language. Although in Cyril the bloodless sacrifice probably refers to the epiclesis, and to the offering of the gifts by means of it, nevertheless, as in Eusebius, its primary and original referent is to prayer. It refers to an offering of thanksgiving and petition, a sacrifice of prayer. This original spiritual sacrifice of prayer as the primary sacrifice of the eucharist is also central to Alexandrian theology, as well as the Alexandrian anaphoras, the Strasbourg Papyrus and MARK. Furthermore, Eusebius's anaphora, like Cyril's, uses the words "heavens, earth, and sun" in the preface, terms peculiar to the Alexandrian and Caesarean anaphoras. The connections that Massey Shepherd indicates among these anaphoras, particularly those of Eusebius and Cyril, demonstrate the interdependence of anaphoral structures and forms among the various sees, in particular the connections of Jerusalem and Cyril to the anaphoral structures and thought of Alexandria and to Eusebius of Caesarea. Eusebius' anaphora bears witness to a primary anaphoral shape that emphasized the church's spiritual worship through prayer, an unbloody sacrifice of prayerful praise with the celestial realms.

In a 1974 article, Geoffrey Cuming made the suggestion that the eucharistic prayer in MC did not have the same structure as the West Syrian anaphoras but as the Egyptian anaphoras, that it was a cousin of MARK.[30] Through comparisons with manuscript evidence for the Alexandrian anaphora—the Strasbourg Papyrus, the Deir Balyzeh Papyrus, and the final redaction of MARK—Cuming found the origins of the Jerusalem anaphora in Egypt. Structurally, Cuming argued that, on the basis of a comparison with the anaphora of John Chrysostom (CHR), Cyril's statement, "when the spiritual sacrifice, the bloodless worship, has been completed" (MC 5.8), referred to the

---

[29]Massey H. Shepherd, "Eusebius and the Liturgy of St. James," *Yearbook of Liturgical Studies* 4 (1963) 109–23; see also Bryan Spinks, *The Sanctus in the Eucharistic Prayer* (New York: Cambridge University Press, 1991) 61–2.

[30]G. J. Cuming, "Egyptian Elements in the Jerusalem Liturgy," *JTS* 25 (1974) 117–24.

completion of the institution narrative. Furthermore, he argued that Cyril followed the Egyptian anaphoras in having an epiclesis before the institution narrative and that Cyril moved the intercessions from their position in MARK before the *Sanctus* to the end of the eucharistic prayer. On the basis of his assumption that the Cyriline anaphora was Egyptian, he argued that it had an anamnesis similar to that of the Deir Balyzeh Papyrus. Furthermore, he posited that certain linguistic constructions in Cyril, such as the singular word "face" in the *Sanctus* and the use of the word "change" in the epiclesis, were borrowed from the Alexandrian anaphora.

In a 1989 article, Bryan Spinks argued against Cuming and contended for the traditional West Syrian origins and structure of the Cyriline anaphora.[31] He believed that the evidence for Egyptian influence was inconclusive. He questioned Cuming's confident use of CHR to interpret Cyril, indicating that, from comparison with the anaphora of Theodore of Mopsuestia, it could as easily be the epiclesis to which Cyril refers when he says that "the spiritual sacrifice, the bloodless worship, has been completed." Furthermore, he argued that the similarities in language between Cyril and the Egyptian anaphoras are due more to the influence of the Septuagint than to a cross-fertilization from Alexandria to Egypt. In addition, as John Fenwick indicates, Cuming's hypothesis demands a complicated procedure of rearrangement, parts of the prayer swapping positions with other parts to construct the anaphora's final shape.[32] Apparently Cuming himself came to realize that. He later asserted that whatever connection existed between Jerusalem and Alexandria had to lie in an augmentation of the Strasbourg Papyrus' form so as to give the shape of the Cyriline anaphora; that is, the Strasbourg Papyrus with the *Sanctus* and epiclesis inserted between its preface and intercessions resulted in the Cyriline anaphora.[33] What Cuming's suggestions have done is indicate that Jerusalem and Alexandria probably began with anaphoras of very similar shape, such as that of the Strasbourg Papyrus, and has indicated the possibility, even probability, of the Alexandrian anaphora's influence upon that of Jerusalem[34] (and vice versa?). Given Alexan-

---

[31]Bryan D. Spinks, "The Jerusalem Liturgy of the *Catecheses Mystagogicae*: Syrian or Egyptian?" *SP* 18/2 (1989) 391–5.

[32]Fenwick, *The Anaphoras of St. Basil and St. James,* 39.

[33]*PEER,* 84; see also Fenwick, *The Anaphoras of St. Basil and St. James,* 38–9.

[34]Even Bryan Spinks admits the possibility, "The Jerusalem Liturgy of the *Catecheses Mystagogicae,*" 394.

dria's theological influence upon Jerusalem and Cyril (as discussed above), such influence seems readily apparent, while not denying the effects of other ecclesiastical centers, especially those of West Syria.

In addition to the core anaphoral outline to which Cyril witnesses, the other sections of his anaphora, including the units added to the core outline, the *Sanctus* and epiclesis, attest to connections with Alexandria, Antioch, and Cappadocia.[35] The preface in Cyril, "After that we commemorate the heavens, the earth and the sea; the sun and moon, the stars, the whole rational and irrational creation, both visible and invisible" (MC 5.6), shows marked similarity to the preface in the Strasbourg Papyrus and MARK, but limits itself to the heavenly creation without mentioning Christ.[36] According to André Tarby, Cyril emphasizes the splendour of the heavenly creation in an attempt to uphold creation's goodness in light of the Marcionite, Gnostic, and Manichaean attacks upon it.[37] It is surprising, given Cyril's interest in opposing the christologies and doctrines of redemption of these heretical groups that Cyril does not incorporate a reference to salvation in Christ into the eucharistic prayer at this point. It demonstrates his conservatism with regard to the anaphora he had received, his unwillingness to tamper with a received tradition, especially with regard to the spiritual, heavenly liturgy of the preface/*Sanctus* section.

The *Sanctus* does serve as a central element in the church's spiritual offering of praise. The form in MC, as Bryan Spinks notes, is rather unique. It is not a hymn of the angels to which the church refers. It is, from the flow of the preface into the mention of the angels in the presanctus,[38] a hymn of creation to the creator. Cyril also

---

[35]These influences probably run in both directions, i.e., from Jerusalem to Alexandria, Antioch, and Cappodocia, and from these sees to Jerusalem.

[36]See Shepherd, "Eusebius and the Liturgy of St. James," 112–3; *PEER*, 83; Arthur H. Couratin, "The Thanksgiving: An Essay," in Bryan D. Spinks, ed., *The Sacrifice of Praise* (Rome: C.L.V.—Edizioni Liturgiche, 1981) 38.

[37]André Tarby, *La Prière Eucharistique de L'Église de Jérusalem*, Théologie Historique 17 (Paris: Beauchesne, 1972) 113–7.

[38]The list of angelic beings is similar to Alexandrian, Antiochene and Cappadocian anaphoras, although the order of the angelic list differs from anaphora to anaphora and the later anaphoras often contain more complex angelologies. Bryan Spinks, *The Sanctus in the Eucharistic Prayer*, 63, rejects Georg Kretschmar's assertion that Psalm 34:3, which Cyril mentions in the presanctus as the equivalent intention of the angelic praise, was part of the presanctus but argues rather that Cyril cites it for catechetical purposes.

makes clear that this song of creation and of the angels is also the song of the church: "It is to mingle our voices in the hymns of the heavenly armies that we recite this doxology which descends to us from the Seraphim" (MC 5.6). The various East Syrian anaphoras (except AM), CHR, the anaphora of St. Gregory, and MC all make explicit that this is the church's song, evidence of another reciprocal relationship, that between Jerusalem and East Syria.

For Cyril, the *Sanctus* (and any other hymns that might have been sung) is not offered purely for its own sake as a sacrifice of praise. As he indicates, the *Sanctus* is in service to what follows: "Next, after sanctifying ourselves by these spiritual songs, we implore the merciful God to send forth His Holy Spirit upon the offering . . .," the epiclesis.[39] As Bryan Spinks indicates, the *Sanctus* apparently served as a way of ensuring the sanctity of the congregation, its spiritual purity as it offers its most spiritual prayer. As Spinks concludes: "The congregation made a 'spiritual ascent' and, having sanctified themselves, standing before God like the seraphim, they then asked for a true communion and the descent of the Spirit, and favours for the living and the dead."[40] The *Sanctus* thus serves in Cyril as the focal point of the ancient notion of the spiritual worship of the people of God and is the means of their attaining to that worship. Likewise, this spiritual worship is the earthly image of the angelic worship in heaven.

After having been sanctified by the spiritual songs, Cyril's rite moves into an explicitly pneumatological and christological section: the epiclesis. In this section Cyril indicates that the people "implore the merciful God to send forth His Holy Spirit upon the offering to make the bread the body of Christ and the wine the blood of Christ. For whatever the Holy Spirit touches is hallowed and changed" (MC 5.7). Cyril's epiclesis is the earliest evidence for such an explicitly consecratory form. Cyril is certainly consistent in espousing such a consecratory view, since he uses the same consecratory language in MC 3.3 and 1.7.[41] As Bryan Spinks notes, Cyril's phraseology is mature in nature, unique in its maturity without displaying any earlier terminology regarding the epiclesis, such as the themes of the Holy

---

[39]MC 5.7; Jasper and Cuming, *PEER*, 82, note a link to MARK in language, "receive . . . our hallowing" (or "sanctification"), and in structure, the epiclesis immediately following the *Sanctus* in MARK as well.

[40]Bryan Spinks, *The Sanctus in the Eucharistic Prayer*, 64.

[41]Stephenson, *The Works of Saint Cyril of Jerusalem* 2:196, n. 24.

Spirit's invocation for the sake of the unity or sanctification of the people.[42] The epicleses of the Coptic version of MARK and the Deir Balyzeh and Louvain papyri are also notably consecratory in nature.[43] The verb that calls down the presence of the Holy Spirit, "send forth" *(exapostello)*, Spinks observes, is found in only two Egyptian anaphoras, MARK and the Manchester papyrus. Spinks concludes that these two Egyptian anaphoras have been influenced by Cyril and that the term "send forth" is the peculiar Jerusalemite term invoking the Spirit.[44]

The phrase by which Cyril proceeds from the epiclesis into the intercessions has been the cause of much controversy among liturgical historians: "Next, when the spiritual sacrifice, the bloodless worship has been completed, over that sacrifice of propitiation we beseech God. . . ." (MC 5.8). In the Strasbourg Papyrus the phrase, "the spiritual sacrifice, the bloodless service," found in the preface, refers to the spiritual and heavenly worship of the people of God, a celestial sacrifice of praise and thanksgiving. However, as demonstrated above, here it refers both to the spiritual offering of prayer and to the offering of the bread and wine as a propitiatory sacrifice. The latter concept predominates in Jerusalem in the fourth century and in the later Antiochene and East Syrian anaphoras. This points to a shift in Cyril's anaphora away from the spiritual sacrifice of praise and thanksgiving, an earthly worship that imitates the heavenly adoration as encountered in Eusebius of Caesarea, toward a decidedly anamnetic and christological worship.

The focal point of this shift is MC 4, which recounts Christ's institution of the Last Supper and the significance of the communion of the

[42]Bryan Spinks, "The Consecratory Epiklesis in the Anaphora of St. James," *SL* 11 (1976) 28–9. Spinks argues that there are essentially three stages in the development of epicletic terminology. Verbs such as "come" and the request for the Holy Spirit's sanctification of the people represent the first stage. These early forms are concerned with the benefits of communion such as the forgiveness of sins, resurrection, and new life. This can be found in the rite upon which Theodore of Mopsuestia comments. Verbs such as "send forth" and "send down" would represent a second stage, and Cyril's rite the third stage, in which the Father is asked to make the bread and wine the body and blood of Christ, without any reference to the sanctification of the communicants.

[43]See *PEER*, 83. The texual parallels with the Deir Balyzeh papyrus are particularly close. Spinks, "The Consecratory Epiklesis," 36, contends that the Deir Balyzeh epiclesis was influenced by the Antiochene rite.

[44]Spinks, "The Consecratory Epiklesis," 32.

newly baptized in Christ's body and blood. Cyril cites Paul's account of the supper's institution in 1 Corinthians at the beginning of his lecture, but the actual institution narrative which he cites in MC 4.1 appears to be a liturgical text. If the institution narrative was verbalized within the eucharistic rite and if Cyril in MC 5 does follow the order of the rite absolutely, why does he depart from the order with regard to the institution narrative? And if the rite does include the institution narrative, does it also include a christological anamnesis?

Three solutions have been proposed to this problem. The first solution suggests that the rite does include the institution narrative/anamnesis and that Cyril, since he discusses it in MC 4, omits any mention of it in MC 5. However, this fails to explain why Cyril would deliberately depart from the rite's order. Georg Kretschmar, espousing a second solution, argued that the growing theology of fear and awe with regard to the eucharist had resulted in the silent recitation of the eucharistic prayer from the *Sanctus* to the epiclesis and that Cyril omitted any mention of this silent section.[45] Although Kretschmar's hypothesis is certainly possible, it is purely conjectural since Cyril provides no indication that any part of the rite was spoken in silence. Furthermore, if the institution narrative/anamnesis block was a part of the prayer, why doesn't he mention its inclusion in the anaphora in MC 4?

Emmanuel Cutrone's solution is to suggest that the rite upon which Cyril was commenting had no institution narrative/anamnesis unit and that Cyril delivered the fourth catechesis to supplement that deficiency.[46] Cutrone believes that Cyril *had* to compensate for that deficiency because of the nature of his sacramental theology, which Cutrone calls an "eikon-mimesis" theology. This theology invokes a new methodology in liturgical interpretation in which the liturgy is seen not only as an antitype of another reality, but actually an imitation of that reality by which the newly baptized are brought into unity with Christ. As Cutrone concludes,

[45]Kretschmar, "Die frühe Geschichte der Jerusalemer Liturgie," *Jahrbuch für Liturgie und Hymnologie* 11 (1956–57) 30–3.
[46]Emmanuel J. Cutrone, "Cyril's Mystagogical Catecheses and the Evolution of the Jerusalem Anaphora," *OCP* 44 (1978) 52–64. Couratin arrives at the same conclusion, "The Thanksgiving," 39–40, as does Fenwick, *The Anaphoras of St. Basil and St. James,* 16. See also Bryan Spinks "The Consecratory Epiklesis" 20, for a summary of the arguments for and against the institution narrative/anamnesis block's inclusion. For arguments favoring the inclusion of this block, see Stephenson, *The Works of Saint Cyril of Jerusalem* 2:194-95, n. 16.

"When this imitation (mimesis) takes place the individual now is an image (eikon) of Christ. This notion of eikon-mimesis focuses on Christ in such a way that the Mystagogue can say that sacramental activity is the place where the individual is identified with Christ to such an extent that what is true of Christ is now also true of the Christian."[47]

Cutrone contends convincingly that the anaphora with which Cyril is familiar does not contain the type of ritual elements and language that lend themselves toward interpretaing the eucharist as incorporation into Christ, the point at which one is united with the central saving activity of Christ. Cyril, in his conservatism unwilling to alter the anaphoral tradition of Jerusalem and add an institution narrative and anamnesis, even though he was probably familar with their use in other anaphoras, opts to explain his theology in a separate lecture. There he utilizes the institution narrative to expound for the newly baptized their incorporation into Christ:

"With perfect confidence, then, we partake as of the Body and Blood of Christ. For in the figure of bread His Body is given to you, and in the figure of wine His Blood, that by partaking of the Body and Blood of Christ you may become of one body and blood with Him. For when His Body and Blood become the tissue of our members, we become Christ-bearers and as the blessed Peter said, 'partakers of the divine nature'" [2 Peter 1:4].[48]

Furthermore, Cyril does emphasize his "eikon-mimesis" theology in MC 5 whenever the possibility arises. The Holy Spirit makes Christ's presence in the eucharist a reality, a presence by which the believer is truly united with him and becomes his image. Thus, the epiclesis is the one moment in the ritual where Cyril's theology fits. In addition, Cutrone observes that Cyril's inclusion of the Lord's Prayer in the anaphora, following directly upon the intercessions, may be a result of his sacramental theology. MC are the first evidence for the inclusion of the Lord's Prayer in an anaphora. For Cyril, as Cutrone observes, sacramental imitation is not a dramatization of Christ's life, but the enactment within the baptized of the salvific realities achieved by Christ during his life. Thus, in a certain respect the anaphora's

---

[47]Cutrone, "Cyril's Mystagogical Catecheses," 53.
[48]MC 4.3.

words and actions can be understood as an imitation of Christ's life. As a result, perhaps he introduced the Lord's Prayer so that it might model Christ's manner of praying as closely as possible.[49]

As persuasive as Cutrone's arguments are, he fails to answer the question of why Cyril cites a liturgically derived institution narrative, not simply one of the biblical texts. Two answers are possible. First, he may have been quoting an institution narrative used liturgically in other anaphoras with which he was familiar, for instance perhaps that of Antioch or Cappadocia, since the narrative he cites is similar to subsequent West Syrian institution texts. On the other hand, the institution narrative actually might have had a liturgical use in the MC—at the point of communion.[50] It would have served as a distribution formula. But why then doesn't Cyril comment upon its use at this point in MC 5? Thus, the first solution, reliance upon an institution narrative from another eucharistic prayer, appears to be the more probable explanation.

Cyril's "eikon-mimesis" theology and his enunciation of it in MC 4 as a solution to the anaphora's deficiencies in espousing such a theology correlate well with Cyril's opposition to Manichee, Gnostic, and Arian devaluations of the divinity of Christ, to which we referred earlier. His inclusion of a theological emphasis upon incorporation into Christ, and specifically into his divinity by participation in his body and blood, balances the purely spiritual view of the eucharist espoused by these heretical groups. He is even countering the type of purely spiritual understanding of the eucharist as enunciated by Eusebius of Caesarea in which there is no emphasis upon participation in the divine life of Christ: the eucharist is the opportunity for a spiritual sacrifice of praise and thanksgiving to God. Rather, central to Cyril's theology is the experience of the eucharist as a direct participation in the divine life through communion in the body and blood of the only-begotten Son of God.[51]

---

[49]See Emmanuel J. Cutrone, "The Lord's Prayer and the Eucharist. The Syrian Tradition," in E. Carr, S. Parenti, A.-A. Thiermeyer, and E. Velkovska, eds., *EULOGEMA: Studies in Honor of Robert Taft, S.J.* Studia Anselmiana 110 (Rome: S. Anselmo, 1993) 105–6.

[50]See Thomas J. Talley, "Word and Sacrament in the Primitive Eucharist," in Carr et al., eds., *EULOGEMA*, 497–510, for a discussion of the institution narrative as a distribution formula.

[51]Cyril's language with regard to communion in MC 5.21-22 likewise reveals his concern to emphasize the presence of Christ in the eucharist, admonishing the

Cyril is not alone in developing a decidedly christological, anamnetic, historical, and sacramentally realistic view of the anaphora. Enrico Mazza has demonstrated how similar concerns govern the theology and anaphoral commentary of Theodore of Mopsuestia (d. 428).[52] Mazza contends convincingly that the ritual upon which Theodore comments is identical in structure to the one upon which Cyril comments.[53] Theodore's commentary reveals an anaphora, the one in use in the last decade of the fourth century in Mopsuestia or Antioch, that is more elaborate in structure and development than the Ordo itself. Yet, the basis for his comments is not the developed ritual but the traditional Ordo. This traditional Ordo included a certain sequence of themes which dictated that sacramental realism be discussed in the first of the two eucharistic homilies. Cyril and Theodore both follow this sequence. Yet, although they comment upon the identical ritual, there are significant differences in their mystagogical method. Cyril does not adopt the allegorizing method of Theodore and interpret the eucharist as the visible dramatization of Christ's death and resurrection. Cyril tempers his own interpretation that focuses primarily on fundamental theological realities that pervade the anaphora, realities which he isolates in each pertinent section of the anaphora.[54] The dramatization/allegorical method not only interpreted the sacramental action vis-a-vis Christ's passion and resurrection, it also interpreted the earthly liturgy as an allegorical dramatization of the heavenly liturgy. Cyril avoids such interpretation. However, it does not mean he withholds comment on the angelic liturgy, such as in the *Sanctus*. As Mazza observes, "The theology of the angelic liturgy and its sanctifying role is fully present in Cyril's *Catecheses,* even though he does not follow the typological method that interprets the earthly liturgy as a *typos* of the angelic liturgy."[55]

---

communicants to "hallow your eyes by the touch of the sacred Body" and "While it [the Blood of Christ] is still warm upon your lips, moisten your fingers with It and so sanctify your eyes, your forehead, and other organs of sense."

[52]See his two books *Mystagogy: A Theology of Liturgy in the Patristic Age* (New York: Pueblo, 1989) 45–101, 150–64, and *The Origins of the Eucharistic Prayer* (Collegeville: The Liturgical Press, 1995) 202–18, 287–330.

[53]The ritual is cited by Theodore at the beginning of his sixteenth homily.

[54]Mazza, *Mystagogy,* 153–4, 164.

[55]Ibid., 154.

Cyril's methodology is a mediating position in the midst of the fourth century. The spiritual worship of praise and thanksgiving, identified with the angelic, heavenly liturgy, is present in the anaphoras of the earliest decades of the century. Within two generations, the paleoanaphoric text, which Mazza identifies as being the same in Egypt, Jerusalem, and Theodore—that which we have previously identified with the anaphoras of Eusebius of Caesarea and the Strasbourg Papyrus—has witnessed two developments in the focus of that offering of praise and thanksgiving: (1) the addition of the *Sanctus* as an image of the heavenly liturgy and the heightened awareness that the church on earth joins in and imitates the praises of the heavenly realm;[56] (2) the interpretation of the liturgy in a christocentric fashion, eventually assigning particular liturgical actions to specific events in the passion and resurrection of Christ. For Cyril these two developments stand side-by-side. In the *Sanctus* the church on earth joins in the praises of the heavenly hosts. The people, having been sanctified by the singing of these heavenly, spiritual hymns of the celestial liturgy, are ready to implore God for the Holy Spirit to make Christ present in the bread and wine. The centrality of the eucharistic rite has moved from the celestial realms to those of earth. The focus is upon Christ's presence in physical means for the sake of the divinization of the body of Christ, the church. This is not for Cyril a dramatic re-enactment of Christ's resurrection. But it is a part of the "spiritual sacrifice, the bloodless worship," no longer only spiritual and heavenly, but carnal, earthly, the presence of the only-begotten Son for the sake of the church's participation in his life.

The movement apparent in the anaphora of Cyril—away from a decidedly spiritual view of the eucharist as the offering of a bloodless sacrifice of prayer, praise, and thanksgiving, mirroring the worship in the heavenly realms, toward a view of the eucharist that is decidedly christological, focusing on the anamnesis of Christ's life, death, and resurrection, centering around his presence in the bread and wine, and offering that bread and wine transformed into his body and blood as the bloodless sacrifice—comes to its culmination in JAS, the successor in Jerusalem to the anaphora of MC. Unlike MC, the redactor of JAS does not hesitate to incorporate into the prayer the christological concerns which Cyril's conservatism in MC prevented him from doing. JAS possesses a postsanctus, an anamnesis, and the insti-

---

[56]Mazza, *The Origins of the Eucharistic Prayer*, 218.

tution narrative. These christological, anamnetic elements dominate the prayer while the spiritual sacrifice of prayer and praise is overshadowed to the point of being unnoticeable. Cyril himself may very well have been the redactor of JAS after having encountered the variety of alterations other sees were making in the traditional anaphoral prayer structure, especially the alterations in Cappadocia under Basil. As Fenwick argues, the redactor of JAS conflated the anaphora of MC with the Ur-anaphora of Basil.[57] Basil's anaphora provided the redactor with exactly the materials that were missing from the MC anaphora: a postsanctus, an anamnesis, and the institution narrative. Thus, Cyril's concern to uphold the believer's incorporation through the eucharist into the only-begotten Son, Jesus Christ, had come full circle: the anaphora of Jerusalem now embodied that very sacramental theology at the center of MC 4 and 5.

[57]Fenwick, *The Anaphoras of St. Basil and St. James*, 303.

John D. Witvliet

7. The Anaphora of St. James

Called by Louis Bouyer "the most accomplished literary monument of the whole of liturgical literature,"[1] the text known as "the liturgy of St. James the brother of the Lord" is crucial both for understanding the textual development of the anaphora in the fourth and fifth century and for probing the theological significance of the eucharistic prayer itself. The anaphora of St. James (JAS) has long been regarded as one of the most significant witnesses to fourth-century eucharistic liturgy in the East, and a key link in establishing lines of influence among Eastern anaphoras. Recent scholarship, especially that of John Fenwick, has suggested that the Jerusalem redaction is, in fact, a theologically astute conflation of Palestinian sources with an early form of the anaphora of St. Basil (BAS).[2]

THE HISTORY OF THE LITURGY

Although the pre-history and redaction of JAS is a complex subject which has warranted intense scholarly attention, the history of its complete text is relatively simple and uncontested.[3] It is generally assumed that JAS was produced for use in the Jerusalem church sometime near the end of the fourth century or the beginning of the fifth. During this period Jerusalem was under the jurisdiction of Antioch, and was probably influenced by Antiochene theology and liturgical practice. Soon after, in the early fifth century, JAS became the primary liturgy of both Jerusalem and Antioch. It probably increased in influence after

---

[1]Louis Bouyer, *Eucharist* (Notre Dame: Notre Dame Press, 1968) 269.

[2]John R. K. Fenwick, *Fourth-Century Anaphoral Construction Techniques,* Grove Liturgical Study 45 (Nottingham: Grove Books, 1986) and *The Anaphoras of St. Basil and St. James,* OCA 240 (Rome: Pontificium Institutum Orientale, 1992).

[3]For other summaries of the history, see B. C. Mercier, *La Liturgie de S. Jacques,* PO 26/2 (Paris: Firmin-Didot, 1946) 123–31; André Tarby, *La Prière Eucharistique de L'Église de Jérusalem,* Théologie Historique 17 (Paris: Beauchesne, 1972) 25–44.

the Council of Chalcedon (451), at which time Jerusalem became the patriarchate over much of Syria. Soon, JAS was supplanted by BAS and the liturgy of St. John Chrysostom (CHR), although in the meantime it may well have exerted influence over the development of both Byzantine and Alexandrine anaphoral traditions.[4] It also continued to be used by Syriac-speaking Monophysites, where it would have its most significant and long-lasting effect. This fact is helpful in the dating of the text, as Louis Duchesne observed: "The fact that the Jacobites have preserved it in Syriac as their fundamental liturgy proves that it was already consecrated by long use at the time when these communities took their rise—that is to say, about the middle of the sixth century."[5] JAS exerted influence over many of the over sixty anaphoras composed in subsequent centuries in the Syrian church.[6]

The medieval period provides only a few references to the use and influence of JAS. Near the beginning of the eighth century, Jacob of Edessa attempted to correct the Syrian text to follow the Greek text more closely.[7] About the same time, the Council of Trullo (692) defended the practice of mixing water with wine at the eucharist on the basis of BAS and JAS.[8] In 860, Charles the Bald referred to JAS in a letter to the clergy of Ravenna, naming it as the rite of the Jerusalem church.[9] The late medieval period provides us with the only extant manuscript evidence for our reconstruction of the genesis and development of the text. It also provides us with numerous examples of

[4]For the possible influence of JAS on later forms of BAS, see B. Botte, "L'épiclèse dans les liturgies syriennes orientales," *Sacris Erudiri* 6 (1954) 48–72. For influence on APSyr, see John R. K. Fenwick, *"The Missing Oblation": The Contents of the Early Antiochene Anaphora*, Alcuin/GROW Liturgical Study 11 (Nottingham: Grove Books, 1989). For the influence on Alexandrine forms, see G. J. Cuming, *The Liturgy of St. Mark*, OCA 234 (Rome: Pontificium Institutum Orientale, 1990).

[5]L. Duchesne, *Christian Worship: Its Origins and Evolution* (London: SPCK, 1931) 67–8.

[6]See J. M. Hanssens, *Institutiones liturgicae de ritibus orientalibus* III, Pars alter (Rome, 1932). At a few key points, JAS appears to resemble lines in the homilies of Severus of Antioch (513–518), indicating that it may in some form have been influential there. See G. J. Cuming, "The Liturgy of Antioch in the Time of Severus (513–518)," in J. Neil Alexander, ed., *Time and Community* (Washington, D.C.: Pastoral Press, 1990) 83–104.

[7]Adolf Rücker, *Die Syrische Jakobosanaphora nach der Rezension de Ja'qob von Edessa. Met dem griechischen Paralleltext* (Münster, 1923).

[8]Canon 32; J. D. Mansi, *Sacrorum conciliorum nova et amplissiam collectio* (Florence, 1737) 11:956.

[9]PL 72:99f.

Roman prayers and practices derived from or, at least, resembling portions of JAS.[10]

The influence of JAS has also extended into the modern period. It has directly influenced two liturgies of the Anglican Communion (the 1718 Scottish Communion Office and the 1922 Bombay Liturgy), the 1940 *Book of Common Order* of the Church of Scotland, and the liturgies of the Church of South India.[11] A version of this prayer is still used by the Mar Thoma Syrian Church of India.

DETERMINING THE TEXT

The brevity of this historical account and the complexity of theories regarding the redaction of JAS are the result of the relatively limited manuscript sources. Manuscripts are extant in five languages. Considered less important (and certainly less accessible) are the manuscripts in Ethiopic,[12] Georgian,[13] and Armenian.[14] These are probably all derivative of earlier Greek and Syriac forms, with the Georgian based on the Greek and the Ethiopic and Armenian on the Syriac. By far the most significant are the sources in Syriac and Greek (hereafter, SyrJAS and GkJAS, respectively). The standard critical edition of the Syriac (with Latin translation) is that of O. Heiming, which is based on thirty extant manuscripts.[15] The standard critical edition of the

[10]Josef A. Jungmann, *The Mass of the Roman Rite* (New York: Benzinger Brothers, 1955). The index provides numerous references to the influence of JAS in various portions of the Roman rite.

[11]Discussions of this influence include G. J. Cuming, *A History of Anglican Liturgy* (London: Macmillan, 1982) 139ff.; E. C. Ratcliff, "The Eucharistic Office and the Liturgy of St. James," in J. C. Winslow, et al, *The Eucharist in India* (London, 1920); T. S. Garret, *Worship in the Church of South India* (Richmond, Va.: John Knox Press, 1958) 9, 19, 26, 29ff.

[12]Sebastian Euringer, "Die Anaphora des hl. Jacobus, des Bruders des Herrn," *OC* 4 (1915) 1–23.

[13]F. C. Conybeare and Oliver Wardrop, "The Georgian Version of the Liturgy of St. James," *Revue de l'Orient chrétien* 18 (1913) 396–410; J. Jedlicka, "Das Prager Fragment der altgeorgischen Jakobusliturgie," *Archiv Orientální* 29 (1961) 183–96.

[14]Anton Baumstark, "Die armenische Rezension der Jakobusliturgie," *OC* 7–8 (1918) 1–32. Fenwick suggests that the Armenian version evidences a "degree of abbreviation and dislocation of material which confirmed the prevailing opinion that it is not a primary form of Jas, but a derivative of Sy-Jas" (*The Anaphoras of St. Basil and St. James*, 66).

[15]O. Heiming, *Anaphorae Syriacae* (Rome, 1953) 2:141-17. An English translation can be found in F. E. Brightman, *Liturgies Eastern and Western* (Oxford: Clarendon, 1896) 69–110.

Greek, prepared on the basis of twenty-nine manuscripts, is that of Mercier.[16] Both these texts are reproduced in English in the anthology of Jasper and Cuming.[17]

The textual problem that bears on the analysis of the history of the redaction concerns the relationship of the Syriac and Greek text. It is assumed that Greek was the original language of the anaphora. About the Syriac version, Bryan Spinks reflects the scholarly consensus that "it may be presumed that the translation was made before the Chalcedonian Council 451, and the split between Melkites and Monophysites."[18] Yet, it is also assumed that neither the Greek nor the Syriac preserves the original form of JAS. André Tarby attempted to determine the text of this original form up to the epiclesis but, as Fenwick points out, this is an extremely difficult task, because "the fact that two independent versions of an anaphora have material in common does not mean that the material concerned is ancient—it may be a late addition in one version which has been borrowed by the other." In addition, "material found only in one version cannot always be assumed to be secondary. Such material may be genuinely ancient but have been lost or replaced in other versions."[19] Thus, the current analysis of JAS relies upon the Syriac and Greek texts, without certain knowledge of which elements of which text came first. Only careful comparisons with other early Eastern anaphoras allows for any judgments to be made about the original form. This limitation makes any conclusion regarding the origins and redaction of the text tentative.

ANALYZING THE TEXT

Careful study of JAS properly begins with a close study of the text itself. The following paragraphs are a quick guided tour of the prayer, with brief comments concerning each section that highlight the prayer's most salient and unique features.

1) The opening of anaphora features the trinitarian blessing (2 Cor 13:13) and *Sursum corda*, common features of Eastern anaphoras.[20]

---

[16]Mercier, *La Liturgie de S. Jacques*, 115–256. The most significant single manuscript in this edition is Vatican 2282, which dates from the ninth century.

[17]*PEER*, 88–99.

[18]Bryan Spinks, "The Consecratory Epiklesis in the Anaphora of St. James," *SL* 11 (1976) 22.

[19]Fenwick, *The Anaphoras of St. Basil and St. James*, 66.

[20]See discussion in Bouyer, *Eucharist*, 269–70.

The trinitarian blessing points to the keen interest in trinitarian formulations throughout the prayer.

2) The preface features three important links with other texts. First, the five (SyrJAS) or six (GkJAS) verbs of praise ("to praise you, to bless you, to hymn you . . .") follow the sequence of those in the *Gloria in Excelsis* (though not the anaphora) of the *Apostolic Constitutions* (AC). Second, the identification of God as "creator of all, visible and invisible" is language identical with that of the *Mystagogical Catecheses* (MC). Third, GkJAS alone includes three additional phrases to identify God: "the treasure of eternal good things, the fountain of life and immortality, the God and Master of all." These phrases vaguely resemble phrases in AC, MARK, and Sarapion, but seem most related to a later form of BAS, though no definitive relationship can be proven.[21]

3) The presanctus calls all the heavenly bodies, all the precincts of earth, the heavenly church, and all angels to praise God, in contrast to prayers that thank God for creation of the heavens and earth. Unlike BAS, but like Eusebius, JAS makes special reference to "the heavenly Jerusalem" (possibly indicating geographical interests) and to "the assembly of the elect, the church of the first-born written in heaven, the spirits of righteous men and prophets, the souls of martyrs and apostles" (cf. Heb 12:22-23).[22] The identification of "angels, archangels, thrones, dominions, principalities and powers, and awesome virtues" relies on language from MC, though in a different sequence. The description of the cherubim and seraphim rely on Isa 6:2-3, as do MC and other Eastern prayers.

4) The *Sanctus* is then sung. Note the tense of the verbs in the *Benedictus:* "He that comes and will come," the latter verb being an addition to the biblical text.[23]

5) The postsanctus opens by echoing the cries of "holy, holy, holy," this time in direct trinitarian reference to the "King of the ages," the "only-begotten Son," and "the Holy Spirit, who searches out all things." The prayer then features a creed-like recital of God's deeds in history. This represents one of the more significant departures from the structure of the anaphora described in MC. Specific mention is made of creation, the fall, the law and prophets of Israel, and the

---

[21]See discussion in Fenwick, *The Anaphoras of St. Basil and St. James*, 81–6.

[22]Ibid., 91–5; Bouyer, *Eucharist*, 270–1; and Massey Shepherd, "Eusebius and the Liturgy of St. James," *Yearbook of Liturgical Studies* 4 (1963) 19–32.

[23]See discussion in Tarby, *La Prière Eucharistique*, 83–5.

incarnation, stopping just short of the institution of the Last Supper according to narrative sequence.[24] The *imago Dei* is mentioned in conjunction with both creation and incarnation, possibly reflecting a significant theological interest of the Jerusalem redactor.[25] In addition, Miguel Arranz has seen the stamp of Galatians 4:4 in this section, based on explicit references to the law, the Spirit, and incarnation.[26] The structure of this part of the prayer clearly resembles E-BAS, though with many textual differences.

6) The institution narrative is recited in its "proper" narrative sequence in the anaphora, that is, after the incarnation and prior to death and resurrection.[27] Special attention is given to Jesus' hands, which are described as "holy, undefiled, blameless, and immortal," a text resembling later versions of BAS.

7) The anamnesis picks up the narrative sequence of Christ's life, featuring creed-like statements regarding his death, resurrection, ascension, session in heaven, and return, all joined by a series of co-ordinating conjunctions.[28] This closely resembles E-BAS. SyrJAS addresses this prayer to Christ ("we remember your death . . ."), while GkJAS addresses the prayer to the Father ("We remember . . . his life-giving suffering").[29] The mention of judgment, as Bouyer points out, leads immediately to a prayer for divine mercy.[30] The second half of the anamnesis, known as the oblation, features a verb of offering in the present tense ("we offer you") and the famous phrase "bloodless sacrifice" that can be traced back to Eusebius and MC.[31] Signifi-

---

[24]Discussion in Fenwick, *The Anaphoras of St. Basil and St. James*, 106–22; Bouyer, *Eucharist*, 271–2; Louis Ligier, "The Origins of the Eucharistic Prayer: From the Last Supper to the Eucharist," *SL* 9 (1973) 183.

[25]Emmanuel J. Cutrone, "Cyril's Mystagogical Catecheses and the Evolution of the Jerusalem Anaphora," *OCP* 44 (1978) 52–74. JAS mentions the notion of *imago Dei* twice in the course of the anaphora, paralelling a reference in AC 8. Such prominence for a relatively minor theme in either the Hebrew or Christian scriptures is conspicuous. See Tarby, *La Prière Eucharistique*, 125–34.

[26]Miguel Arranz, "L'economie du Salut: dans la prière Post-Sanctus des anaphores de type antiochéen," *La Maison-Dieu* 106 (1972) 46–75.

[27]See discussion in Fenwick, *The Anaphoras of St. Basil and St. James*, 137–46.

[28]Ibid., 162–6; Bouyer, *Eucharist*, 272–4.

[29]Josef A. Jungmann, *The Place of Christ in Liturgical Prayer* (Collegeville: The Liturgical Press, 1989) 55–68, esp. 57–8.

[30]Bouyer, *Eucharist*, 274.

[31]See discussion in Kenneth Stevenson, "Anaphoral Offering," *EL* 94 (1980) 209–28; *Eucharist and Offering* (New York: Pueblo, 1986) 42–4; and Robert F. Taft,

cantly, this section of the prayer does not correspond to anything in BAS. This section is also marked by a decidedly penitential tone, with its references to human sinfulness and its quotation from Psalm 102:10: "deal not with us after our sins nor reward us according to our iniquities."[32]

8) The epiclesis is one of the most studied sections of the prayer.[33] Its begins with a three-fold "have mercy on us" that continues the penitential flavor, and includes a relatively lengthy identification of the Spirit as Lord. This reflects the doctrinal interests of the late fourth century, and even the particular credal phraseology of the Council of Constantinople (381): "the Lord and giver of life," "who spoke through the prophets," and "consubstantial and co-eternal." This doctrinal language is supplemented by narrative language, which derives from MC, with particular reference to the Spirit's work through the law and prophets, the baptism of Jesus, and Pentecost.

Remarkably, the prayer features two verbs (*exapostello*, "send out," and *katapempo*, "send down") that call upon the Holy Spirit, in effect making for two discrete epicleses. Bryan Spinks argues that it is likely that "*exapostello* is peculiar to Cyril and James, and may be, therefore, the particular Jerusalem terminology for the invocation of the Spirit," while "*katapempo* represents an Antiochene Epikletic word."[34] The second epiclesis also bears resemblance to the Greek Anaphora of St. Gregory.[35] As in E-BAS, both verbs of sending call for the Spirit to be sent both "upon us and upon these gifts," reflecting a typical pattern of late fourth-century prayers. The epiclesis concludes with a long, rhetorically-colorful extension, unique to JAS, that asks for the strengthening of the church.

10) The intercessions are by far the largest portion of the anaphora, comprising nearly two-thirds of the full prayer. Bouyer concluded that they were "the most elaborate . . . found in any liturgy of the

"Understanding the Byzantine Anaphoral Oblation," in Nathan Mitchell and John F. Baldovin, eds., *Rule of Prayer, Rule of Faith: Essays in Honor of Aidan Kavanagh, O.S.B.* (Collegeville: The Liturgical Press, 1996) 32–55.

[32]Massey Shepherd links this with Eusebius: "Eusebius and the Liturgy of St. James," 116.

[33]See discussion in Fenwick, *The Anaphoras of St. Basil and St. James*, 185–91; Bouyer, *Eucharist*, 274; Spinks, "The Consecratory Epiklesis," 19–39.

[34]Spinks, "The Consecratory Epiclesis," 32, 33.

[35]Botte, "L'épiclèse dans les liturgies syriennes orientales"; Fenwick, *The Anaphoras of St. Basil and St. James*, 187–9.

patristic age."[36] Fenwick's analysis has demonstrated that the structure of the intercessions in JAS closely resembles that of E-BAS, with some particular prayers drawn from MC.[37] The intercessions are linked by their common verb of petition, "remember." Eucharist thus involves not only a remembrance of God's deeds, but a plea for God to remember the church. The intercessions are marked by a significant ecclesiological concern that is already begun at the end of the epiclesis. Of particular interest is the first intercession for Zion and the holy places, which reflects the geographical setting of the text. This emphasis is echoed six intercessions later with a reference to "your holy and royal city." Several intercessions, including those for the priests, bishop, and all worshipers, highlight the sacrificial aspect of the eucharist. The prayer for the gathered priests specifically refers to "the offering of the holy and bloodless sacrifice," language that echoes the earlier oblation. Also, the prayer for the bishop continues the penitential theme of the anaphora ("your humble, sinful, and unworthy servant . . . since sin abounded in me").

11) The concluding doxology is entirely different in the Greek and Syriac forms of JAS.[38] The Syriac doxology focuses on the glorification of the divine name, while the Greek text follows directly after an appeal for forgiveness from sin.

CHARACTERISTICS OF THE PRAYER AS A WHOLE

On the basis of this brief analysis, we can identity the salient features of JAS. First, as we have noted, the prayer clearly reflects geographical interests, with numerous references to Jerusalem, the holy places in Jerusalem, and to the kingdom of God as "the heavenly Jerusalem." At the end of the fourth century, Jerusalem was a city of increasing ecclesiastical influence that attracted numerous pilgrims, thanks in part to Constantine's aggressive building of churches at the sites of events in Jesus' life. JAS reflects this importance, and provides a liturgical monument to parallel the structural monuments of the city.

Second, JAS is marked by a distinct concern for doctrinal precision. For one, it reflects an unmistakable trinitarian structure. In some

[36]Bouyer, *Eucharist*, 277.
[37]See discussion in Fenwick, *The Anaphoras of St. Basil and St. James*, 271–83; Bouyer, *Eucharist*, 274–8.
[38]See discussion in Fenwick, *The Anaphoras of St. Basil and St. James*, 294–5.

Eastern prayers, trinitarian theology is reflected in one or more small blocks of text that name the Father, Son, and Holy Spirit in succession. This is found in only one instance in JAS, at the opening of the postsanctus. But as Fenwick concludes: "The Redactor of James . . . creates his Trinitarian shape by devoting the Preface to the Father, the Postsanctus and Anamnesis to the Son . . . and the much amplified Epiclesis to the Holy Spirit."[39] The trinitarianism in JAS is thus conceived on a broad, structural scale. Bouyer, though appreciative of the trinitarian emphasis, does identify a "defect" in the prayer, consisting of a "schematicism to reserve creation alone to the Father, redemption to the Son, and sanctification to the Spirit."[40] This reflects the so-called doctrine of appropriations by which divine persons are associated with particular dimensions of salvation history. Classical trinitarianism, however, would not see this as opposed to the equally strong claim that all works in the economy of salvation are the works of the undivided Trinity. In addition, the prayer shows concern for doctrinal precision with its reference to Christ as "consubstantial, co-eternal" and to the Spirit as the "Lord and giver of life." Finally, JAS also reflects the tinkering with prepositions in doxologies which Jungmann has linked with the development of trinitarian orthodoxy. Prayers are offered not only through Christ, but also to Christ. Praise is offered to not only the Father, but also the Son and the Spirit.[41] Each of these points evidences the inter-relation of credal, doctrinal, and liturgical language at the end of the fourth century.

Third, JAS evidences a propensity for textual elaboration and literary refinement. Comparison with nearly every earlier anaphora demonstrates the unmistakable process of elaboration, which reflects one of the basic "laws" or patterns of early liturgical development. JAS is a classic witness to this process of elaboration, with its two oblations, two epicleses, the extension to the second epiclesis, and its very lengthy intercessions. This length is not the result of careless additions. Rather, the additions are crafted into a refined, highly-structured prayer. This literary refinement can be noticed in the smooth transitions between sections of the prayer: The presanctus

[39]Fenwick, *The Anaphoras of St. Basil and St. James*, 82; also Bouyer, *Eucharist*, 278; Tarby, *La Prière Eucharistique*, 90–108.

[40]Bouyer, *Eucharist*, 279.

[41]See Jungmann, *The Place of Christ in Liturgical Prayer*, 193, although he also speaks of "a considerable reserve towards the liturgical prayer to Christ" in JAS (236), with most prayers directed to the Father (62).

identifies all of creation as joining in the venerable hymn of praise, the postsanctus begins with acclamations of "holiness" that flow from the *Sanctus* itself, and the intercessions flow naturally from the ecclesiologically-oriented conclusion to the epiclesis. For these reasons, Bouyer described JAS as having a "well thought-out structure, that remodeled the traditional materials with hardly believable daring."[42]

Fourth, the prayer reflects a decidedly penitential flavor, with references to human sinfulness and pleas for divine forgiveness scattered throughout the anaphora.

TEXTUAL SOURCES AND THE PROCESS OF REDACTION
The central question in twentieth-century scholarly analysis of JAS concerns its relationship to other Eastern anaphoras. There is sufficient structural and textual similarity among these anaphoras to posit some mutual influence, though not enough to establish any definitive statement regarding the process of development. In determining the place of JAS in the development of fourth-century anaphoras, we must assess the text in terms of its relationship with six other extant sources: the writings of Eusebius of Caesarea, the descriptions of liturgical practice found in MC, the anaphora in AC 8, MARK, and the early and late form of BAS. This section will briefly review the current state of scholarship on each of these relationships.

First, JAS bears slight but significant resemblance to the writings of Eusebius of Caesarea. At issue is the dedication sermon preached by Eusebius at the consecration of the cathedral built by Bishop Paulinus at Tyre c. 315, in which Massey Shepherd saw "unmistakable parallels" to JAS.[43] A first parallel is a reference in Eusebius to Hebrews 12:22-23, which is reflected in the preface of JAS. Second, and more significant, is the reference in the oblation to the eucharist as an "unbloody sacrifice." Shepherd notes that these words are not found in a reference specifically to the eucharist by any Christian author prior to Eusebius. In the fourth century, this theologically-redolent phrase appears in both Palestinian and Alexandrian, but *not* Antiochene eucharistic rites. It may be uniquely Palestinian eucharistic language that was continued in the redaction of JAS.

---

[42]Bouyer, *Eucharist*, 246.
[43]Shepherd, "Eusebius and the Liturgy of St. James," 109.

Second, JAS reflects an unmistakable relationship with MC. This is not in any way surprising, given their common point of origin in Jerusalem. This relationship is marked by common phraseology in several portions of the eucharistic prayer. Phrases from MC are found in the preface, presanctus, institution narrative, anamnesis, epiclesis, and intercession of JAS, as described above. These common phrases are generally assumed to be part of the traditional Jerusalem liturgy, which was maintained in some form in the redaction of JAS. These common phrases, however, do not imply a common structure, and JAS features the dramatic addition of a full anamnesis and institution narrative to the structure of MC. Other textual parallels must be sought for this section of the prayer.

Third, the structural differences between JAS and MC have often been assumed to result from the influence of the Antiochene anaphora, of which the anaphora of AC 8 is a prime example. Spinks, for example, suggested that "a possible explanation might be that the influence of AC caused a thanksgiving for redemption, Institution Narrative and an Anamnesis to be inserted into the Liturgy at Jerusalem, the final synthesis being St. James."[44] Though this suggestion has been superseded by the work of Fenwick, as we shall see, there are, in fact, a few significant points of resemblance between AC 8 and JAS. As mentioned above, the praise verbs in the preface to JAS reflect the exact sequence of the *Gloria in Excelsis* in AC. The second imperative in the epiclesis of JAS, *katapempo*, is found in AC and in a few other Antiochene anaphoras. In addition, both AC and JAS refer to the creation of humanity in the image of God in their recital of salvation history. Though these similarities do not account for a large portion of the prayer, it is not out of the question that the Jerusalem redactor was aware of several Antiochene-type prayers, one of which may have been AC.

Fourth, JAS also evidences some similarities to Egyptian anaphoras. Geoffrey Cuming was most interested in this relationship, arguing that "the Jerusalem rite, though showing clear signs of Syrian influence, is basically akin rather to the Egyptian *Liturgy of St. Mark*."[45] More specifically, Cuming suggested that "St. Mark and St. James probably had a common ancestor. . . . If we had a papyrus

[44]Spinks, "The Consecratory Epiclesis," 21.
[45]G. J. Cuming, "Egyptian Elements in the Jerusalem Liturgy," *JTS* 25 (1974) 117–24.

fragment of St. James, it would probably contain something very like the Strasbourg Papyrus of St. Mark."[46] The most tantalizing potential link between Palestinian and Egyptian prayers is the presence of the phrase "unbloody sacrifice" in Egyptian sources. In addition, some non-anaphoral portions of the prayer, such as the litanies, feature apparent structural and textual similarities.[47] There is no doubt that JAS resembles the final form of MARK, particularly in its anamnesis and epiclesis, though it is most often assumed that JAS influenced MARK and not the other way around.[48] There simply is not substantial extant early textual evidence to confirm Cuming's claim regarding a common source for MARK and JAS.[49]

Fifth and most significantly, JAS appears to have significant lines of interdependence with at least early and possibly late forms of BAS. What has come to be a standard view was suggested by Gregory Dix: "There is a relationship between St. James . . . and the equivalent parts of the Liturgy of St. Basil, which is not close enough to describe as 'borrowing' on either side but which is nevertheless unmistakable in places. It might well be accounted for by their being independent versions of the same common original."[50] More recently, John Fenwick has argued that JAS actually reflects the conflation of an early form of BAS with the one known to the author of MC. Fenwick's thesis is that

"the similarities between Basil and James are not due in any substantial way to the influence one upon the other of the developed forms in which we now know them . . . but rather to the fact that *each represents an independent reworking of a common original*, an original which is preserved most faithfully in the Egyptian version of the Liturgy of St. Basil."[51]

[46]G. J. Cuming, "The Shape of the Anaphora," *SP* 20 (1987) 341.

[47]Cuming's studies of the non-anaphoral portions of the prayer include: "The Litanies in the Liturgy of St. James," *Ecclesia Orans* 3 (1986) 175–80; "The Missa Catechumenorum of the Liturgy of St. James," *SL* 17 (1987) 62–71; "Further Studies in the Liturgy of St. James," *SL* 18 (1988) 161–9. See especially "The Litanies," 180.

[48]See Cuming, *The Liturgy of St. Mark.*

[49]Unless, of course, this source is E-BAS, as discussed by Fenwick.

[50]Gregory Dix, *The Shape of the Liturgy* (London: Dacre, 1945) 204.

[51]Fenwick, *The Anaphoras of St. Basil and St. James,* xxiv. The resemblance of JAS to BAS was also explored in H. Lietzmann, *Mass and Lord's Supper* (Leiden: Brill, 1953–1979) 27, 44, 116; and in Cuming, "The Shape of the Anaphora."

Fenwick supports his thesis by painstaking analysis of both the structure and phraseology of JAS and BAS. Two observations are particularly striking: first, the sequence of the anaphoral intercessions, where material from MC is clearly incorporated within the structure of intercessions found in E-BAS; and second, the fact that texts from BAS are found in JAS in those sections which have no equivalent in MC.[52] Thus, Fenwick contends that JAS was the result of a conflation of the material in the MC with an early form of BAS.

On the basis of this analysis, Fenwick presents a thoughtful conjecture regarding the context of this Jerusalem conflation. "It seems very likely," Fenwick muses, "that the Redactor of Jas undertook his task because he felt that the Jerusalem anaphora which he had inherited was in some respects inadequate." A new model was needed, yet "it was important that it contain sufficient of the familiar traditional phraseology to ensure its rapid acceptance by the Jerusalemite clergy and people . . . a synthesis was needed,"[53] Thus, the Redactor synthesized the most prominent phrases from the earlier Jerusalem rite with the best available model, which was the prayer associated with the name Basil: "All a Jerusalem Redactor had to do was to conflate his traditional material with this highly esteemed anaphora to create a new prayer which was distinctly Jerusalemite yet contained all the best features of the currently popular Cappadocian form."[54] The textual resources for this project, and the motivation for carrying it out, may well be accounted for by Jerusalem's status at the end of the fourth century as a "liturgical showpiece to the whole Christian world."[55]

In sum, it is generally agreed that JAS is a significant link in the development of Eastern anaphoras. Eusebius and MC are widely assumed to antedate and to have influenced the development of JAS. AC 8 and MARK each have structural and textual similarities with JAS that warrant continued comparison. But the closest and most provocative data arise out of comparing JAS with BAS in its various stages of development.

---

[52]See Fenwick, *Fourth Century Anaphoral Construction Techniques*, 26–9, and *The Anaphoras of St. Basil and St. James*, 301–9.

[53]Fenwick, *The Anaphoras of St. Basil and St. James*, 44–5.

[54]Ibid., 305.

[55]Ibid., 5.

DATING THE TEXT

The precise dating of JAS is not possible with the extant evidence. Yet the following six factors help us narrow the range of dates in which the conflation of the Jerusalem anaphora likely took place. First, the dating of JAS depends in part on the dating of MC. JAS almost certainly represents a later textual stratum than does MC, incorporating elements of the earlier Jerusalem anaphora in a more fully developed structure. Conjectures regarding the dating of MC vary widely, from 340–80. Second, if Fenwick's theory is correct, the dating of JAS depends upon the date when a version of BAS, such as E-BAS, would have available for use by the Jerusalem redactor. This also points to the end of the fourth century. Third, there is the slight complication of the credal material in the anaphora, which curiously Fenwick does not discuss. Of particular significance is the reference to the Spirit as "Lord and giver of life . . . who spoke by the prophets." This language was not formally adopted as creed until the Council of Constantinople (381). It is perhaps possible that the credal formulation was used liturgically before its adoption as creed. Or it is possible that this material was added after the original conflation of JAS in an effort to refine the doctrinal precision of the epiclesis. But this text could not have been added much before 381.[56] Fourth, the conflation of JAS had to have been complete (or nearly so) prior to the time in which it influenced other Eastern anaphoras, including (possibly) the Ryland Manuscript of MARK (400), as well as later mss of MARK (425), and the anaphora of the Twelve Apostles (c. 400). This points to the likelihood that the conflation of JAS was complete near the end of the fourth century. In any case, it had to have been completed and translated into Syriac by the mid-fifth century, as discussed above. Thus, the dating of JAS is very dependent on the dating of other Eastern anaphoras, as well as on hypotheses regarding lines of mutual influence among these prayers. Fenwick's conclusion that JAS was likely written c. 370, possibly by Cyril, is as good a conjecture as any thus far.

[56]In the same manner the reference to "theotokos" may well have been added even later. This issue is also significant for determining whether, as Fenwick has suggested, Cyril may have himself produced the conflation of JAS. J.N.D. Kelly, *Early Christian Doctrines* (London: A & C Black, 1968) 256–8, observes that Cyril was a moderate in the fourth-century theological debates, affirming the deity of the Spirit, but shying away from the formal terminology *homo-ousios*. Either Cyril did not add the material or Kelly's assessment must be revised.

In sum, it appears as though sometime between 370 and 400 that a literarily and theologically astute Jerusalem redactor worked with a number of extant prayer texts and credal formulations to produce a highly refined anaphoral prayer, that in turn influenced a number of subsequent Eastern anaphoras.

NEW DIRECTIONS IN THE STUDY OF JAS

As this brief overview points out, JAS has been extensively studied from a variety of angles by some of the leading liturgical scholars of this century. Without the discovery of new textual evidence, the days of making ground-breaking discoveries regarding this text are perhaps largely in the past. Nevertheless, I suggest two brief notes—one theological and one regarding textual sources—that may refine our understanding of the development and significance of this text.

Narrativity and Eschatology

First, JAS reflects a remarkable awareness of the entire sweep of salvation history and a strong sense of the forward movement of salvation history toward eschatological fulfillment. Traditional analysis of eucharistic prayers begins by identifying and comparing what had, by the end of the fourth century, become standard structural components: preface, presanctus, *Sanctus*, postsanctus, institution narrative, anamnesis, oblation, epiclesis, intercessions, doxology. This analysis, while helpful for pointing to the structural evolution of Eastern anaphoras, may obscure the most salient feature of JAS, its remarkable narrative unity.

Viewed as a whole, the anaphora sketches the entire sweep of salvation history. Following the opening salvo of praise, it continues with specific references to creation, the fall, the law and prophets of Israel, the incarnation (postsanctus), the Last Supper (institution narrative), Christ's death, resurrection, ascension, session (anamnesis), Pentecost (epiclesis), the life of the Church (intercessions), and the praise of God in the coming kingdom (doxology). Seen in this way, the entire prayer has an anamnetic quality.[57] That is, while the so-called "anamnesis" section of the prayer remains focused as a recital of key events in the history of salvation, this in no way exhausts the

[57]Cutrone, "Cyril's Mystagogical Catecheses and the Evolution of the Jerusalem Anaphora," 61.

anamnetic dimension of the prayer. The entire prayer is structured as an expansive narrative of creation and salvation history.

Certainly the innovation of placing the institution narrative in the sequence of events in Christ's life is the most obvious step in realizing this narrative sequence. But it is not the only one. Another is the extension of the epiclesis to focus on the present life of the church, which, in turn, is echoed throughout the intercessions. Yet another is the narrative sequence of the second half of the intercessions, which petitions God to remember the faithful departed of ancient Israel, Mary, the apostles, the martyrs, and the bishops, teachers, and councils of the early church. Yet another is the way in which this recital of past historical events has the feel of driving toward an eschatological resolution.[58] Eschatological references are scattered throughout the rite, reaching a climax at the end of the intercessions, where the praise of God is acclaimed "now and always and to ages of ages."

In his analysis of the prayer, Bouyer spoke of the "redistribution of material" in the prayer that occurred through "analysis of each idea in its parts" and eventual synthesis "of themselves into one general idea,"[59] though he said little about what this might be. I am suggesting that this large time-eschatology structure may be the conceptual framework which governed the textual adaptation of the various parts of the anaphora.

Textual Sources

Second, regarding textual sources, it may well be the case that the redactor of the Jerusalem anaphora had a sense of the variability of BAS. More specifically, based on Fenwick's own presentation of BAS and JAS, it is apparent the redactor of JAS may have been influenced by both early and late sources of BAS. Fenwick suggests that "it is reasonable to suppose the Redactor of Jas, rather than extracting material from a number of anaphoras, chose one in order to provide both material for his missing sections and an overall framework."[60] I

---

[58]Thus, JAS, along with other Eastern anaphoras, serves as important evidence in Geoffrey Wainwright's study of the eschatological horizen of eucharistic celebration in *Eucharist and Eschatology* (New York: Oxford University Press, 1980) 52, 63, 84, and other pages cited in the index. See also Dix, *The Shape of the Liturgy*, 205.

[59]Bouyer, *Eucharist*, 249.

[60]Fenwick, *Fourth-Century Anaphoral Construction Techniques*, 15.

am suggesting that the redactor worked with more than one text, or, at the very least, with more than one version of a text of BAS.

The basis for my contention is my analysis of the text provided in Fenwick's *Anaphoras of St. Basil and St. James*, where he prints in four parallel columns the text of E-BAS (the earliest known form of BAS), Ω-BAS (a hypothetical reconstruction of a late form of BAS, prior to its further adaptation in Greek and Armenian), SyrJAS, and GkJAS. This format allows one to compare fairly easily both early and late versions of BAS for their potential influence on JAS.

Suppose we grant that BAS in some form exerted influence on JAS, as Fenwick has suggested, but reserve judgment as to which version of BAS it was. In this case, our attention is drawn to any text that appears in one form of BAS but not the other, and in at least one form of JAS. (Extant texts from both versions of BAS and JAS would not help us decide which version the redactor of JAS might have used.)

The relevant texts are as follows.[61] First, there are some texts that appear in E-BAS and in a version of JAS, but do not appear in Ω-BAS. These include scattered phrases in the presanctus ("and all their powers"), postsanctus (the reference to transgressing "your commandment"; the reference "our Lord Jesus Christ" following the text "only begotten Son"; the reference "from the Holy Spirit"; and the name "Mary"), institution narrative (he mixed "wine and water"), the epiclesis (the phrase "for the sanctification of souls and bodies"), and intercessions (the reference to "confessors" in the petition just prior to the remembrance of Mary, and the phrase "whence pain, sorrow, and sighing have fled away" following a reference to Abraham, Isaac, and Jacob near the end of the intercessions). These texts support Fenwick's thesis that the redactor of JAS worked with an early form of BAS.

Second, there are also several texts that appear in Ω-BAS and a version of JAS, but not in the earlier form of E-BAS.[62] These texts include

---

[61]Readers are invited to underline these words in *PEER* in order to sense the flow of this argument. These references are based on Fenwick's presentation of the Greek and Latin translation of the Syriac texts. The following are the references in Fenwick's apparatus (chart number. line number): II.7; III.34, 79, 80, 83; 100–3; VI.59; X.102–3; XV.360, 594–5.

[62]The following are the references in Fenwick's apparatus (chart number. line number): I.6, 18–9, 24, 43–4, 70, 72; II.1, 22–3, 33–42; III. 26, 57; VI.9–10, 23–31, 46, 68–71, 76, 92–3; X.67–8, 78–9; XV.33–4, 71–86, 194–8, 249–61, 276–9, 328, 335–43, 382–3, 399–400, 499, 639–43; XIII.27–9.

scattered phrases in the preface (the words "suitable," *"to praise you, to hymn you,"* "to give thanks to you," "of all creation," *"of eternal good things,"* and *"the fountain"*), presanctus ("you are hymned," *"thrones, dominions,"* "which cover their own faces . . . silent hymns of praise"), postsanctus (*"after your image,"* "for you are good"), institution narrative ("voluntary and *life-giving*," "in his holy, undefiled, blameless, and immortal hands . . . and showed it to you, his God and Father; he gave thanks," "broken," "to his *holy* . . . disciples and apostles," "of the new covenant," and *"resurrection we confess"*), epiclesis ("this bread . . . the body" and "this cup the blood"), intercessions ("divide the word of truth in orthodoxy," *"Remember, Lord, according to the multitude of you pity, me also, your humble, sinful, unworthy servant,"* "Remember, Lord, the emperor . . . subject to him all the . . . barbarous nations . . . that we may lead a quiet and peaceful life in all piety and gravity," *"end the divisions in the churches, speedily put down the uprisings of the heresies,"* "abundance of fruit," "the crown of the year," *"Remember, Lord, those who have brought and bring forth fruit in your holy churches, O God, those who remember the poor," "give them heavenly things for earthly, imperishable for perishable, eternal for temporal,"* "Holy John . . . baptist," and "Holy Stephen . . . first martyr"), and doxology (*"now and always and to the ages of ages"*). These texts seem to suggest a relationship of textual dependence between Ω-BAS and JAS.

At first glance, it appears the relationship between Ω-BAS and JAS is stronger than that between E-BAS and JAS. There simply is more text in common with the former than with the latter. It is not, however, quite as clear as this suggests. First, the references in the presanctus to "all creation" and "which cover their own faces. . . ." and the intercession for the emperor also appear in MC, which we can assume was their immediate source. Second, some of these texts appear in only one form of JAS, usually GkJAS (these are italicized in the preceding paragraph). These may be a later accretion, added after JAS was translated into Syriac in the mid-fifth century, or they may have been in the original conflation of JAS and dropped in later Syriac revisions.[63] Thus they should be considered as ambivalent evidence. Yet

---

[63]Here we can recall Fenwick's comment that "material found only in one version cannot always be assumed to be secondary. Such material may be genuinely ancient but have been lost or replaced in other versions" (*Anaphoras of St. Basil and St. James*, 66).

there are still other significant phrases common to Ω-BAS and JAS, but not to E-BAS.

Third, it is possible that these phrases were first in JAS, which then influenced the later form of BAS, instead of the other way around. However, the relevant texts, in every case where they are slightly different, are slightly longer in JAS than in Ω-BAS. This would seem to point to the phrases in JAS having been adapted from Ω-BAS, and suggest, albeit tentatively, that JAS was, in fact, influenced by a later form of BAS. This hypothesis is certainly not conclusive. The evidence consists of relatively few phrases out of the entire prayer and relies upon the "liturgical law" that later texts are more elaborate, which need not be true in every instance.

Nevertheless, if we assume that some form of BAS influenced JAS, then Ω-BAS appears to be as strong a contender as E-BAS for the role. I do not wish to contest Fenwick's carefully articulated thesis that the Jerusalem redactor worked with some form of BAS. But I do wish to suggest that the redactor was influenced by a later form of BAS, a form something like Fenwick's Ω-BAS.[64] Perhaps the most complete hypothesis would posit that the Jerusalem redactor worked with both forms of BAS. This would suggest the anaphoral construction techniques in use in Jerusalem at the end of the fourth century involved a process of refinement, pursued in light of any available liturgical text.

This slight revision to Fenwick's thesis can helpfully be pictured graphically. In his study, Fenwick produced this chart:

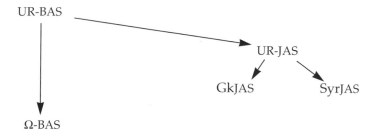

[64]This directly opposes Fenwick's statement that of the material in Ω-BAS, "none is found in both versions of Jas," which is the basis for his claim that this is "insufficient to support the possibility that it was Ω-Basil with which the anaphora of MC.V was conflated" (ibid., 303).

My own contention is that the following analysis of the relation-ship between BAS and JAS is more satisfactory:

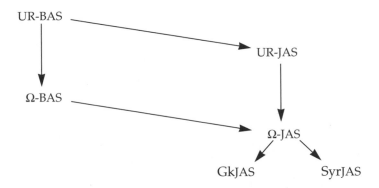

This analysis may also influence the dating of JAS. Perhaps, as Fen-wick suggests, the influence of E-BAS on JAS occurred relatively early (even c. 370), that is, before Ω-BAS was known in Jerusalem (c. 370–??), and a subsequent redaction of JAS incorporated elements of Ω-BAS at a slightly later date. Perhaps the whole process went through several stages of development, such that E-BAS was worked in about 370 and Ω-BAS about 380, credal material added about 390, and a stray *theotokos* inserted even later.[65] In any case, it is clearly the case that the Jerusalem anaphora is part of a much larger puzzle involving each of the anaphoras discussed in this volume.

[65]It cannot be ruled out, however, that the Jerusalem redactor may have worked with both early and late texts at a single time.

Raphael Graves

8. The Anaphora of the Eighth Book of the Apostolic Constitutions

From the earliest attempts to discern the origins of the eucharistic prayer, the anaphora of the pseudo-Clementine liturgy found in the Eighth Book of the *Apostolic Constitutions* (hereafter AC) has held a particular fascination for liturgical historians.[1] Among early eighteenth-century liturgists who accepted AC genuinely apostolic, the Clementine liturgy was regarded as the original pattern of the primitive eucharist. The importance of AC for liturgiologists was hardly diminished, however, when it was recognized to be a fourth-century compilation. Not long after liturgical scholars put aside their belief in the genuine apostolic authorship of the work, some began to posit a link between certain prayers in AC and the liturgy of the Jewish synagogue. AC was such a key piece of evidence for theories seeking to trace the origin of Christian liturgical practice back to the synagogue that for many liturgiologists its anaphora retained a central place for understanding the development of the eucharistic rites.

This first portion of this essay will review a number of theories put forward concerning the composition of the anaphora of AC 8. These theories fall into two broad approaches. One seeks to trace elements in the anaphora of AC 8.12 back through the prayers of AC 7.33–38 to the liturgy of the Jewish synagogue. The second approach centers on the redactor's use of other early anaphoral sources. The latter part of the essay will look in greater depth at how the redactor employed these sources to compose his anaphora.

Since the view that AC is a fourth-century compilation gained wide acceptance a century ago, a consensus of scholarly opinion has formed on a few points regarding the composition of its anaphora. Structurally the anaphora is of the West Syrian type, and like the

[1] ET in *PEER*, 103–3.

remainder of the pseudo-Clementine liturgy in which it is embedded, it reflects liturgical practice in the region of Antioch in the last quarter of the fourth century. Furthermore, it is agreed that the hand of the redactor of AC has left a distinct mark on the character of the text. Thirdly, it is recognized that Book Eight as a whole has been structured around the framework of the document commonly referred to as the *Apostolic Tradition* of Hippolytus (AT) and that the anaphora itself contains small blocks of material which are derived from this source. Beyond these few points, there is little broad agreement about the composition of this eucharistic prayer or its place in the history of the development of anaphoras in general.

CONNECTIONS WITH THE LITURGY OF THE SYNAGOGUE

AC has been a continuous focus of attention in the literature on the Jewish roots of Christian liturgy since the turn of the century, when Kaufmann Kohler recognized the collection of prayers in AC 7.33–38 as a version of the Seven Benedictions of the synagogue liturgy for the Sabbath.[2] While Kohler's main interest was this collection of so-called Jewish prayers in AC 7, he also noted the resemblance of sections of AC 8.12 with portions of these prayers.[3] Anton Baumstark initiated the investigation for a Jewish source behind AC 8 among Christian liturgiologists.[4] He claimed to have "proved from the later Biblical literature and Apocryphal writings that both this prayer of the *Jôzêr* as well as the many forms of the Christian anaphoric prayer are the echo of a type of prayer which belongs to the worship of the post-exilic Temple."[5] This type of euchological pattern is found pre-eminently in the anaphora of AC 8. Another scholar to argue for a Jewish source for a number of prayers from AC 7 and 8 was Wilhelm

[2]Kohler first made this suggestion in "Ueber die Ursprünge und Grundformen der synagogalen Liturgie," *Monatschrift für die Geschichte und Wissenschaft des Judentums* 37 (1893) 441–51, 489–97. He developed the idea in the entries "Didascalia" and "Essenes," in I. Singer, ed., *The Jewish Encyclopedia* (New York: Funk and Wagnals, 1903) 4:592–94, 5:224f.; and in "The Essene Version of the Seven Benedictions as Preserved in the vii Book of the Apostolic Constitutions," *Hebrew Union College Annual* 1 (1924) 410–25.

[3]Kohler, "Essenes," 224–31.

[4]"Das eucharistische Hochgebet und die Literatur des nachexilischen Judentums," *Theologie und Glaube* 2 (1910) 354–70.

[5]A. Baumstark, *Comparative Liturgy* (London: Mowbray, 1958) 50.

Bousset.[6] Bousset also noted parallels between AC 7.34 and AC 8.12.9–20, but argued that the two prayers were not the work of the same redactor. He was convinced that the differences between the two prayers were so great that they must be independent reworkings of a common hellenistic Jewish source.[7]

Over the course of the century since the first of these articles appeared, numerous scholars have sought to develop further the theories set forth by Kohler, Baumstark, and Bousset.[8] While each of these seminal studies argued for a Jewish source behind portions of the anaphora of AC 8, there were significant differences in the approaches taken by Bousset and Baumstark which have led to separate lines of research. Bousset was primarily interested in the collection of prayers in AC 7.33–38, and the aim of his study was to explore the Jewish background of the prayers rather than the development of the Christian liturgy. Baumstark on the other hand was chiefly interested in the anaphora of AC 8 and in coming to an understanding of the evolution of the eucharistic prayer. While most subsequent scholars have undoubtedly been aware of both lines of research, the two approaches have persisted to the present.[9]

Bousset's work was taken up by E. R. Goodenough, who not only affirmed that all the prayers Bousset suggested might be Jewish in origin actually were, but claimed to find even more Jewish prayers in AC.[10] Goodenough maintained that these Jewish prayers were evidence that Philo's "mystical Judaism" was widespread throughout the diaspora.[11] Goodenough represents an extreme, but his inclination

[6]"Eine jüdische Gebetssammlung im siebenten Buch der apostolischen Konstitutionen," *Nachrichten von der königlichten Gesellschaft der Wissenschaften zu Göttingen: Philologisch-historische Klasse, 1915* (1916) 483–5. Bousset was apparently ignorant of both Baumstark's article and the work of Kohler.

[7]Ibid., 455–7.

[8]The best summary of the this literature is David Fiensy, "The Hellenistic Synagogal Prayers: One Hundred Years of Discussion," *Journal for the Study of the Pseudepigrapha* 5 (1989) 17–27.

[9]Fiensy, "Hellenistic Synagogal Prayers," describes Bousset's approach as belonging to the history of religions school, while Baumstark employed the approach of comparative liturgy.

[10]E. R. Goodenough, *By Light, Light: The Mystic Gospel of Hellenistic Judaism* (New Haven: Yale, 1935) 336.

[11]M. Simon, *Verus Israel* (Paris: Bocard, 1948) 74–82, also saw in the Jewish prayers of AC evidence that post-70 diaspora Judaism continued to make use of hellenistic philosophical and ethical ideas.

to view the prayers of AC 7 and 8 as only slightly Christianized versions of Hellenistic Jewish synagogue prayers was a common tendency in much of the early scholarship. Even Baumstark believed that the "Greco-Jewish" liturgy was preserved in prayers of AC 7.33–38 under "the light veneer of a somewhat superficial Christian revision."[12]

This line of research has recently been given a much needed corrective through the work of David Fiensy.[13] Fiensy's goal was to recover the original Jewish layer behind the alleged Jewish prayers of AC 7 and 8. Unlike Bousset and Goodenough, Fiensy employs a rigorous, redactional critical methodology, which he argues has enabled him to discern the material belonging to the Jewish core from the work of the redactor. As a result of his analysis he maintains that only the collection of prayers in AC 7.33–38 can with any certainty be said to have derived directly from a Jewish source. AC 8.12.6–27 is in his opinion the redactor's reworking of AC 7.34, and contains little of the core Jewish strata.[14]

The line of investigation that Baumstark initiated was carried forward by Baumstark himself as well as by other liturgiologists.[15] Hans Lietzmann found support for his theory of two types of eucharistic prayer in Bousett's hypothesis that the sections of the anaphora of AC 8 prior to the postsanctus represented a Christian reworking of prayers derived from the liturgy of the Jewish synagogue. In his opinion, the contents of the anaphora through the *Sanctus* are, with the exception of certain interpolations, not specifically Christian in character, while the postsanctus represents a version of the Christian *eucharistia*. Lietzmann perceived no connection between the first portion of the anaphora and the anaphora of AT, while the later sections of the anaphora down to the intercessions cover the same ground as AT and even show verbal dependance at times.[16]

---

[12]Baumstark, *Comparative Liturgy*, 11–12.

[13]*Prayers Alleged to be Jewish: an Examination of the Constitutiones Apostolorum* (Chico, Calif.: Scholars Press, 1985).

[14]Ibid., 153, 172–6. Fiensy provides a valuable chart on pp. 189–97 with the prayers of AC 7.34 and 8.12 in parallel columns.

[15]The extensive bibliography on this subject includes: F. Gavin, "Rabbinic Parallels in Early Church Orders," *Hebrew Union College Annual* 6 (1929) 55–67; C. P. Price, "Jewish Morning Prayers and Early Christian Anaphoras," *Anglican Theological Review* 43 (1961) 153–68; E. R. Hardy, "Kedusha and Sanctus," *SL* 6 (1969) 183–8; P. Sigal, "Early Christian and Rabbinic Liturgical Affinities: Exploring Liturgical Acculturation," *New Testament Studies* 30 (1984) 63–90.

[16]Hans Lietzmann, *Mass and Lord's Supper* (Leiden: Brill, 1955) 102, 107.

Louis Bouyer's interpretation of the structure of the anaphora of AC 8 also builds on Baumstark's theory that two strata were combined in the fully developed eucharistic anaphoras, both with Jewish roots. The first of these is the Jewish table blessing after meals; the second stratum consists of elements drawn from the synagogue liturgy.[17] According to his theory, in the old Alexandrian tradition represented by the anaphora of St Mark, the two strata follow one another sequentially, while the West Syrian type anaphora represents a fusion of these two strata into a single well-ordered and logical whole.[18] Bouyer attempts to trace the *Sanctus* and anaphoral intercessions in particular back to the synagogue liturgy. The prayers of AC 7.33–38 are interpreted as evidence of an intermediate stage prior to the interpolation of these elements from the synagogue liturgy into the developed anaphora. The precise nature of the connection between the prayers of 7.33–38 and the anaphora in AC 8.12 is therefore central to his hypothesis.

A few scholars have offered theories concerning a Jewish source that differ from the general trend to trace the connection back through the synagogue morning service. Louis Ligier, investigating one particular feature of the euchological tradition described by Baumstark, the sin of Adam and the expulsion from paradise, comes to the conclusion that the Jewish background for the *Sanctus*/salvation history portion of the Christian eucharistic prayer is not to be sought in the *Yotzer*, but in the *Seder abodah* of the Day of Atonement, whose structure presents a clearly recognizable resemblance to the anaphora of AC 8.[19]

While the portion of the anaphora of AC 8 for which a Jewish source is alleged has been subjected to more scholarly attention than the parts which precede and follow, more questions than answers remain. Much of the analysis has been flawed by allowing some grand theory on the relationship of the eucharist to the synagogue service to dictate the methodology employed. One consequence is often a

---

[17]Baumstark, *Comparative Liturgy*, 48–51.

[18]*Eucharist* (Notre Dame: Notre Dame Press, 1968) 244–52. Bouyer gives a concise statement of his hypothesis in "The Different Forms of Eucharistic Prayer and their Genealogy," *SP* 8 (1966) 156–70.

[19]L. Ligier, "Autour du sacrifice eucharistique, Anaphores orientales et anamnèse juive de Kippur," *Nouvelle revue théologique* 82 (1960) 40–55; *Péché d'Adam, Péché du Monde—Bible, Kippur, Eucharistie* (Paris: Aubier, 1961) 2:295–6; "Anaphores orientales et prières juives," *Proche-Orient Chrétien* 23 (1963) 99–113.

failure to consider this block of material within its setting in the entire anaphora of AC 8, and thus in relation to the development of the anaphora in general. The picture is more complex than has usually been admitted. While a strong case can be made that the redactor employed the Jewish prayers of AC 7 as a source for AC 8, it is probable that these were reworked in light of the customary content of this section of the anaphora, perhaps even integrating the material from AC 7 with one or more other anaphoras.[20]

OTHER ANAPHORAL SOURCES BEHIND
THE ANAPHORA OF AC 8

Other scholars have paid less attention to a hypothetical connection with the synagogue liturgy, and have focused instead upon the possibility that the redactor was employing other eucharistic prayers as sources for his own composition. F. E. Brightman already recognized that AC 8 contains materials related to what was soon afterwards to be identified as AT.[21] While it is not difficult to ascertain that the overall plan of Book 8 has been taken from this source, there is little apparent resemblance between much of the anaphora of AC 8 and any of the surviving versions of the eucharistic prayer of AT. Only in the anamnesis and epiclesis did the compiler of AC make use of AT in a substantial manner. Apart from these two sections, elements of AT have been detected in three other places: (1) "angelum voluntatis tuae . . . per quem omnia fecisti" appears to lie behind ἄγγελον τῆς μεγάλης βουλῆς σου and δι 'αὐτοῦ τὰ πάντα πεποίηκας; (2) "voluntatem tuam complens" behind τὸ θέλημά σου ἐπλήπθσε; and (3) "ut a passione liberet . . . ut mortem solvat et vincula diaboli dirumpat" behind ἵνα πάθους λύσῃ . . . καὶ ῥήξῃ τὰ δεσμὰ τοῦ διαβόλου.[22] As scant as these parallels are, there is little doubt that a version AT was one source employed by the redactor of AC 8.

However, it is difficult to account for the anaphora of AC 8 as an expansion of AT alone. The lack of correspondence between the

---

[20]This is essentially the conclusion to which Fiensy (*Prayers*, 154, 175) comes in his study of the alleged Jewish prayers of AC 7 and 8. However, he does nothing to investigate the connection of either AC 7.33–38 or AC 8.12 to early Christian liturgical traditions.

[21]F. E. Brightman, *Liturgies Eastern and Western* (Oxford: Clarendon, 1896) xxx.

[22]W. H. Bates, "The Composition of the Anaphora of Apostolic Constitutions VIII," *SP* 13 (1975) 343–4.

anaphoras of AT and AC 8 has prompted some scholars to posit that the redactor was also employing one or more additional sources. For example, after examining the manner in which AT had been worked into the structure of AC 8, W. E. Pitt developed a hypothesis that AC 8 was the fusion of the AT anaphora with one that resembled the Cyriline anaphora of Jerusalem.[23] He was not able to stop there, however, for he also noticed that AC 8 appeared to contain two anamneses, one prior to the institution narrative and one immediately following the narrative. This oddity led him to conjecture that there was a second AT-type prayer, though one without a full institution narrative, contained within AC 8. Pitt offers no conjectures about the identity of this second AT-type anaphora. In particular he does not explore the possibility that this second prayer might have been an early form of the anaphora of St. Basil (BAS), though he does observe that the Basiline anaphoras show indications of not having had a full institution narrative at one time. Nor does Pitt consider the possibility that the prayer might have been a version of the early Antiochene anaphora.

W. H. Bates comes very close to suggesting that an early form of BAS was a second source. He too begins with an examination of the redactor's use of AT. The few rather brief borrowings which he is able to establish lead him to assert that AT was at most a formal framework used by the constitutor "providing the bones for the flesh of later elaborations."[24] Bates then asks whether AC 8 is then largely the creation of the compiler's imagination or whether it may not have drawn on other sources. He argues for the second view and devotes the remainder of the article towards ascertaining what those sources might have been.

Bates examines evidence from the writings of John Chrysostom, BAS, and JAS to suggest that the compiler of AC 8 was following a customary pattern for the contents of the eucharist.[25] For instance, he

---

[23]W. E. Pitt, "The Anamnesis and Institution Narrative in the Liturgy of Apostolic Constitutions Book VIII," *JEH* 9 (1958) 1–2.

[24]Bates, "Composition," 344.

[25]Bates is apparently dependent on J. H. Srawley, *The Early History of the Liturgy* (Cambridge: CUP, 1949) 88, who states: "Further, the thanksgiving in *A.C.*, when compared with the quotations of Chrysostom and the corresponding parts of the liturgies of St James and St Basil, exhibits certain parallels of language and ideas, which suggest that the author has drawn upon the Syrian thanksgiving existing in his time."

draws attention to Chrysostom's use of the concept of divine providence, picking up on a suggestion first made by Brightman, who pointed to the homily *Ad eos qui scandalizanti sunt.* Brightman had gone so far as to say that the homily was "a spacious paraphrase of this section of the anaphora."[26] Bates is more cautious but notes a number of parallels with AC 8. Both develop the concepts of God's *philanthropia* and *pronoia,* both mention the Old Testament figures Cain and Abel, Abraham, and Joseph.[27]

In addition to the similarities with Chrysostom's homilies, Bates also notes a number of points of contact with ideas found in BAS and JAS. For instance, following the first mention of the cherubim and seraphim, the anaphora of AC 8 begins a rehearsal of salvation history beginning with the creation, the introduction of humankind into paradise, and continuing with the subsequent disobedience and banishment. Had the *Sanctus* been joined with this mention of the heavenly hosts, the pattern would have been very similar to that of BAS and JAS. He goes so far as to suggest that AC 8 is an early cousin to BAS and JAS, stating that "while there is little verbal similarity between the three, all show a general community of pattern and sequence."[28] Although Bates sensed the direction in which future study of the anaphora of AC 8 needed to move, he did not pursue his own suggestions as thoroughly as he might have done.

The most recent contribution to the discussion of the composition of the anaphora of AC 8 has been made by John Fenwick.[29] Employing the same theory of fourth-century anaphoral construction techniques that he developed from his study of the relationship between BAS and JAS, Fenwick has proposed that the anaphora of AC 8 was constructed around the framework of the old Antiochene anaphora that was the common ancestor of the anaphora of St. John Chrysostom (CHR) and the Syriac anaphora of the Twelve Apostles (APSyr). As a full textual comparison is difficult on account of the much greater length of AC 8, Fenwick omits those large blocks of material which have no apparent relation to CHR. These are mainly found in the rehearsal of old covenant salvation history that precedes the *Sanc-*

---

[26]Brightman, *Liturgies Eastern and Western,* 479.

[27]Bates, "Composition," 350.

[28]Ibid., 351.

[29]John R. K. Fenwick, *'The Missing Oblation': The Contents of the Early Antiochene Anaphora,* Alcuin/GROW Liturgical Study 11 (Nottingham: Grove Books, 1989).

tus. An analysis of the remainder of the anaphora of AC 8 reveals "a significant number of points of similarity in structure, content, and wording" precisely for those portions of the anaphora that correspond to the conjectured structure of the Antiochene ancestor of APSyr and CHR. Furthermore, there is a lack of agreement in the oblation and intercessions, which he argues supports his thesis that these elements were absent from the structure of the common ancestor.

There are two portions of the anaphora where the similarities are of particular interest. One of the oft-noted oddities of the anaphora of AC 8 is the apparent duplication of both the presanctus and anamnesis material, creating what Fenwick describes as a "false" presanctus and "false" anamnesis in addition to the true presanctus and anamnesis. This doubling strongly suggests the use of at least two sources. Based on a significant number of verbal parallels, Fenwick argues that one of these sources is the common ancestor of APSyr and CHR.

On the basis of the overall structural similarity and the verbal parallels, Fenwick asserts that AC 8, APSyr, and CHR are three independent reworkings of a common anaphora. APSyr appears to have been created by conflation with material from the Syriac version of JAS, while CHR incorporates material found in the Byzantine version of BAS. In the case of AC 8, Fenwick is more reticent to specify the additional sources: "AC has been created by greatly expanding the original core, with large amounts of rhetorical and biblical material, and with liturgical material derived from other prayers."[30] Despite the massive reworking, he believes he has shown that characteristic phrases of the original Antiochene anaphora survive, especially in the false presanctus and false anamnesis.

MULTIPLE SOURCES BEHIND THE ANAPHORA OF AC 8

In the preceding review of the literature at least four sources have been posited by one scholar or another to lie behind the text of the anaphora of AC 8: (1) AT, (2) the version of the Jewish synagogal prayers preserved in AC 7.33–38, (3) an early form of BAS, and (4) the common ancestor of CHR and APSyr. However, no one scholar has yet attempted to integrate the various hypotheses concerning these sources. The remainder of this essay will attempt to show that such an endeavor would indeed be worthwhile for understanding the

[30]Ibid., 34.

place of the Clementine anaphora within the history of the early eucharistic prayers. The constraints of space will necessitate that we
examine only those sections of the anaphora up to and including the
Sanctus. This portion of the anaphora is most critical, however, because it contains those sections which many scholars believe were
derived from Jewish sources.

To facilitate analysis, this portion of the anaphora may be divided
into four blocks: (1) ascription of praise to the Father and the Son
(8.12.4–8); (2) thanksgiving for creation (8.12.9–17); (3) thanksgiving
for the old covenant (8.12.18-26); (4) presanctus and *Sanctus* (8.12.27).
We will examine each one in turn.

Ascription of Praise to the Father and Son
The anaphora opens in a manner typical of classical eucharistic
prayers with the repetition of the *axios kai dikaios* of the introductory
dialogue followed by an infinitival praise-verb. In the following lines
three phrases occur which may possibly have been derived from AT
(angelum voluntatis tuae), BAS (τὸν ὄντως ὄντα θεὸν), and APSyr/CHR
(ἐκ τοῦ μὴ ὄντος εἰς τὸ εἶναι παρήγαγες). However, in the case of the
phrase in common with AT we are dealing with a biblical allusion
(Isa 9:5, LXX), while the latter two phrases are possibly drawn from
the stock of customary formulaic expressions for prayer.[31] Thus, the
evidence for dependence on these three anaphoras is inconclusive for
this section.

Far more significant are the parallels between this section and the
opening lines of the prayer for the ordination of a bishop from AC
8.5.1. Eleven nouns or adjectives are common to the two prayers and
with one exception the shared vocabulary appears in the same
order.[32] The common vocabulary constitutes over a third of the text of
AC 8.12.6–7 between the appearance of the first and last of the terms.

In regard to the links between 8.5.1 and 8.12.6–7, Thomas Kopecek
has pointed to a number of parallels between 8.5.1 and 7.35.9. In the
latter we find a string of phrases employing alpha-privatives, including "invisible by nature . . . whose life is without need . . . whose
habitation is inaccessible . . . whose knowledge is without begin-

---

[31]For instance, the phrase ἐκ τοῦ μὴ ὄντος εἰς τὸ εἶναι occurs in the early
anaphora of Egyptian provenance found in the Barcelona papyrus.

[32]The eleven words are: ὁ μόνος ἀγέννητος, ἀβασίλευτος, [ἀδέσποτος], ὁ ἀνενδεὴς,
πάσης αἰτίας καὶ γενέσεως κρείττων, ἡ γνῶσις ἄναρχος.

ning" (ἀόρατος τῇ φύσει, οὐ ἀνενδεὴς ἡ ζωὴ, ἀπόσιτος ἡ κατιοκία, ἄναρχος ἡ γνῶσις). Each of these is paralleled in the string of alpha-privatives in 8.5.1: "without any need . . . invisible by nature, whose knowledge is without beginning . . . inaccessible" (ὁ πάντη ἀνενδεὴς . . . ὁ τῇ φύσει ἀόρατος, οὗ ἡ γνῶσις ἄναρχος . . . ὁ ἀπρόσιτος).[33] The order of the phrases is different, and the form of two members of the group has been altered slightly, but the parallels suggest that the same redactor had a hand in composition of both prayers. The links between 8.5.1 and 7.35 are all the more interesting since the latter also has extensive connections with 8.12. Not only does 7.35 contain a version of the *Sanctus* and associated material which have made this prayer the focus of attention among scholars who seek to link AC with the liturgy of the Jewish synagogue, but there are links with this opening section of the anaphora as well. Of the four phrases mentioned above from 7.35.9, two also have parallels in 8.12.6-7: τὸν ἀνενδεῆ, . . . ἡ ἄναρχος γνῶσις. It would appear that the redactor has either borrowed these phrases from 7.35 and incorporated them into both the episcopal ordination prayer in 8.5 and this opening section of the anaphora, or that he has introduced the same phrases into all three prayers.

Thanksgiving for Creation
Following the praise of the Father and Son, the anaphora of AC 8 moves to giving thanks for the created world, both invisible and visible. The section dealing with the invisible realm of heavenly beings is relatively brief, consisting of little more than a list of the angelic orders. This description of the heavenly hierarchy is so strongly reminiscent of the typical introduction to the *Sanctus* that it has sometimes been termed a "false presanctus." Consideration of this block of material should therefore be deferred until we evaluate the true presanctus.

Next in the order of creation is the visible world. Here the redactor becomes his most expansive, introducing into his prayer a lengthy block of material which has no close parallel in any other extant early anaphora. Although the description of the created world presented here is ultimately based on biblical sources, the most probable direct

[33]Thomas Kopecek, "Neo-Arian Religion: The Evidence of the *Apostolic Constitutions*," in R. Gregg, ed., *Arianism: Historical and Theological Reassessments* (Philadelphia Patristic Foundation, 1985) 161–2.

source of this block is AC 7.34. It is beyond doubt that some relationship exists between 7.34 and 8.12.9–20, but the precise nature of this
relationship is the matter of considerable debate.

Both 7.34 and 8.12.9–20 are broadly based on the biblical creation
account of Gen 1 and the poetic reflection on the creation of Psalm
104. Neither, however, follows the precise sequence of the biblical
account as this chart, reproduced from Fiensy,[34] shows:

7.34	8.12
1. order (day one)	1. heaven arched, firmament (day two)
2. firmament, heaven arched (day two)	2. night, day, light, darkness, sun, moon, stars (day four)
3. stars, light, sun, moon, night, day (day four)	3. water, air, fire
4. dry land (day three)	4. dry land (day three)
5. sea described (Job 38:11)	5. animals in the sea and on land (days five and six)
6. earth became green, plants (day three)	6. plants (day three)
7. luminaries for signs, seasons, and years (day four)	7. abyss and seas (Job 38:8)
8. animals (day six)	8. rivers, herbs, living creatures, circuits of years and winds described
9. man (day six)	9. man (day six)
10. weather described	10. resurrection promised
11. resurrection promised	

Not only does the structure of the two prayers show clear similarities, but there are points of verbal correspondence as well. These include not only those words which would be expected from a common
reliance on Gen 1, but also the following words and phrases: "heaven
as a vault" (οὐρανὸς δὲ ὡς καμάρα/τὸν οὐρανὸν ὡς καμάραν), "for consolation in darkness" (σκότους παραμυθίαν), "living things small and
great" (ζώοις μικροῖς καὶ μεγάλοις), "painted" (καταγράψας) and
"multicolor" (ποικιλῶν), "cosmopolitan" (κοσμοπολίτην), "by/to your
Wisdom" (τῇ σῇ Σοφίᾳ), "presenting him an ornament of the world"
(κόσμου κόσμον αὐτὸν ἀναδείξας), "from the four elements" (ἐκ μὲν
τῶν τεσσάρων σωμάτων/στοιχείων), "from nothing" (ἐκ τοῦ μὴ ὄντος),
"fivefold sense perception" (πένταθλον . . . αἴσθησιν). Finally there is

[34]Fiensy, *Prayers*, 172–3.

a more extended passage at the close of the section: "but making (mankind) sleep for a little while, you called them into rebirth by an oath, you loosed the bonds of death" (χρόνῳ δὲ πρὸς ὀλίγον αὐτὸν κοιμίσας ὅρκῳ εἰς παλιγγενεσίαν ἐκάλεσας, ὅρον θανάτου λύσας).

Verbal similarities between this portion of the anaphora and other prayers in AC are not limited to 7.34 alone. Kopecek has pointed to a small number of parallels between 7.35 and this portion of 8.12 which either do not occur in 7.34 or are used in the same manner as in 8.12 but in a different manner in 7.34. In both 7.35 and 8.12 the earth is said to stand "upon nothing" (ἐπὶ μηδενὸς/ἐπ᾽ οὐδενὸς), and the stars are "a choir" (χορὸν τῶν ἀστέρων). And while in 7.34 it is the stars that are a "consolation in darkness," in both 7.35 and 8.12 it is fire which offers this comfort.[35] These parallels with 7.35 raise further questions about the relationship of the prayer in 7.34 and 8.12.

A Reconsideration of the Relationship of 7.34 and 8.12.9–20
The nature of the relationship between these two prayers continues to be a thorny question about which no consensus has yet developed. In support of a common source or redactor Fiensy notes that in both prayers the creation of the stars is mentioned out of place as compared with Genesis, that both employ Job 38 when speaking of the sea, both employ a web of Stoic ideas, and both emphasize that man was created by God and Wisdom.[36] Yet there are significant differences between the two prayers. These differences were great enough to lead Bousset to conclude that the two were independent reworkings of a common source. Fiensy rightly rejects this view and concludes that both prayers come from the hand of the redactor of AC, who was reworking Christian liturgical tradition, and that the Jewish core behind 7.34 is minimal. Fiensy does not explore what the liturgical tradition might have been.

The expanded description of creation in the anaphora of AC 8 has no precedent in any other surviving early anaphora. Thus, it would appear unlikely that the redactor of AC 8.12 drew directly from another anaphoral source for this part of the prayer. So while he may have been reworking Christian liturgical tradition in a broad sense, it is not unwarranted to conclude that he went beyond the customary anaphoral patterns in this detailed description of the creation. The

[35]Kopecek, "Neo-Arian Religion," 179, n. 26.
[36]Fiensy, *Prayers*, 173.

prayer of 7.34, whatever the path of its development from the original Hebrew core which Fiensy has identified, was a praise for the wonders of creation before it reached the hands of the redactor. Taking these two points together, the most probable source for this section of the anaphora is 7.34, whether in its final redacted form or as it came to the hands of the redactor. Although the precise nature of the relationship cannot be determined with certainty, based on the parallels between 8.12 and 7.35, it would seem more probable that 7.34 and 35 were composed prior to 8.12 even if all three prayers are largely the work of the same redactor.

Thanksgiving for the Old Covenant
The anaphora of AC 8 contains a lengthy rehearsal of the events of salvation history under both the old and new covenants. This salvation history narrative forms nearly a third of the entire anaphora. While certain other early West Syrian anaphoras such as BAS have extensive rehearsals of salvation history, AC 8 is unique in the detailed coverage it gives to the events and persons of the old covenant. Much of this distinctive material appears to be the work of the redactor himself. As is the case with the praise of the Father and Son which forms the first portion of the anaphora, those aspects of the old covenant history that are distinctive to the anaphora of AC 8 have parallels in other portions of AC. This is most notable in the sequence of old covenant figures referred to in the anaphora. In the section encompassed by paragraphs 20–26 the following figures are mentioned: Abel, Seth, Enos, Enoch, Noah, Lot, Abraham, Melchizedek, Job, Isaac, Jacob, Joseph, Moses, Aaron, and Joshua. A virtually identical sequence of figures is named in the ordination prayer found in 8.5, and partial parallels are found in two of the so-called Jewish prayers in AC 7 and in the directions for catechetical instruction in AC 7.39, as may be seen in the table below.

7.37.2ff.	7.38.2	7.39.3	8.5.3	8.12.20–26
Abel			Abel	Abel
		Seth	Seth	Seth
	Enos and	Enos	Enos	Enos
	Enoch	Enoch	Enoch	Enoch
Noah		Noah	Noah	Noah
				Lot
Abraham		Abraham and descendants		Abraham

7.37.2ff.	7.38.2	7.39.3	8.5.3	8.12.20–26
		Melchizedek	Melchizedek	Melchizedek
		Job	Job	Job
			Abraham and	
Isaac			the rest	Isaac
Jacob			of the	Jacob
			patriarchs	Joseph
Moses	Moses and	Moses	Moses	Moses
Aaron			Aaron	Aaron
Joshua	Joshua	Joshua and		Joshua
		Caleb		
		Phineas	Eleazar and	
Gideon	the		Phineas	
Manoah	judges			
Sampson				
Jephthah				
Barak				
Samuel	Samuel,		Samuel	
	Elijah			
	the			
	prophets,			
David	David and			
	the kings			
	. . . .			

Based on a comparison of these lists it would appear that the redactor has conflated the less complete lists found in AC 7.37, 38, and 39 to form the nearly identical catalogue of figures in AC 8.5.3 and 8.12.20ff. While the narrative is filled out more extensively in AC 8.12.20ff. than in these other locations, themes such as divine providence, deliverance from adversity, and the provision of priestly ministers also form the background for the other lists. Ultimately, however, each of these lists of old covenant figures harken back to the catalogue of heroes of faith of Hebrews 11, which in turn appears to have been modeled on similar catalogues in Sirach 44–50 and 1 Maccabees 2:51-60.[37] Because it is impossible to ascertain the extent to

---

[37]Such catalogues of old covenant figures may have been a standard element in catechetical instruction passed down in the summary of apostolic teaching. An list almost identical with that in AC 8.5 and 8.12 is found in such a summary

which the redactor's hand has shaped the lists found in the Jewish prayers, it is difficult to assert with certainty that the redactor drew upon the lists of AC 7.37 and 7.38 as he found them. As the list of 7.39 is found within the redactor's reworking of the baptismal instructions of the *Didache*, that list is more likely to have been from his hand.

The portions of the salvation history that surround this extensive rehearsal of the old covenant follow closely the typical West Syrian pattern, which leaves open the possibility that this material was derived from other anaphoras. The similarities of portions of the salvation history in the anaphora of AC 8 with that in BAS has been noted by several scholars. The parallels with BAS are especially notable in the opening paragraphs, which recount the creation and fall of the human race. The elements common to both anaphoras include the following: (1) humankind created in the image of God; (2) Adam and Eve placed in "the paradise of pleasure"; (3) the promise of immortality as a reward for obedience to God's commandment; (4) the disobedience of Adam and Eve as a result of "the deceit of the serpent"; (5) God's just judgment in driving the parents of the human race out of paradise; (6) the goodness of God in not completely abandoning his creature; (7) deliverance from death by "rebirth"; (8) the giving of the law and sending of the prophets to recall the human race to the way of salvation, and (9) the guardianship of the angels over the human race. This sequence very nearly encompasses the whole of this portion of BAS, which then moves to the incarnation of Christ as the culmination of God's provision of salvation. In AC 8.12 this sequence of ideas is interrupted by the detailed recounting of old covenant history. The parallels with BAS resume only after the *Sanctus*, where we find in 8.12.30 the mention of the giving of the law and prophets and the guardianship of the angels just prior to the introduction of the coming of Christ into the world.[38]

---

contained in Origen's *De Principiis* 1.4: Adam, Abel, Seth, Enos, Enoch, Noah, Shem, Abraham, Isaac, the twelve patriarchs, Moses, and the prophets.

[38]Although it is beyond the scope of the portion of the anaphora being examined here, it might be noted that in the remainder of the salvation history section few distinct parallels between AC 8.12 and BAS are to be found. Both anaphoras recount similar aspects of the Lord's ministry, passion, and resurrection, and both contain numerous phrases which recall the language of the early baptismal creeds, but the parallels are too imprecise to warrant making a direct connection between the two.

To summarize, the thanksgiving for the old covenant therefore appears to be partially based upon BAS, and partially the redactor's own work inspired by similar catalogs of old covenant figures in AC 7.37, 7.38, 7.39 and 8.5. This detailed retelling of the events of old covenant history is unique among surviving early anaphoras, but has been interpolationed into a section that presents themes related to the creation and fall of the human race, and God's subsequent merciful dealings with humanity, themes which are well developed in BAS but not limited to that anaphora alone.

The Presanctus and Sanctus

As noted above, the anaphora of AC 8 contains two lists of heavenly beings, the first in 8.12.8 and the second in 8.12.27. The second leads into the *Sanctus*; the first would seem to be doing so, but does not, and is therefore sometimes referred to as the false presanctus. These lists of angelic powers have close parallels with the lists found in the Basiline anaphoras and in APSyr/CHR, as well as with the list found in conjunction with the *Sanctus* of AC 7.35, as the following table shows:

BAS	CHR	AC 7.35.3	AC 8.12.8[a]	AC 8.12.27[b]
		seraphim		
		six-winged		
		cherubim		
angels		angels	angels	angels
archangels		archangels	archangels	archangels
thrones		thrones	thrones	thrones
dominions		dominions		dominions
rulers		rulers	rulers	rulers
authorities		authorities	authorities	authorities
powers		powers	powers	powers
			armies	eternal
				armies
			aeons	(see below)
	thousands			
	archangels			
	myriad			
	angels			
many-eyed			seraphim	
cherubim	cherubim		cherubim	cherubim
six-winged				six-winged

189

BAS	CHR	AC 7.35.3	AC 8.12.8	AC 8.12.27
seraphim	seraphim			seraphim
				feet
faces				heads
feet				thousands
				of
				thousands
				archangels
				myriad of
				myriad
				angels

^aFalse presanctus, listed in reverse order
^bTrue presanctus

Several observations may be made. First, the order of the false presanctus list is reversed not only from that encountered in AC 7.35.3
and AC 8.12.27, but from the sequence typically found in the
anaphoral presanctus. The most probable explanation for this reversal is that the redactor's purpose was to list the invisible heavenly
powers in a descending hierarchy from the unbegotten Father and
only-begotten Son, through the seraphim and cherubim, the other
lesser orders according to their ranks, and ending with the archangels and angels.[39] In the redactor's cosmology the creation of the
visible world is located after that of the invisible heavenly order, and
this list of heavenly beings serves as a bridge from the praise of the
Father and Son to the thanksgiving for the manifold wonders of the
visible creation, with which the redactor commences immediately.

Secondly, the list in the true presanctus would therefore appear to
run in ascending order from angels and archangels to cherubim and
seraphim. However, there is an anomaly in the second mention of the
angels and archangels at the conclusion of the list of heavenly
powers. In this second instance the numeric modifiers "thousands of
thousands" and "myriad of myriad" are added, and as in CHR,
which also employs these modifiers, the archangels are mentioned
first in order that the number of angels should not be greater than the
number of archangels. In all the extant versions of the early Eastern

---

[39]This interpretation is reinforced if we accept the reading of Vat. gr. 1506 as authentic, since it adds the Spirit to the list as the first among the created heavenly
powers. However, this heterodox reading is found only in this single manuscript.

anaphoras, CHR and AC 8.12.27 are unique in this use of the two numeric modifiers thousands and myriads with the archangels and angels respectively and the resulting reversal from the normal order, angels and archangels. The second mention of the angels and archangels and the close parallel with CHR suggests that two sources are being combined here, one of which was the *Urform* of CHR. At the very least the two anaphoras contain a customary Antiochene formula.[40] Apart from the duplication of the angels and archangels and the absence of the expanded description of the seraphim and cherubim, the list of heavenly powers in the true presanctus is virtually identical with that in the false presanctus. The most notable difference is the addition of dominions to the list between thrones and rulers, and the conflation of armies and aeons into a single rank, eternal armies. The list in the true presanctus is also largely identical with the list in AC 7.35.3, which differs mainly in the absence of any equivalent to the eternal armies found in the list of the presanctus. The similarity of the three lists might be interpreted as indicating either that the redactor was being influenced by a conventional formula, or that he borrowed this sequence from another source. Apart from the mention of the seraphim and cherubim to whom the singing of the *Sanctus* is specifically attributed in AC 7.35.3, the list of angelic beings there appears to be a Christian interpolation, and so possibly from the hand of the redactor.

One early anaphora which follows the core of the sequence found in AC 7.35.3 and 8.12.27 very closely is Byzantine BAS. This constitutes yet another parallel between the Basiline anaphoras and the anaphora of AC 8. The list in Byzantine BAS differs from the list in AC 8.12.27 in the addition of the modifier many-eyed to cherubim, and in the details of the description of the manner in which the seraphim employ their wings. In Byzantine BAS, as in all the Basiline anaphoras, the seraphim cover their faces and feet, while in AC 8.12.27 it is their feet and heads which are covered. Among the extant early anaphoras AC 8.12 presents the only instance of the seraphim covering their heads rather than their faces, and this unusual reading may simply reflect an idiosyncratic view of the redactor.

---

[40]Fenwick (*Missing Oblation*, 17) also adduces the summing up phrase ὑπὲρ ἁπάντων σοι ἡ δόξα δέσποτα παντοκράτορ that introduces the true presanctus as further evidence of a connection with CHR/APSyr, which employ the phrase ὑπὲρ τουτῶν ἁπάντων εὐχαριστουμεν σοι in a similar fashion.

The *Sanctus* in the anaphora of AC 8.12 has two distinguishing features. First, rather than the customary later form "heaven and earth are full of *your* glory," we find "heaven and earth are full of *his* glory." An Antiochene homily of John Chrysostom also supports this use of the third person in the *Sanctus*.[41] Secondly, the form of the *Sanctus* lacks the customary Matthean *Benedictus* found in the fully developed anaphoras. Instead it concludes with the phrase "Blessed [be] you to the ages." The form of the *Sanctus* in AC 7.35, following the form found in the *Yotzer* of the synagogue liturgy, quotes Ezekiel 3:12, "Blessed [be] the glory of the Lord from this place." This acclamation is placed on the lips of the lesser orders of angelic beings, a christianized list of which has replaced the *ophanim* and *chayoth* found in the *Yotzer*. The form of the *Sanctus* in AC 7.35 is clearly shaped by its Jewish source, but what of the form in AC 8.12? If the Antiochene anaphora known by the redactor already possessed a *Sanctus*, as the evidence cited above concerning the presanctus suggests, it is possible that the form of the *Sanctus* in AC 8.12 is that which was current in the region of Antioch during the last quarter of the fourth century.

The Relationship Between the Sanctus *in AC 7.35 and AC 8.12*
A number of scholars who have argued that the *Sanctus* had its origin in the *Qedusha* of the synagogue liturgy have attempted to trace the anaphoral *Sanctus* of AC 8.12 through the form of the *Sanctus* found in AC 7.35 back to the liturgy of the synagogue. However, if the redactor of AC was making use of existing anaphoras which already contained the *Sanctus*, then its presence in the anaphora of AC 8 is best accounted for by tracing it through those sources rather than through the enigmatic prayers of AC 7.

The presence of the *Sanctus* in AC 7.35 is possibly a coincidence with only minor significance for our understanding of the introduction of the *Sanctus* into the eucharistic prayer. It seems that the redactor of AC was unfamiliar with any liturgical use for the prayers in AC 7.33–38. Alone of all the prayer texts found in AC they are not placed in a liturgical setting, but as models of personal prayer for the initiated. The redactor is hostile towards Judaism, and thus it seems

[41]*In illud: Vidi Dominum, hom.* 1.3 (PG 56:100); cf. F. van de Paverd, *Zur Geschichte der Messliturgie in Antiochia und Konstantinople gegen Ende des vierten Jahrhunderts*, OCA 187 (Rome: Pontificium Institutum Orientale, 1970) 276–87.

unlikely that he himself was responsible for the appropriation of prayers from the synagogue for inclusion in a church order.[42] It appears more likely that these prayers had already been incorporated into the *Didache* source which the redactor used. The most plausible scenario it perhaps the following. The remote origin of the prayers in 7.33-38 is in the synagogue service for the Sabbath. At some point a Jewish Christian community adapted these prayers, possibly for liturgical use. This christianized version of the prayers then found their way into a recension of the *Didache* which eventually comes into the hands of the redactor of AC. Elements from certain of these prayers, which the redactor takes to be part of ancient Christian tradition, are adapted for use in the anaphora. This is most notably the case with 7.34 and certain sections of 7.35. The redactor also encounters the *Qedusha* in the prayer of 7.35 and accepts it as a version of the *Sanctus* with which he is familiar from the anaphora. Perhaps the redactor was responsible for certain modifications which assimilated the form of the *Qedusha/Sanctus* and its introduction to the customary form of the eucharistic anaphora with which he was familiar, but it is also possible that these modifications had already been made prior to the redactor getting hold of the text. In either case it appears unlikely that the form of the *Qedusha* in 7.35 was the direct source for the *Sanctus* in the anaphora of AC 8.12.

In asserting that the source of the *Sanctus* in AC 8.12 is not to be sought in the form of the *Qedusha* preserved in AC 7.35, it is not my intention to deny the possibility that the presence of the *Sanctus* in the anaphora had its remote origins in the *Qedusha* of the synagogue liturgy. Rather, I am only arguing that form of the *Qedusha* preserved in AC 7.35 is not the direct source of the *Sanctus* in AC 8.12, and that therefore the Jewish prayers of AC 7.33-38 are not the clear evidence for the influence of the synagogue liturgy on the contents or form of the eucharistic prayer which some have argued. The presence of the synagogal prayers in AC 7 remains a mystery. While there is no reason to doubt that at one time a version of these prayers had a place in the liturgy of a Jewish-Christian community, it is unwarranted to assume that their use was widespread or that it lasted until the period in which AC was redacted. Yet the case that the *Qedusha* of the synagogue liturgy was the source of the *Sanctus* in AC 8.12 rests upon these assumptions.

[42]AC 2.60–61; 5.17; 6.26, 27.

CONCLUSION

The preceding analysis of the anaphora of AC 8.12 has shown that the redactor of AC may have employed elements from other anaphoras in composing his eucharistic prayer. In the portion of the anaphora examined here the parallels with BAS are the most significant. Not only do these two anaphoras exhibit the same overall structure, but the contents of the salvation history section of AC 8.12 bear a marked similarity to the equivalent portion of BAS. In addition there are a couple of significant points of contact with CHR in the presanctus. However, much of the content of the anaphora of AC 8 has no close parallel in any other surviving early eucharistic prayer. These portions of the anaphora have close similarities to other prayers and doctrinal passages within AC. These other passages also shows signs of expansion and alteration at the hands of the redactor such that if these other portions of AC are described as sources behind the anaphora, it would be the case that the redactor has largely borrowed from his own work in composing the anaphora of AC 8.

Robert F. Taft, S.J.

9. St. John Chrysostom and the Byzantine Anaphora that Bears His Name*

THE CHRYSOSTOM LITURGICAL FORMULARY

The Liturgy of St. John Chrysostom (CHR), with the Liturgy of St. Basil (BAS), is one of the two eucharistic formularies of the Byzantine churches.[1] Employed according to present usage on all but ten days of the Byzantine liturgical year,[2] CHR is by far the most widely-used eastern eucharistic anaphora. It is also one of the oldest, for I shall argue that it was introduced into Constantinople from Antioch, probably by St. John Chrysostom in 398.[3]

---

*I resume here material treated in far greater detail in R. F. Taft, "The Authenticity of the Chrysostom Anaphora Revisited. Determining the Authorship of Liturgical Texts by Computer," *OCP* 56 (1990) 5–51, reprinted with corrections and further notes in R. F. Taft, *Liturgy in Byzantium and Beyond* (London: Variorum, 1995) ch. III; and idem, "The Byzantine Anaphora of St. John Chrysostom," to appear in a companion volume to the 2nd ed. of A. Hänggi & I. Pahl, eds., *Prex eucharistica,* Spicilegium Friburgense 12 (Fribourg, 1968).

[1]I adopt the convention of using "formulary" to designate a complete liturgical text—e.g., the Liturgy of St. James—which comprises numerous individual "formulas" or particular euchology texts, e.g., the anaphora. A third Byzantine eucharistic formulary, the Liturgy of the Presanctified, is not a real eucharist but a communion service from the reserved eucharist for aliturgical days when the full liturgy may not be celebrated. JAS, though sometimes celebrated by Byzantine churches, is a hagiopolite, not a Byzantine formulary. The Syriac Anaphora of St. John Chrysostom (ed. H. G. Codrington, *Anaphorae Syriacae* [Rome: Pontificium Institutum Orientale, 1939–] I.2:149–201) "has nothing in common with the Byzantine liturgy of Chrysostom" (ibid., 151).

[2]BAS is used on Sundays of Lent, Thursday and Saturday of Holy Week, the vigils of Nativity (Dec. 25) and Theophany (Jan. 6), and the feast of St. Basil (Jan. 1). If a vigil coincides with Sunday, some adjustments are made.

[3]Taft, "The Authenticity of the Chrysostom Anaphora," 27–38, 48–51.

Since local churches with more than one anaphora usually insert them into a fixed common framework comprising those parts chanted aloud (diaconal exclamations, doxologies and other ekphoneseis, the people's responses and chants), when CHR was introduced into Constantinople it was assimilated to the already existing framework of BAS, and later, other common elements were added to both formularies.[4] By the eleventh century CHR had superseded BAS as the main eucharistic formulary of the Byzantine Orthodox Church.[5]

An anaphoral prayer not only of great antiquity but also of profound beauty and simplicity, it is understandable that CHR, along with BAS, JAS, Addai and Mari, and Maronite *Sharar,* has attracted more considerable scholarly attention. One reason for this scholarly interest in CHR lies in its debated provenance.

[4]G. Wagner, *Der Ursprung der Chrysostomusliturgie,* LQF 59 (Münster: Aschendorff, 1973) 45–47; H. Engberding, "Die Angleichung der byzantinischen Chrysostomusliturgie an die byzantinische Basiliusliturgie," *OS* 13 (1964) 105–22. I prescind here from the various redactions of the CHR anaphora, which present some emendations, mostly minor and not always an improvement: cf. A. Jacob, "La tradition manuscrite de la Liturgie de S. Jean Chrysostome (VIIe–XIIe siècles)," in *Eucharisties d'orient et d'occident* II, Lex orandi 47 (Paris: Cerf, 1970) 109–38; S. Parenti & E. Velkovska, eds., *L'Eucologio Barberini gr. 336 (ff. 1–263),* Bibliotheca *Ephemerides Liturgicae* Subsidia 80 (Rome: C.L.V.-Edizioni Liturgiche, 1995); S. Parenti, "Osservazioni sul testo dell'Anafora di Giovanni Crisostomo in alcuni eucologi italo-greci (VIII–XI secolo)," *EL* 105 (1991) 120–54; idem, "Fonti ed influssi italo-greci nei frammenti dell'Eucaristia bizantini nei 'Fogli slavi' del Sinai (XI sec.)," *OCP* 57 (1991) 145–77; R. F. Taft, *The Byzantine Rite. A Short History,* American Essays in Liturgy (Collegeville: The Liturgical Press, 1992) ch. 5.

[5]Jacob, "La tradition," 109–38, esp. 113; cf. R. F. Taft, *The Great Entrance. A History of the Transfer of Gifts and Other Preanaphoral Rites of the Liturgy of St. John Chrysostom,* OCA 200 (Rome: Pontificium Institutum Orientale, 2nd ed. 1978) xxxi–ii.

[6]A. Baumstark, "Die Chrysostomosliturgie und die syrische Liturgie des Nestorios," in *XPYCOCTOMIKA. Studi e ricerche intorno a S. Giovanni Crisostomo, a cura del comitato per il XV^0 centenario della sua morte, 407–1907* (Rome: Pustet, 1908) 771–857; idem, "Zur Urgeschichte der Chrysostomosliturgie," *Theologie und Glaube* 5 (1913) 299–313; idem, "Antwort an Th. Schermann," *Theologie und Glaube* 5 (1913) 394–95; Th. Schermann, "Die griechische Chrysostomusliturgie. Einleitung," in *Die griechischen Liturgien,* Bibliothek der Kirchenväter 5 (Kempten-Müchen: Kosel, 1912) 198–204; idem, "Zur Herkunft der Anaphora der Chrysostomusliturgie," *Theologie und Glaube* 5 (1913) 392–3; I. E. Rahmani, *I fasti della Chiesa patriarcale antiochena,* Conferenza d'inaugurazione tenuta in nome dell'Istituto Pontificio Orientale li 18 gennaio 1920 da Ignazio Efrem II Rahmani, Patriarca Antiocheno dei Siri, con la pubblicazione in Appendice di varii

PROVENANCE

The origins of CHR have long been an object of speculation.[6] Modern studies[7] have discredited documents claiming CHR to be an abbreviation of BAS,[8] and identified the Syriac Anaphora of the Twelve Apostles I (APSyr) as closely related to CHR.[9] Fenwick has argued that AC 8.12, APSyr, and CHR are all independent derivatives of a single prayer.[10] More likely, as I shall argue, CHR/APSyr are elaborations of the same Urtext, generally identified with the Greek Anaphora of the Apostles (AP) referred to by Leontius of Byzantium c. 543.[11]

The CHR anaphora has been attributed to St. John Chrysostom with unwavering consistency throughout the Greek ms. tradition,[12] beginning with the earliest euchology ms. *Barberini Greek 336*, a beautiful mid-eighth-century uncial codex preserved in the Vatican Library, of which we at last have a modern critical edition by two of my former students, the husband-and-wife team Stefano Parenti and Elena Velkovska.[13] But in ancient texts, attribution and authenticity are far from synonymous and, with regard to religious texts, skepticism in the face of attributions of authorship is the prudent attitude. And skepticism is what has generally greeted the attribution of CHR to St. John Chrysostom. Is that skepticism justified?

---

antichissimi documenti inediti (Rome: Accademiadei Lincei, 1920); A. Raes, "L'authenticité de la Liturgie byzantine de S. Jean Chrysostome," *OCP* 24 (1958) 5–16; G. Khouri-Sarkis, "L'origine syrienne de l'anaphore byzantine de saint Jean Chrysostome," *L'Orient syrien* 7 (1962) 3–68; most recently, Wagner, *Der Ursprung der Chrysostomusliturgie*; Taft, "The Authenticity of the Chrysostom Anaphora."

[7]Full review of sources and literature in Taft, "The Authenticity of the Chrysostom Anaphora."

[8]F. J. Leroy, "Proclus, 'de traditione Missae': un faux de C. Palaeocappa," *OCP* 28 (1962) 288–99.

[9]H. Engberding, "Die syrische Anaphora der zwölf Apostel und ihre Paralleltexte einander gegenübergestellt und mit neuen Untersuchungen zur Urgeschichte der Chrysostomosliturgie begleitet," *OC* 34 (1938) 213–47, esp. 241ff.; idem, "Zur griechischen Epihaniusliturgie," *Le Muséon* 74 (1961) 135–42, esp. 139, 141.

[10]J.R.K. Fenwick, *"The Missing Oblation": The Contents of the Early Antiochene Anaphora*, Alcuin/GROW Joint Liturgical Study 11 (Nottingham: Grove Books, 1989) 5, 34–35, and passim.

[11]*Libri tres contra Nestorianos et Eutychianos* 3.19 (PG 86/1:1386C = CPG 6813); cf. Taft, "The Authenticity of the Chrysostom Anaphora," 11–15.

[12]I summarize the evidence in Taft, "The Authenticity of the Chrysostom Anaphora," 9–11.

[13]Parenti-Velkovska, *L'Eucologio Barberini*.

The question is imperative, for computer scanning has revolutionized all textual study within the past decade. The manipulation of Greek liturgical texts by computer, when applied to one precise issue in the history of the liturgies of Late Antiquity, the authentication of texts, can now provide results that are scientific and free of the inevitable subjectivity that has usually plagued such work in the past. Here I can only summarized the problems involved in testing supposed authorship, the methods adequate for solving them, and how computers have revolutionized the latter. I shall illustrate all this via one sample-text, the presanctus of CHR, a translation of which is presented here, in parallel columns with the corresponding text from the related Syriac Anaphora of the Apostles (APSyr).[14]

THE TEXTS
The following arrangement of our paradigm-text, the earliest extant redaction of the presanctus of Greek CHR,[15] placed in parallel with APSyr,[16] shows at a glance the relationship between the two texts. The need to illustrate the parallelism between the two texts has required, at times, a literal translation preserving even the word order of the original Greek of CHR. Italicised sections of text are peculiar to the respective redaction and have no doublet in the other.

CHR	APSyr
1. It is fitting and right	1. It is fitting and right
2. to praise you	
3. *to thank you*	
4. to adore you	4. to adore you
	2. to praise you

---

[14]The results of my study of the CHR presanctus appear in Taft, "The Authenticity of the Chrysostom Anaphora." There I review the full dossier of previous scholarly writing concerning the point at issue. That study presents but a small section of my application of computer analysis to the entire CHR anaphora, the results of which will appear in R. F. Taft, *A History of the Liturgy of St. John Chrysostom* III: *The Anaphora* (OCA, Rome: Pontificium Institutum Orientale, in preparation). Two volumes of this projected 5-volume history of CHR have already appeared as II: *The Great Entrance;* IV: *The Diptychs,* OCA 238 (Rome: Pontificium Institutum Orientale, 1991).

[15]Parenti-Velkovska, *L'Eucologio Barberini,* no. 32.10 = F. E. Brightman, *Liturgies Eastern and Western* (Oxford: Clarendon, 1896) 321–3 = Hänggi & Pahl, *Prex eucharistica,* 224.

[16]*Anaphorae Syriacae* I.2:215 = Hänggi & Pahl, *Prex eucharistica,* 265–6.

CHR

5. *in every place of your dominion*
6. for you are God,
7. *ineffable, inconceivable, invisible, incomprehensible,*
8. *always existing, ever the same,*
9. you and your only-begotten Son and your Holy Spirit.
10. You brought us from non-existence into being,
11. and when we had fallen you raised us up again,
12. and have not ceased doing everything to lead us to heaven
13. and to bestow on us your future kingdom.
14. For all these things we thank you
15. and your only-begotten Son and your Holy Spirit
16. *for all the things we know and do not know,*
17. *your seen and unseen*
18. *benefits accomplished for us.*
19. *We thank you also for this liturgy which you deign to receive from our hands*
20. though there stand before you *thousands of archangles and myriads of angels,*
the Cherubim
and the Seraphim, six-winged *and many-eyed, soaring aloft,*
21. the triumphal hymn

22. singing, proclaiming, crying out, and saying: Holy, holy, holy . . .

APSyr

6. for you are *truly* God,

9. and your only-begotten Son and Holy Spirit.
10. You brought [us] from non-existence into being,
11. and when we had fallen you raised [us] up again,
12. and have not ceased doing everything to lead us to heaven
13. and to bestow on us your future kingdom.
14. For all these things we thank you
15. and your only-begotten Son and Holy Spirit

20. though there stand before you

the Cherubim, *four-faced,*
and the Seraphim, six-winged,

21. the praise of majesty,
*with mouths not silent
and voices not quiet,
with all the heavenly powers,*
22. singing, proclaiming, crying out, and saying: Holy, holy, holy . . .

CHR	APSyr
23. *With these holy powers, O Master, we too cry out and say,* holy are you and all-holy,	holy are you and all-holy,
24. you and your only-begotten Son and your Holy Spirit;	24. you and your only-begotten Son and your Holy Spirit;
25. holy are you and all-holy, and magnificent is your glory,	25. holy are you and all-holy, and the magnificence of your glory
26. who so loved the world that you gave your only-begotten Son, so that all who believe in him might not perish, but have eternal life;	26. who so loved the world that you gave your only-begotten Son *for it,* so that all who believe in him might not perish, but have eternal life;
27. who, when he had come and fulfilled the whole economy for us,	27. who, when he had come and fulfilled the whole economy for us,
28. on the night on which he was betrayed,[17]	28. on the night on which he was betrayed,
29. he took bread in his holy *and pure and immaculate* hands, gave thanks *and* blessed, broke, and gave it to his *holy* disciples and apostles, saying:	29. he took bread in his holy hands, gave thanks, hallowed, broke, and gave it to his disciples and apostles, saying:
30. Take, eat,	30. Take, eat *of this all of you,*
this is my body which is broken for you	this is my body which is broken for you *and for many, and given*
for remission of sins.	for remission [of sins] *and for eternal life.*
31. Likewise the chalice, after having supped,	31. Likewise the chalice, after they had supped, *mixing wine and water, he gave thanks, blessed, sanctified, and*

[17]From the eleventh century, mss of CHR interpolate here "or rather gave himself up for the life of the world," not found in the early mss.

CHR	APSyr
	after having tasted of it, gave it to his disciples the apostles,
saying:	saying:
	Take,
Drink of this all of you, this is my blood of the new covenant, for you and many shed	drink of this all of you, this is my blood of the new covenant, for you and many, shed *and given*
for the remission of sins.	for the remission of sins.
	32. *Do this in memory of me.*
	33. *For as often as you eat this bread and drink the chalice, you announce my death and confess my resurrection until I come.*
	34. *Your death, O Lord, we commemorate and your resurrection we confess and your second coming we await. Mercy and indulgence we ask of you, and we implore the remission of sins. May your mercy be upon us all.*
35. Remembering, therefore,	35. Remembering, therefore, *O Lord,*
this saving command and all that was done for us: the cross, *the tomb,* the resurrection on the third day, the ascension into heaven, the sitting at the right hand,	this saving command and your whole *economy* that was done for us: the cross,
	the resurrection on the third day, the ascension into heaven and sitting at the right hand *of the Father's majesty, and your* second glorious coming,
the second *and* glorious coming *again,*	
	in which you will come in glory to judge the living and the dead and to reward all men according to their works with philanthropy, for your church supplicates you, and

CHR	APSyr
	your flock, and through you and
	with you your Father, saying:
	Have mercy on me, have mercy on
	us!
36. *(aloud) offering you your own*	
from what is yours,	
37.	37. *We too, Lord, giving thanks,*
	confess you
for everything and in every way	for everything and in every way
38. *(people)* We praise you,	38. we praise you,
we bless you,	we bless you
we thank you, O Lord,	
and we pray you, O our God!	and we pray you, our God,
	be propitious, o Good One, and
	have mercy on us.
	39. *In silence and fear . . .*
40. *Again we offer you this reason-*	40. *Then, indeed,*
able and unbloody worship and we	
invoke and pray and beseech you,	we pray you,
	Lord almighty and God of the holy
	powers, falling on our faces before
	you,
send down your Holy Spirit.	that you send down your Holy
	Spirit.
upon us and	
upon these offered gifts,	upon these oblations that are
	offered
41. and *make* the bread	41. and *show* this bread [to be]
the precious body of	the venerable body of
your Christ,	*our Lord Jesus* Christ
42. *changing [it] by your Holy*	
Spirit, amen,[18]	
43. and *what is in*	43. and
this chalice the *precious* blood of	this chalice the blood of
your Christ,	*our Lord Jesus* Christ
44. *changing [it] by your Holy*	
Spirit, amen,	

[18]The new redaction of CHR in use today has this change petition (**42, 44**) only
once for both species, after the blessing of the chalice (**44**).

CHR	APSyr
45. so that they might be, for those receiving [them],	45. so that they might be for *all* those who receive of them *life and resurrection and*
for sobriety of soul, for remission of sins, *for communion in your Holy Spirit,* *for fullness of the kingdom,*	remission of sins
	and health of soul and body, and enlightenment of mind,
for filial confidence before you, *not unto judgement or damnation.*	*and a good answer before the dread tribunal of your Christ . . .*

The CHR/APSyr parallelism I am illustrating does not concern the commemorations/intercessions, which tend to be strongly influenced by local usage and undergo notable modifications even in borrowed anaphoras. In CHR these intercessions follow the epiclesis:

46. Again we offer you this reasonable worship for those who have gone to their repose in the faith: the forefathers, fathers, patriarchs, prophets, apostles, preachers, evangelists, martyrs, confessors, ascetics, and for every just soul who has died in the faith.

47. *(Aloud)* Especially for our most holy, most pure, most blessed and glorious Lady the Theotokos and ever-virgin Mary [incipit of the diptychs of the dead].[19]

48. Again we beseech you, remember, Lord, the whole Orthodox episcopate . . . [intercessions for the clergy].

49. Again we offer you this reasonable worship for the whole world, for the holy, catholic and apostolic Church, for those living in purity and honor, for the civil authorities . . . [intercessions for the living continued].

[19]Taft, *The Diptychs,* 9–10, 100–2, 118–20. This Marian commemoration was introduced in the fallout from the Theotokos controversy at Ephesus (431). Originally CHR had sanctoral commemorations only by category, not by proper name. Later this Theotokos ekphonesis, plus the commemoration of St. John the Baptist and the saint of the day, were inserted at this point in the text in imitation of BAS, beginning with the earliest mss from southern Italy (Parenti-Velkovska, *L'Eucologio Barberini,* no. 36.3 = Brightman, *Liturgies Eastern and Western,* 331–2): G. Winkler, "Die Interzessionen der Chrysostomusanaphora in ihrer geschichtlichen Entwicklung (II)," *OCP* 37 (1971) 333–54.

50. *(Aloud)* First of all remember, O Lord, our bishop N . . . [incipit of the diptychs of the living].[20]

51. Remember, Lord, this city in which we live, and every city and country place, and the faithful dwelling therein . . . [intercessions for the living concluded].

CHR AND APSYR COMPARED

1. Methodological Principles

Two principles govern the comparative liturgical analysis of related liturgical texts:

1. One must discount as evidence of commonality all textual parallels which can be otherwise explained—e.g., citations from Sacred Scripture or obvious Formelgut material, that corpus of stereotyped phrases common to parallel liturgical units across the traditions.
2. Conversely, divergences attributable to another source must be discounted as evidence against commonality—e.g., passages of APSyr that derive from the common framework of Syro-Jacobite anaphoras borrowed from SyrJAS; passages in CHR that derive from the Byzantine Greek anaphoral setting common to CHR and BAS.

2. The CHR-APSyr Relationship

Those who have examined the structure of the parallel texts of CHR and APSyr[21] (and not only in our presanctus paradigm), have noted the following coordinates and dissonances:

1. The core segments of all constitutive parts of both texts are in quasi-total agreement.
2. In such core segments where the two recensions are in substantial agreement, manifesting only minor redactional variants of the same basic text, APSyr gives the shorter recension: whatever is found in APSyr is also in CHR—but not vice-versa.
3. APSyr departs substantially from CHR in two areas:
   [a] in those units of the Antiochene anaphoral structure traditionally most subject to local developments: the institution narrative, the anamnesis, and the epiclesis.

---

[20]Taft, *The Diptychs,* 11–2, 134–40, 158.

[21]Especially Engberding, "Die syrische Anaphora"; Wagner, *Der ursprung der Chrysostomusliturgie.*

[b] in those parts of the anaphora proclaimed aloud. These ek-phoneseis constitute the common anaphoral framework of the local church, as with CHR and BAS, substantially different texts which are, nevertheless, *practically identical in all chanted parts, including those of the anaphora itself.*

4. Sections of text where APSyr differs from CHR show clear signs of the influence of SyrJAS.
5. Where CHR departs from APSyr, the added material is largely:
[a] *stylistic:* rhetorical developments, such as the multiplications of epithets and synonyms, the smoothing out of transitional passages, etc.
[b] *theological:* echoes of the Eunomian controversy, explicitation of the epiclesis as consecratory.

From these data, certain provisional results may be formulated:

1. In both anaphoras, the agreement of the principal segments of all constituent parts is such that this could not have resulted from the common use of a third source, or from Formelgut material.[22] *Hence CHR and APSyr must be considered different redactons of one and the same text.*
2. The fact that CHR is *longer* in parallel passages where the two texts agree substantially, renders less probable Wagner's thesis that APSyr is a later redaction of CHR.[23] Rather, since in the parallel passages common to CHR-APSyr, everything contained in APSyr is also in CHR; and the Syriac text is *shorter* where it *agrees* with the Greek and *longer* where the difference is so substantial that the passages in question are obviously not variant redactions of a common source; it would seem:
[a] that the Syriac recension was translated from an earlier Greek text of which CHR is a later, elaborated redaction. I have called this earlier Urtext AP. When the Syriac version which lies behind APSyr was made, this AP Urtext did not contain the later interpolations peculiar to CHR, additions which characterize those common passages where CHR shows a more developed text than APSyr;
[b] that this Syriac version of AP was inserted into a West Syrian—i.e., Syro-Antiochene or Syrian Jacobite—liturgical framework

[22]Engberding, "Die syrische Anaphora," 236.
[23]Wagner, *Der Ursprung der Chrysostomusliturgie,* 6–10, 49–51.

(above, no. 3), which is the source of the Jacobite elaborations found in APSyr but not in CHR.[24]

So in CHR and APSyr we are faced with two independent reworkings of an earlier text, which can probably be identified with the Anaphora of the Apostles (AP) referred to by Leontius of Byzantium c. 543 AD.[25]

3. Conclusion

One may conclude at this point:

1. That the Chrysostom anaphora is a later redaction of a no-longer extant Greek anaphora (AP).
2. That APSyr is a later Jacobite reworking of a Syriac translation of this AP Urtext independent of CHR.

In its present form, APSyr is both similar and dissimilar to CHR. Now we know that West Syrian anaphoras have generally been conformed to a common framework derived from SyrJAS. Consequently, if we exclude from APSyr whatever is obviously from SyrJAS and not in CHR; and exclude from CHR whatever it has in common with BAS, and whatever is not in APSyr; the remaining least common denominator should go back to the common Greek Urtext of both, i.e., AP.

DETERMINING AUTHORSHIP

Where, when, and by whom was this lost AP composed, and its two extant recensions, CHR and APSyr, redacted? Comparative structural analysis alone furnishes no reply to these questions. So we must turn to the text and its contents.

1. Internal Indices of Authenticity

The *external* evidence is clear: the CHR text is indeed attributed to St. John Chrysostom (d. 407). Our task is to test by *internal* evidence the validity of this attribution. This consists in identifying in the text it-

---

[24]Wagner, *Der Ursprung der Chrysostomusliturgie*, 47–50, believes this occurred after the point when the anaphora came to be recited in secret. Though possible, that is by no means demonstrated by what was just said above in 2b. The existence of a traditional local framework of key transitional passages and vocal signals introducing popular exclamations is not dependent, strictly speaking, on the rest of the anaphora being said silently.

[25]Note 11 above.

self such internal indices of authenticity as similar style and the repetition of vocabulary, doublets, and favored scriptural loci. The first, style, is the most intangible and the least convincing. It is of more use negatively, in showing what is *not* authentic, than positively, in proving what is. The recurrence of vocabulary is much more decisive. Certain authors betray themselves by using common words with uncommon frequency, or by employing rare expressions more than once. Some authors also cite certain scriptural passages with unaccustomed frequency. This strange frequency of usual terms, or unusual appearance of strange terms, is even more convincing if the contexts in which they emerge closely resemble one another—what are called "doublets," characteristic phrases repeated almost word for word in several demonstrably authentic texts as well as in the text(s) being scrutinized.

Such indices may not be forceful enough to restore to an author a work which the mss place under another's name, for writers of the same epoch and school share common traits, and borrowing and even plagiarism were common coin, especially among homilists and later Byzantine writers. But internal indices can offer convincing confirmation of an already existing, solid tradition of attribution, as in the case of CHR.

2. Problems Peculiar to Liturgical Texts

In the case of liturgical texts, and especially anaphoras, the process of authentication is beset by problems peculiar to the genre. First of all, *liturgical texts are living texts,* subject to growth and change, and later changes can obscure the traces of the original author's hand.

Second, *liturgical texts are stereotypical.* Their composers were not free to follow untrammelled the vagaries of their personal thought patterns, vocabulary, and style, but were constrained by the nature of the genre to accepted patterns and an established vocabulary, replete with topoi.

Third, for that very reason *the most important liturgical texts may be the hardest to authenticate.* Obviously, all the above problems are magnified in the case of frequently used prayers like an anaphora, especially an anaphora like CHR. Such long-lived, mainline compositions are by their very nature representative of orthodox liturgical tradition, and hence far more liable to standardization and doctrinal updating than some offbeat, little-used text gathering dust in the cupboard.

Finally, even when internal indices have established a close relationship between a prayer and the authentic writings of an author, there remains the problem which source is prior. Already from the fourth century, the anaphora had developed an established convention of stereotypical structure, style, and vocabulary in each of its fixed components, all ordered in a preordained sequence within each of the three traditional eastern anaphoral shapes (Antiochene, Alexandrian, East Syrian). One would expect both eucharistic anaphoras and the Fathers of the Church to draw their liturgical vocabulary from this Formelgut font, that common stock of traditional phrases, just as both would draw from Scripture, when speaking of things the eucharist is concerned with: praise and thanks for creation and salvation, sin and redemption, Last Supper and cross, etc. In the case of an anaphora certainly known to and used by the author whose presumed authorship is being tested, literary similarities are of no help in indicating the *direction of the influence.* For if a eucharistic text was used frequently by its presumed author, the similarities between the style and vocabulary of the prayer and his other writings could perfectly well have originated in his repeated use of the prayer rather than from his common authorship of both. Consequently, all doublets attributable to another source, or common to several authors and anaphoras, and hence possibly Formelgut, must simply be discounted as indices of dependence.

3. The Special Case of Chrysostom

Proving or disproving authenticity is nowhere so daunting as in the case of CHR, for two reasons. First of all, in his preaching Chrysostom cites liturgical texts more frequently than any other patristic author. This marked interest in and easy familiarity with the texts of the liturgy increases the probability that the liturgy influenced Chrysostom as much as he influenced it. Secondly, Chrysostom was one of the most prolific and popular patristic authors, with the result that his name has attracted to it more spuria than are attributed to any other writer of Christian Antiquity. Obviously, until these spuria and genuina are sorted out, and until we have critical editions of all certainly authentic works of St. John, the process of authenticating his anaphora will be built partially on sand, since one end of the comparison will remain incomplete.

ENTER THE COMPUTER

The vastness of the Chrysostom corpus, real or supposed, provides a basis for comparison so huge that only via computerization can one get a relatively complete picture of the relatedness of vocabulary, the author's theological and ascetical nomenclature, recurring thought patterns, parallel passages, hapax legomena, rare terms and their frequency, all served up by this programming. In all this it is not one indication but the convergence of many that confirms—though cannot prove—attribution.[26]

Though we do not yet have fully computerized the vast and still far from definitively sifted and critically edited corpus of Chrysostomica, a quantum leap forward was made by the recent appearance of the *Thesaurus Linguae Graecae* data-base (hereafter *TLG*).[27] This CD-ROM[28] data-bank already contains over 8,000 works by almost 3,000 Greek authors from classical antiquity and the patristic period.

Computerized scanning of the TLG data-bank adds to what we have known hitherto about the relationship of CHR and Chrysostom four new qualities: (1) speed, (2) completeness, (3) accuracy, and (4) (relative) exclusivity, of which the last is crucial. Exclusivity shows not only what is found in Chrysostom, but *what is not found anywhere else*. We have long known that there are numerous parallels between the anaphora and the authentic writings of Chrysostom. We can now prove that in certain instances, not only are there doublets in

---

[26]On these methods see M. Aubineau, *Les homélies festales d'Hesychius de Jérusalem*, Subsidia Hagiographica 59.1–2 (Brussels: Societé des Bollandistes, 1978–1980) I:xxx–xli, II:608–14; idem, "«Hesychius redivivus.» Un prédicateur hiérosolymitain de la première moitié du Vᵉ siècle," *Freiburger Zeitschrift für Philosophie und Theologie* 28 (1981) 254–64, reprinted in idem, *Chrysostome, Sévérien, Proclus, Hésychius et alii. Patristique et hagiographie grecques. Inventaires de manuscrits, textes inédits, traductions, études*, Variorum Reprints Collected Studies 276 (London, 1988) ch. XXVII.

[27]The history and characteristics of the *TLG* are recounted in the Preface and Introduction to the program's accompanying volume listing the works in the data-bank: L. Berkowitz & K. A. Squitier, with technical assistance from W. A. Johnson, *Thesaurus Linguae Graecae. Canon of Greek Authors and Works* (New York/Oxford: Oxford University Press, 2nd ed., 1986). See also the extremely useful information-updating in R. A. Kraft, ed., "Offline: Computer assisted Research for Religious Research," *Bulletin of the Council of the Society for the Study of Religion*, appearing regularly since vol. 17/1 (February 1988) 20–2. I am grateful to Marina B. Smyth, Librarian of the Medieval Institute at the University of Notre Dame, and Professor Maxwell E. Johnson of St. John's University, Collegeville, for introducing me to the *TLG* and helping me to exploit it.

[28]I.e., compact-disk read-only memory, which can be read, scanned, printed, etc., but not changed or added to by the user.

Chrysostom's writings, but that such doublets exist in no other writings in the data-bank.

CHRYSOSTOMIAN DOUBLETS IN THE CHR TEXT

Let us apply the methods discussed to a sample of CHR and its perceived parallels in the anaphoral tradition and in the writings of John Chrysostom, with a view to adjudicating, if not definitively then at least with greater assurance than was hitherto possible, the long disputed question of its authenticity.

1. The Apophatic Credo (7)

The first text I wish to examine begins at number 7 of the CHR text in the left column. I skip over variants 3 and 5. Since the former is Formelgut, and the latter from Psalm 102:22, neither can provide any grist for the authenticity mill. But 6–7 is another matter. It reads:

"For you are God, ineffable, inconceivable, invisible, incomprehensible, always existing, ever the same, you and your only-begotten Son and your Holy Spirit."

Here, the simple divine address in APSyr, "qui vere es deus," has been expanded considerably in the Greek text by a series of alpha-privative epithets, and by the phrase "always existing, ever the same," affirming God's eternity and unchangeableness.

Of course other early anaphoras have apophatic epithets in the presanctus, especially in Egypt.[29] But they are not *exactly these epithets, in this order.* Only such true doublets will serve our purposes in this testing, and I have found this apophatic confession in no anaphora but CHR.

---

[29]E.g., E-BAS (Hänggi & Pahl, *Prex eucharistica,* 232); the fourth-century Greek Anaphora of Sarapion of Thmuis (Maxwell E. Johnson, *The Prayers of Sarapion of Thmuis. A Literary, Liturgical, and Theological Analysis,* OCA 249 [Rome: Pontificium Institutum Orientale, 1995] 46, cf. 200–1 = Hänggi & Pahl, *Prex eucharistica,* 128); the Alexandrian Greek Anaphora of St. Gregory (A. Gerhards, *Die griechische Gregoriosanaphora. Ein Beitrag zur Geschichte des eucharistischen Hochgebets,* LQF 65 [Münster: Aschendorff, 1984] 22.18–20); and related Sahidic anaphoral fragments (H. Quecke, "Das anaphorische Dankgebet auf den koptischen Ostraka B.M. Nr. 32 799 und 33 050 neu herausgegeben," *OCP* 37 [1971] 393–4, line 8; idem, "Das anaphorische Dankgebet auf dem koptischen Ostrakon Nr. 1133 der Leningrader Eremitage neu herausgegeben," *OCP* 40 [1974] 52–4, lines 12–3).

It is precisely here, in these epithets peculiar to CHR and not found in APSyr, that we encounter our first close parallels between the liturgical text and the authentic writings of Chrysostom. The time is shortly after Chrysostom's ordination to the presbyterate, at the beginning of his decade-long preaching career in Antioch (386–397), when the Anomean heresy, a strict form of late Arianism, was being vigorously defended by its chief propagator Eunomius (d. 394).[30] Chrysostom attacks the Anomeans especially for their teaching on the knowability of God's essence. From the literature of this controversy originated an entire vocabulary of apophatic theology, including the four alpha-privatives of CHR: [1] ineffable *(anekphrastos)*, [2] inconceivable *(aperinoêtos)*, [3] invisible *(aoratos)*, [4] incomprehensible *(akatalêptos)*.

Before Chrysostom and CHR, most of these expressions are found already in Gnostic writings, in Philo, in the New Testament, and in Clement of Alexandria, and they are common to the anti-Eunomian treatises of Basil the Great and his brother Gregory. So the epithets in question are not peculiar to Chrysostom. But he does use all four of them in the body (i.e., excluding the titles) of his five Antiochene homilies *On the Incomprehensibility of God,* as follows: (1) only once, (2) twice, (3) three times, and (4) his favorite, *akatalêptos,* "incomprehensible," twenty-seven times (plus five more times in the titles, which are doubtless not from Chrysostom himself).[31]

Once, however, in *Hom. 3,* 54–55, Chrysostom employs all four epithets in combination, and, strikingly, on that occasion he not only uses all four, and only these four epithets; he does so in *exactly the same sequence as in CHR:* "Let us call upon him, then, the ineffable, the inconceivable God, the invisible, the incomprehensible . . ."[32]

[30]Sozomen witnesses to how threatening the heresy was viewed in Antioch and elsewhere throughout this period: *Church History* 4.12–30, ed. J. Bidez, GCS 50 (Berlin: Akademie-Verlag, 1960) 154–87 passim. On the whole question see F. Cavallera, *Le schisme d'Antioche (IVe–Ve siècle)* (Paris: Picard, 1905); E. Cavalcanti, *Studi eunomiani,* OCA 202 (Rome: Pontificium Institutum Orientale, 1976) 1–22; M. Simonetti, *La crisi ariana nel IV secolo,* Studia Ephemerides «Augustinianum» 11 (Rome: Institutum Patristicum Augustinianum, 1975) passim, esp. 251–9, 462ff., 502–3; R.P.C. Hanson, *The Search for the Christian Doctrine of God. The Arian Controversy 318–381 AD* (Edinburgh: T. & T. Clark, 1988) passim, esp. 611–36.

[31]Jean Chrysostome, *Sur l'incompréhensibilité de Dieu (Homélies 1–5)* ed. A.-M. Malingrey, SC 28bis (Paris: Cerf, 1970) index, 332–34 (= CPG 4318).

[32]Ibid., 190. The first, *anekphrastos,* is very rare. Chrysostom himself uses it but twice, only once in combination with all three other apophatic epithets. The TLG

Even more significant is the fact that *among all Greek writers in the TLG*, no one but Chrysostom uses all four epithets together, and no one but Chrysostom uses them in the exact order in which they are found in CHR.[33]

So we can conclude the following:

1. Chrysostom knew these four epithets in the liturgical order as given in CHR.
2. It is probable that he knew them as part of a prayer invoking God.
3. Since the doublets in question are not found in APSyr, and hence were not in AP; and since computer scanning provides no secure basis for ascribing to Chrysostom the texts common to CHR-APSyr, i.e., that least common denominator we have attributed to AP, the doublets do not show Chrysostom to be the author of AP.
4. Since whatever is almost certainly attributable to Chrysostom is an addition to AP, this narrows our question to whether Chrysostom, even if not the author of AP (and therefore of CHR) in the modern sense of the term, could at least have been responsible for this later, Byzantine redaction that has come down to us as CHR.
5. Apart from the authenticity issue, what we have seen so far concerning the historical context of the apophatic confession provides a relatively secure context for locating this later elaboration of AP to the period during or after the anti-Eunomian polemic, which raged from c. 355.

---

scan gives only two other sources as using *anekphrastos* in conjunction with one of the other three epithets: Theophilos of Antioch, *Ad Autolycum* I.3 (c. 160), text and trans. R. M. Grant (Oxford: Clarendon, 1970) 4; Theophile d'Antioche, *Trois livres à Autolycus*, ed. G. Bardy, SC 20 (Paris: Cerf. 1948) 62; and Eusebius, *Demonstratio evangelica* 5.1.5, ed. I. A. Heikel, *Eusebius* 6, GCS 23 (Leipzig: Hinrichs, 1913) 151b.

[33]The relevant texts, all cited in Greek and analyzed in Taft, "The Authenticity of the Chrysostom Anaphora," 31–2, are: [1] *De incomprehensibili Dei natura, hom. 3*, 54–5 (Antioch before 398), SC 28bis, 190 (= *CPG* 4318); [2] *In Mt hom. 2*, 2 (Antioch), PG 57:25D (= *CPG* 4424), cf. Wagner, *Der ursprung der Chrysostomusliturgie*, 76–7; [3] *In illud 'Pater si possibile est'* 3, PG 51:37A (= *CPG* 4369), cf. Wagner, *Der Ursprung der Chrysostomusliturgie*, 76–7; [4] *Ad eos qui scandalizati sunt* II.18 (in exile 404–7), Jean Chrysostome, *Sur la providence de Dieu*, ed. A.-M. Malingrey, SC 79 (Paris: Cerf, 1961) 70–2 (= *CPG* 4401); [5] *Hom. de capto Eutropio* 9 (Constantinople 398–404), PG 52:404A, of doubtful authenticity: *CPG* 4528; J.A. de Aldama, *Repertorium pseudochrysostomicum*, Documents, études, et répertoires publiés par l'Institut de recherche et d'histoire des textes 10 (Paris: 1965) 170.

6. That, in turn, would place the composition of the AP Urtext back to at least mid-fourth century as an anaphora in use in the metropolis of Antioch.

* * *

Let us return now to the main question as narrowed by these conclusions: is John Chrysostom the author of Byzantine CHR? Chrysostom's writings so abound in apophatic epithets[34] that it is only on the basis of a strict correspondence of doublets, as in the case of this apophatic confession of CHR, that any real argument for a liturgical parallel can be developed. Does this parallel argue for Chrysostom himself as the redactor of the elaborated text of the CHR presanctus?[35] I would consider this conclusion the only reasonable one under the circumstances.

Note well that the argument is not based just on the doublets in Chrysostom and CHR, but on them *plus the complete absence of similar doublets in any other Greek Christian writer then, before, or after*. With the expression "God the ineffable, the inconceivable, the invisible, the incomprehensible, always existing, ever the same," we are, then, dealing with a "Chrysostomism" verified nowhere else.

This, in turn, permits us to argue as follows:

1. The text in question is not found in APSyr, and hence most probably was not in AP.
2. but it is found in the later Greek redaction of AP, which we know as CHR.
3. Further, it is an expression clearly derived from the anti-Eunomian polemic raging in Antioch from c. 355.
4. In this polemic, John Chrysostom played a major role.
5. The text, in its liturgical form in CHR, is a Chrysostomian hapax found in no other writer.
6. So either Chrysostom borrowed the expression from the liturgy, or the liturgy got it from him.

Did Chrysostom himself personally redact this expanded recension of the liturgical text? And if so, when? Since it is difficult to imagine a young presbyter even of Chrysostom's obvious gifts meddling with

---

[34]See indices, SC 28bis:314; SC 79:281–2.
[35]Cf. Wagner, *Der Ursprung der Chrysostomusliturgie,* 76.

the anaphora of a major see, one might prefer to think that the anaphora influenced the preacher, not vice-versa, and thus was a text well-known to Chrysostom from frequent use, and not a recent innovation. Our main proof text, *On the incomprehensibility of God, homily 3*, was, after all, preached at a eucharist in Antioch,[36] and it would be quite natural that at its conclusion, where the text in question appears, the homilist exhort his hearers to pray God in the words of the imminent anaphora—*if those words were, in fact, part of the anaphora at that time.*

This is the sticking point, and there is no sure way to resolve it. But it seems to me fairer to the true weight of the objective evidence to attribute the apophatic epithets to Chrysostom, but to conclude that they were added to Antiochene AP by him, or at this direction, only after being ordained bishop of Constantinople on February 26, 398. The reasons for this are twofold:

1. We find the apophatic confession in Chrysostom's homilies in Antioch *before they appear in the liturgy*, or at least before Chrysostom would have borrowed them from the liturgy after going to Constantinople. For the absence of the expression in APSyr, I have argued, means it was not part of the AP as it would have been known to Chrysostom during his Antiochene period.
2. So one can infer that the liturgy got the apophatic confession from Chrysostom, not vice-versa.

2. Confirmatory Evidence

As I have shown elsewhere, all of the above is confirmed by other texts of CHR.[37] For instance, everything said above concerning the apophatic epithets applies, mutatis mutandis, to the expression "always existing, ever the same" (**8**). It, too, comes out of the Anomean controversy; it, too, is a favorite of Chrysostom. Indeed, if taken verbatim, it is a hapax found thus nowhere but in CHR and Chrysostom, who *not only has it twice, but both times he uses it in conjunction with our alpha-privative epithets.*

Likewise, the segment of the anaphora (**16–18**), where CHR expands the original, common conclusion of the thanksgiving (**14–15**) by a further thanksgiving for hidden benefits: "For all the things we

---

[36]SC 28bis:58.
[37]Taft, "The Authenticity of the Chrysostom Anaphora," 36ff.

know and do not know, your seen and unseen benefits accomplished for us," is a Chrysostom hapax *pace* Engberding, who wrongly dismisses these additions as Formelgut.[38] The TLG data-base scan shows that Chrysostom not only uses the vocabulary, and even the antitheses "known, unknown/seen, unseen." especially the latter. He is also *the only Greek writer in the TLG data-bank to use the expression "benefits known and unknown," and each time he does so in the genitive plural exactly as in CHR.*[39]

[38]Engberding, "Die syrische Anaphora," 239. Its presence in the Anaphora of Nestorius (Hänggi & Pahl, *Prex eucharistica*, 388) is clearly dependent on CHR and can be discounted. Its absence in APSyr is not surprising for, as Ligier has pointed out, in liturgical language "things known and unknown, manifest and hidden," are usually sins, not divine gifts, particularly in Jewish and Syriac prayers: L. Ligier, "Pénitence et eucharistie en Orient. Théologie sur une interférence de prières et de rites," *OCP* 29 (1963) 21–4, 51–3. Ligier cites GkJAS (B. C. Mercier, *La Liturgie de S. Jacques*, PO 26/2 [Paris: Firmin-Didot, 1946] 222.2–3); and the Syriac anaphoras of Cyril (*Anaphorae Syriacae* I.3:357); SyrJAS and Gregory John (*Anaphorae Syriacae* II.2:168–69, 227); Clement of Rome, Gregory Abul Farag, and John the Scribe (E. Renaudot, *Liturgiarum orientalium collectio* [Frankfurt/London, 2d ed. 1847) II, 196, 464, 482.

[39]The following passages in particular recall this anaphoral text: *In Gen hom. 26, 5* (reminiscent of the idea if not the vocabulary), PG 53:238 (= CPG 4409); *Ad Stagirium a daemone vexatum liber 1, 5*, PG 47:437 (= CPG 4310); *In Eph hom. 19, 2*, PG 62:130 (= CPG 4431). In addition, Wagner, *Der Ursprung der Chrysostomusliturgie*, 92–95 cites an impressive array of texts, mostly from Chrysostom's Antiochene period, proving that this theme of the hidden benefits received from God's bounty is another favorite of Chrysostom, who often employs 1 Cor 2:9, citing Is 64:5 and 65:17, to the effect that "No eye has seen, nor ear heard, nor heart of man conceived, what God has prepared for those who love him." The most extensive passage, and closest to the liturgical text of CHR, is from Chrysostom's Constantinopolitan sermon *In Col hom. 10, 2–3*, PG 62:368–9 (= CPG 4433). On this text see Wagner, *Der Ursprung der Chrysostomusliturgie*, 94–96; S. Antoniadis, *Place de la liturgie dans la tradition des lettres grecques* (Leiden: Sijthoff, 1939) 160; F. van de Paverd, *Zur Geschichte der Meßliturgie in Antiocheia und Konstantinopel gegen Ende des vierten Jahrhunderts. Analyse der Quellen bei Johannes Chrysostomos*, OCA 187 (Rome: Pontificium Institutum Orientale, 1970) 494. By way of a corollary, the fact that this Constantinopolitan homily does provide doublets for CHR, whereas Chrysostom's Antiochene sermon *In Mt hom. 25/26, 3–4*, PG 57:331–2 (= CPG 4424), which refers explicitly to the eucharistic prayer, and to God's benefits past, present, and future recalled in the *eucharistia* as the motive of our thanksgiving, does not, confirms rather than undermines the line of argument taken thus far regarding Chrysostom's authorship of CHR but not AP, and about his effecting this redaction of CHR in Constantinople between 388–404.

CONCLUSION

From what we have seen concerning the text of presanctus of CHR in relation to APSyr and the writings of Chrysostom, I would draw the following conclusions:

1. Because CHR has textual elaborations dictated by theological concerns that cannot antedate the anti-Eunomian polemic in Antioch from c. 355, and these additions are not found in APSyr, at least some passages of APSyr seem to present an older redaction than CHR of an earlier Antiochene Greek anaphora, which I have called AP.

2. For the same reason, this no longer extant AP without the anti-Eunomian emendations most probably dates from before the start of that crisis c. 355.

3. Conversely, the present redaction of the Greek CHR that does have those additions must, perforce, be later than that date.

4. The authentic writings of John Chrysostom have numerous exact doublets to precisely these later emendations, but not to passages of AP. Hence this redaction of CHR is most probably the work of John Chrysostom himself.

5. Chrysostom probably did this revision of AP between 398–404, as bishop of Constantinople. According to this admittedly hypothetical scenario, he would have introduced into the rite of the Great Church an existing Antiochene Greek anaphora, AP, inserting it, with his own redactional emendations, into the already existing anaphoral setting of the Great Church.

6. APSyr is a Syriac translation of the same anaphora, adapted to the traditional Syro-Antiochene anaphoral setting modelled on SyrJAS. No one challenges this. The only issue is whether APSyr is a later, abbreviated translation of CHR itself, or a translation of what I have called AP, independent of CHR and for that reason lacking CHR's later emendations of AP.

7. I have opted, against Wagner, for the latter hypothesis—i.e., that Chrysostom is the redactor of CHR on the basis of AP, but not the author of AP-become-CHR, because:
   [a] In passages common to both, and hence part of the shared Ur-text, CHR is more developed than APSyr, and I see no reason why the Syriac translator would have cut the orginal Greek text so drastically if it contained the passages in question—as, indeed, according to Wagner's scenario, it must have.

[b] My computer scan of APSyr and CHR shows that there are no strict doublets in the authentic writings of Chrysostom to any elements peculiar to the text of APSyr. Those similarities between Chrysostom's writings and AP Urtext passages common to CHR-APSyr, though at times notable, are not real doublets. And besides, they are patient of another explanation: some of them are at least partly Formelgut material or scriptural resonances. In such cases Chrysostom himself could have been influenced by the common liturgical language, or even directly by AP. All true doublets turned up by the scan are found exclusively in the CHR elaborations of AP not found in APSyr. This makes it highly improbable that the AP text underlying APSyr and CHR is a later abbreviation of an authentic CHR, rather than, as I have said, CHR representing Chrysostom's expanded redaction of AP, elements of which, once we exclude the passages referred to above in the methodological principles, are still embedded in the later Jacobite reworking of AP which APSyr represents.

8. All this, when joined with the total silence of all sources before c. 750 concerning a Chrysostom Liturgy, and with the explicit mention by Leontius of a Liturgy of the Apostles, makes it more plausible, it seems to me, to conclude that John Chrysostom took an already existing Antiochene anaphora, which I have called AP, and reworked it into what we know as CHR.

STRUCTURE AND CONTENT

CHR follows the classic Antiochene-type anaphoral order of presanctus "Vere dignus" praise (1–19), *Sanctus* bloc (20–22), postsanctus with christological economy and institution narrative (23–31), anamnesis (35), oblation (36), epiclesis (40–45), followed by the commemorations/intercessions and diptychs (46–51). Its primitive undifferentiated structure[40] mingles throughout praise, remembrance, thanksgiving, and oblation themes, with christological material both before and after the *Sanctus*.[41]

---

[40]The term is from L. Ligier, "Célébration divine et anamnèse dans la première partie de l'anaphore ou canon de la messe orientale," *Gregorianum* 48 (1967) 225–52, esp. 228–32.

[41]This raises the question whether the *Sanctus* was added to an already existing text, an issue to which there is no definitive solution: R. F. Taft, "The Interpolation of the *Sanctus* into the Anaphora: When and Where? A Review of the Dossier,"

1. Presanctus

The presanctus concludes with a thanksgiving for all benefits (14),[42] which some commentators consider to be the original conclusion of the anaphora before the interpolation of the *Sanctus* and the explicit incorporation of the institution-anamnesis embolism.[43] As we saw, CHR extends this thanksgiving with the Chrysostomism, "for all the things we know and do not know, your benefits seen and unseen" (16–18). The trinitarian gloss "You and your only-begotten Son and your Holy Spirit," repeated twice in the presanctus (9, 15) and again at the beginning of the postsanctus (24), betrays redactional reworking provoked by the Arian crisis and its fallout.[44]

2. The Sanctus

The incipit of the transition to the *Sanctus,* a thanksgiving "for this liturgy which you have deigned to receive from our hands," is a hapax in CHR and its clone, the East Syrian Anaphora of Nestorius.[45] Though there are resonances in the apocrypha,[46] it is unique for an anaphora to thank God for the very thanksgiving we are offering him. The *Sanctus* material itself is drawn largely from the classic Septuagint and apocryphal texts on which *Sanctus* Formelgut traditionally depends.[47]

3. The Postsanctus and Institution Narrative

Noteworthy in the postsanctus is the absence of any developed "oratio christologica" or account of the saving economy of Jesus, which is

---

OCP 57 (1991) 281–308; 58 (1992) 82–121; B. D. Spinks, *The Sanctus in the Eucharistic Prayer* (Cambridge: Cambridge University Press, 1991).

[42]As in AC 8.12.27 (Hänggi & Pahl, *Prex eucharistica,* 88); similarly the *Birkat ha-mazon* (ibid., 11, 27, cf. 53); Wagner, *Der Ursprung der Chrysostomusliturgie,* 91.

[43]Taft, "Sanctus" I (note 41 above) 289–90.

[44]See E. Lanne, "Gli incisi trinitari nell'anafora di San Giovanni Crisostomo e nelle anafore imparentate," in E. Carr, S. Parenti, A.-A. Thiermeyer, E. Velkovaska, eds., *EULOGEMA. Studies in Honor of Robert Taft, S.J.,* Studia Anselmiana 110 = Analecta Liturgica 17 (Rome: S. Anselmo, 1993) 269–83.

[45]Hänggi & Pahl, *Prex eucharistica,* 388.

[46]Acts of Peter 5 (c. A.D. 200), *Acta apostolorum apocrypha,* ed. R. A. Lipsius & M. Bonnet (Leipzig: Mendelssohn, 1891–1898) I, 51:3–11; also 50:7–10; cf. R. Ledogar, *Acknowledgment. Praise-Verbs in the Early Greek Anaphora* (Rome: Herder, 1968) 39–40.

[47]Is 6:103; Dan 7:9-10; Ez 1:5-11; 10:20-21; Mt 21:9 (= Ps 118:26); Rev 4:8; 5:11; cf. 1 Enoch 39:12; 40:1 in R. H. Charles, *The Book of Enoch or 1 Enoch* (Oxford: Clarendon, 2nd ed., 1912) 76–7; 1 Clement 34.6.

compressed into the passage cited from Jn 3:16, "Who so loved your world that you gave your only-begotten Son . . ." (**26**). This leads directly to the institution narrative (**27–31**), which in later mss—though not in the earliest CHR text—has undergone assimilation to BAS.[48]

4. The Anamnesis (**35**)

CHR omits the customary "command to repeat"—some form of "Do this in memory of me"[49]—but the explicit reference to "this saving command" in the anamnesis incipit (**35**), and the presence of the command in APSyr (**32**),[50] make it likely that AP had the command too.[51] The traditional Antiochene anamnesis picks up from the command to repeat with the incipit "remembering," the sequence being "in remembrance/remembering therefore."[52] The extension of the list of mysteries commemorated beyond the death and parousia, an orientalism foreign to the Latin West, may reflect an accommodation of

[48]Compare Brightman, *Liturgies Eastern and Western,* 327:23ff. (left and right), 385:22–5. For a detailed study of liturgical institution texts, see F. Hamm, *Die liturgischen Einsetzungsberichte im Sinne der vergleichenden Liturgieforschung untersucht,* LQF 23 (Münster: Aschendorff, 1928); J.R.K. Fenwick, *The Anaphoras of St. Basil and St. James. An Investigation into their Common Origin,* OCA 240 (Rome: Pontificium Institutum Orientale, 1992) ch. 10. The later text departs from the Pauline "On the night on which he was betrayed he took bread . . ." of 1 Cor 11:23, preferring to stress the self-giving of Jesus as in Gal 2:20; Eph 5:2; cf. Gal 1:4; 1 Tim 2:6; Tit 2:14; 1 Jn 3:16; Jn 10:17-18; Wagner, *Der Ursprung der Chrysostomusliturgie,* 108. This emphasis goes back to the earliest anaphoral tradition in AT 4 (Hänggi & Pahl, *Prex eucharistica,* 81); see also MARK (ibid., 112).

[49]Its most traditional liturgical form comprises Lk 22:19/1 Cor 11:24b plus 1 Cor 11:26, e.g., AC 8.12.37, BAS, E-BAS, GkJAS, SyrJAS, APSyr, MARK (G. J. Cuming, *The Liturgy of St. Mark,* OCA 234 [Rome: Pontificium Institutum Orientale, 1990], 41–43), Coptic Cyril/Mark, the Anaphora of St. Gregory (Gerhards, *Die griechische Gregoriosanaphora,* 34), the Anaphora of Nestorius (Hänggi & Pahl, *Prex eucharistica,* 92, 112, 137, 235, 248, 266–67, 271, 350–352, 365, 390); ES-BAS (J. Doresse & E. Lanne, *Un témoin archaïque de la liturgie copte de S. Basile,* Bibliothèque du *Muséon* 47 [Louvain, 1960] 18–9). But one finds other forms: the Deir Balyzeh fragment has only 1 Cor 11:26 (Hänggi & Pahl, *Prex eucharistica,* 126) the Roman Canon Missae gives only 1 Cor 11:25b (ibid., 434); cf. AT 4, the Anaphora of Theodore of Mopsuestia (ibid., 81, 383).

[50]Hänggi & Pahl, *Prex eucharistica,* 266.

[51]Unless, as Fenwick suggests (*"The Missing Oblation,"* 24), the CHR anamnesis incipit, "Remembering, therefore, this saving command," could refer to the "Take, eat . . . drink of this all of you . . ." command of the institution narrative.

[52]On anamnesis types see B. Botte, "Problèmes de l'anamnèse," *JEH* 5 (1954) 16; Ledogar, *Acknowledgment,* 29ff.

the liturgical texts to the creeds.[53] The CHR/APSyr anamneseis remain unique especially for the sobriety of their anamnetic mystery-lists and the summary phrase "and all that was done for us" in place of the more usual recalling of the passion.[54]

5. The Oblation and Hymn (36–37)
The anamnesis concludes with an ekphonesis that introduces the hymn of the people and forms one grammatical unit with the anamnesis and hymn:

"Remembering . . . offering you yours from what are yours, always and in every way we praise you, we bless you, we thank you, Lord, and we pray to you, our God."

This sequence—remembering, we offer, <praise,> and/or give thanks, and ask you to send the Spirit—appears to reflect an ancient anaphoral format, though CHR/APSyr betray signs of substantial reworking to fit the framework of their respective local traditions. Problematic are the double oblation in CHR (**36, 40**) and none whatever in APSyr.[55]

The oblation ekphonesis incipit (**36**) "Yours from what are yours *(Ta sa ek tôn sôn)*"—i.e., "Your own gifts from what are your own gifts"—derived from the Septuagint 1 Paralepomenon (Chron) 29:14,[56] was liturgical Formelgut already by the sixth century, and

---

[53]Botte, "Problèmes de l'anamnèse," 17–8, 20–1. The expanded list is characteristic of almost all eastern anaphoras save Addai and Mari: W. F. Macomber, "The Oldest Known Text of the Anaphora of the Apostles Addai and Mari," *OCP* 32 (1966) 369; cf. H.-J. Schulz, *The Byzantine Liturgy. Symbolic Structure and Faith Expression* (New York: Pueblo, 1986) 142–59, esp. 156–57; idem, *Ökumenische Glaubenseinheit aus eucharistischer Überlieferung* (Paderborn: Bonifacius-Drurkerei, 1976) 24–45, 48–53. Far from being "eschatological," as some maintain, this extended catalogue of mysteries is an historicization in which the paschal mystery itself becomes but one in a list of saving events. See G. Dix, *The Shape of the Liturgy* (London: Dacre, 1945) 264ff.; Schulz, *The Byzantine Liturgy*, 10–2, 15–20, 154–9.

[54]Cf. AC 8.12.38, JAS, BAS (Hänggi & Pahl, *Prex eucharistica*, 92, 236, 248). This is a favorite expression of John Chrysostom: texts in Taft, "The Authenticity of the Chrysostom Anaphora," 46–8.

[55]Cf. Fenwick, *"The Missing Oblation,"* 12–3. I consider the reprise of the oblation in **45** as just an extension of **40** and not another oblation.

[56]It is reflected c. AD 185 in Irenaeus, *Adv. haereses* 4.18.5, Sancti Irenaei episcopi Lugdunensis, *Libros quinque adversus Haereses*, ed. W. W. Harvey (Cambridge,

had probably entered the liturgy even earlier.[57] The absence of the oblation formula in AC 8.12:38 and APSyr, however, would seem to indicate that it was not a fixed part of the Antiochene tradition when AP was redacted in Antioch before the middle of the fourth century. The presence of the formula in the same form and context in both CHR and BAS shows assimilation of CHR to BAS.

The transition from anamnesis to epiclesis (**34–40**) has been disrupted in CHR by later reworking and interpolations to make room for the oblation/hymn sequence (**36–37**),[58] which is probably a later interpolation into the Antiochene anaphoral structure.[59] Later reworking of the text necessitated a reprise of the oblation in the new incipit "Again we offer you. . . ." (**40**).

1857) II:105 = PG 7:1028; and found in BAS (Hänggi & Pahl, *Prex eucharistica,* 236); in the Roman Canon's "offerimus praeclarae maiestati tuae de tuis donis ac datis hostiam puram . . ." (ibid., 434); and, with variants, in ES-BAS (Doresse-Lanne, *Un témoin archaïque,* 18–21); E-BAS (Hänggi & Pahl, *Prex eucharistica,* 352); the Anaphora of St. Gregory (Gerhards, *Die griechische Gregoriosanaphora,* 34 = Hänggi & Pahl, *Prex eucharistica,* 364); MARK (Cuming, *The Liturgy of St. Mark,* 44 = Hänggi & Pahl, *Prex eucharistica,* 114; the doubling of the phrase in some mss of MARK [Cuming, *The Liturgy of St. Mark,* 43.6–9] is a later Byzantinization); Coptic Mark/Cyril (Hänggi & Pahl, *Prex eucharistica,* 114).

[57]It is witnessed to in evidence from Palestine, Egypt, and throughout the provinces of Asia Minor, in both Chalcedonian Orthodox and Monophysite sources. That could indicate a date before the Council of Chalcedon in 451 for the interpolation, which at any rate certainly occurred before the fusion of hagiopolite and Antiochene elements in the anaphoras of the Syro-Jacobite tradition after 518. For witnesses to the text, see K. Weitzmann & I. Ševčenko, "The Moses Cross at Sinai," *Dumbarton Oaks Papers* 17 (1963) 393–95. Especially relevant here is the inscription around the rim of the altar of Hagia Sophia, dating from the restoration after the earthquake of May 7, 558: G. Cedrenus, *Historiarum compendium,* ed. I. Bekker, Corpus Scriptorum Historiae Byzantinae I (Bonn: Weber, 1838) 677 = PG 121:737; cf. A. Boeck & J. Franz, *Corpus inscriptionum graecorum IV* (Berlin: Akademie-Verlag, 1877) no. 8643; M. Amelotti et al., *Le costituzioni Giustineanee,* Legum Iustiniani Imperatoris Vocabularium, Subsidia 1 (Milan: A. Giuffrè, 1972) 111, no. 20; also found in some mss of the *Narratio de structura templi S. Sophiae* 17, Th. Preger, ed., *Scriptores originum Constantinopolitanarum,* Bibliotheca Scriptorum Graecorum et Romanorum Teubneriana, Scriptores Graeci (Leipzig, 1901) 96; and later sources: cf. C. Mango, *Materials for the Study of the Mosaics of St. Sophia at Istanbul,* Dumbarton Oaks Studies 8 (Washington, D.C., 1962) 123–4.

[58]Fenwick, *"The Missing Oblation,"* esp. 12–3.

[59]Neither the oblation nor the hymn are found c. 380 in the Antiochene Greek anaphora of AC 8.12.38-39 (Hänggi & Pahl, *Prex eucharistica,* 92).

The oblation is the crux interpretum.[60] CHR and BAS have two oblations—offering (36)/we offer (40)—whereas APSyr has none. Since it is not found in AC 8.12:37–39,[61] the oblation/hymn combination now common in Antiochene-type anaphoras is probably a late fourth- or early fifth-century interpolation.

So I would conclude that the post-anamnesis structures of CHR and APSyr are independent. Since the elements common to both are embedded in a different framework, in CHR of oblation, in APSyr of thanksgiving, they do not go back to AP but were added to CHR and APSyr independently from another source(s). This means that the early Antiochene post-institution anaphoral material—and hence AP from which both CHR and APSyr derive—had no oblation at all but rather an anamnesis-thanksgiving-epiclesis structure.[62] (Since the oblation in AC 8.12:38 is derived from AT 4 it can be discounted). So the shape of CHR results from assimilation to BAS: hence its *remembering/offering you yours from what are yours/always and in every way we praise you/epiclesis* sequence. And the shape of APSyr results from assimilation to SyrJAS: hence its *remembering/giving thanks/always and in every way we praise you/epiclesis* sequence.

6. The Epiclesis (40–45)

The classical Antiochene epiclesis is a tripartite prayer which asks the Father [1] to send the Holy Spirit (on us and) on the offered gifts (40), [2] to make the bread and wine the body and blood of Christ by the power of the Holy Spirit (41–44), [3] so that they might be unto salvation for those who receive them in communion (45). Section 2 (41–44) is doubtless a later development. The entire change petition (42, 44) where CHR departs from APSyr, I would consider a later interpola-

---

[60]For a detailed discussion of this very complex question of textual development, see R. F. Taft, "The Oblation and Hymn of the Chrysostom Anaphora. Its Text and Antecedents," in *Miscellanea di studi in onore di P. Marco Petta per il LXX compleanno*, vol. IV = *Bolletino della Badia Greca di Grottaferrata* n.s. 46 (1992) [published 1994] 319–45; idem, "Some Structural Problems in the Syriac Anaphora of the Apostles I," A Festschrift for Dr. Sebastian P. Brock, *ARAM Periodical* 5.1-2 (1993) [published 1996] 505–20; idem, "Understanding the Byzantine Anaphoral Oblation," in Nathan Mitchell & John F. Baldovin, eds., *Rule of Prayer, Rule of Faith: Essays in Honor of Aidan Kavanagh, O.S.B.* (Collegeville: The Liturgical Press, 1996) 32–55. Cf. also Fenwick, "The Missing Oblation," 12–3, 24–5.

[61]Hänggi & Pahl, *Prex eucharistica*, 92.

[62]Fenwick, "The Missing Oblation," 12–3, 24–5.

tion not found in AP. The primitive epiclesis, directed at the sanctification of the communicants, not of the gifts, was a prayer for the sanctification of the ecclesial communion, not for the sanctification of its sacramental sign, the Holy Communion. Hence modern commentators distinguish between a more primitive "communion epiclesis" and the "developed" or "consecratory epiclesis" containing explicit petitions, as in CHR, for the hallowing of the gifts and their change into the body and blood of Christ.[63]

The fruits of the eucharist are traditionally enumerated in the pristine communion epiclesis. These benefits of the Supper of the Lord, like those of any meal, are received by those who eat and drink.[64] In CHR (45) the six fruits prayed for are both negative [1–2, 6] and positive [3–5].[65]

7. Commemorations/Intercessions (46–51)

The anaphoral commemorations/intercessions flow from the epiclesis in Antiochene-type anaphoras, where the petition for the fruits of the eucharist (45) provides a natural transition to further petitions for the living and the dead, the latter including the saints too.[66] Unique to BAS/CHR is the order of the intercessions, with the dead before the living. In CHR this is doubtless the result of assimilation to BAS,

---

[63]On this see R. F. Taft, "The Epiclesis Question in the Light of the Orthodox and Catholic Lex orandi Traditions," in Bradley Nassif, ed., *New Perspectives on Historical Theology. Essays in Honor of John Meyendorff* (Grand Rapids, Mich.: Eerdmans, 1996) 210–37.

[64]This is the testimony of most early eucharistic prayers from 1 Cor 11:26 to AT 4, AC 8.12.39, Sarapion, MARK, JAS, SyrJAS, APSyr, CHR, BAS, E-BAS, the Roman Canon (Hänggi & Pahl, *Prex eucharistica*, 81, 92, 114, 122, 130, 226, 238, 250, 267, 271, 352, 435) and ES-BAS (Doresse-Lanne, *Un témoin archaïque*, 21–3). Among the early texts, only *Testamentum Domini* I.23 leaves it implicit (Hänggi & Pahl, *Prex eucharistica*, 221), and Addai and Mari expresses it outside the epiclesis, in the preceding kuššapa, which is not part of the Urtext (Hänggi & Pahl, *Prex eucharistica*, 409); cf. W. F. Macomber, "The Oldest Known Text of the Anaphora of the Apostles Addai and Mari," *OCP* 32 (1966) 368–9.

[65]See R. F. Taft, "The Fruits of Communion in the Anaphora of St. John Chrysostom," in I. Scicolone, ed., *Psallendum. Miscellanea di studi in onore del Prof. Jordi Pinell i Pons, O.S.B.*, Analecta Liturgica 15 = Studia Anselmiana 105 (Rome: S. Anselmo, 1992) 275–302.

[66]The basic study is G. Winkler, "Die Interzessionen der Chrysostomusanaphora in ihrer geschichtlichen Entwicklung," *OCP* 36 (1970) 301–36; 37 (1971) 333–83. See also the references in the next two notes.

where the passage from the epiclesis petition for communion in the Holy Spirit and communion with the saints leads directly to their commemoration and that of the dead.[67]

In CHR the saints were simply named as chief among the deceased. The notion that we pray *for* the dead but *to* the saints, a later refinement based on theological reflection, is foreign to the original text of CHR, which in the earliest mss had no commemoration of saints by name.[68]

LITERARY AND THEOLOGICAL CHARACTERISTICS
CHR is a prayer of great moderation, economy, and restraint,[69] even austere by comparison with the occasionally exaggerated rhetorical expansiveness in some other Greek anaphoras, the remarkable compression and symmetry of its text exhibiting, though with considerably greater economy than comparable Greek anaphoras, many of the features of artistic prose, especially of the Second Sophistic.[70]

---

[67]Hänggi & Pahl, *Prex eucharistica,* 238; H. Engberding, "Das anaphorische Fürbittgebet der byzantinischen Chrysostomusliturgie," *OC* 45 (1961) 26–29; van de Paverd, *Zur Geschichte der Meßliturgie,* 521–4; idem, "Anaphoral Intercessions, Epiclesis and Communion Rites in John Chrysostom," *OCP* 49 (1983) 331–2; G. Winkler, "Einige Randbemerkungen zu den Interzessionen in Antiochien und Konstantinopel im 4. Jahrhundert," *OS* 20 (1971) 55–61; J.R.K. Fenwick, "The Significance of Similarities in the Anaphoral Intercession Sequence in the Coptic Anaphora of St. Basil and Other Ancient Liturgies," *SP* 18/2 (1989) 361; full review of the question in Taft, *The Diptychs,* 173–83.

[68]Winkler, "Die Interzessionen der Chrysostomusanaphora," (I) 305–8; (II) 333–4, 342–4; Taft, *The Diptychs,* 24, n. 3, 40–2. On the theological question cf. also C. Vogel, "Prière ou intercession? Une ambiguïté dans le culte paléochrétien des martyrs," in B. Bobrinskoy et al., *Communio sanctorum. Mélanges offerts à Jean-Jacques von Allmen* (Geneva: Labor et Fides, 1982) 284–90; R. F. Taft, "Praying to or for the Saints? A Note on the Sanctoral Intercessions—Commemorations in the Anaphora: History and Theology," in M. Schneider & W. Berschin, eds., *Ab Oriente et Occidente (Mt 8,11). Kirche aus Ost und West. Gedenkschrift für Wilhelm Nyssen* (St. Ottilien: EOS, 1995) 439–55.

[69]This is noted throughout CHR by D. J. Sheerin, "The Anaphora of the Liturgy of St. John Chrysostom: Stylistic Notes," in D. Jasper & R.C.D. Jasper, eds., *Language and the Worship of the Church* (New York: St. Martin's Press, 1990) 44–81, esp. 50, 54–5, 57–8, 61–2, 79.

[70]Ibid., passim, esp. 62–5, 76–7. Sheerin employs over twenty technical Greek rhetorical terms in his analysis of the style of CHR. See Rosemary Radford Ruether, *Gregory of Nazianzus, Rhetor and Philosopher* (Oxford: Clarendon, 1969) 59–70: "Figures of Language"; S. S. Averincev, *Poetika rannevizantijskoj literatury*

The extreme simplicity of the eucharistic theology expressed in CHR betrays its antiquity.[71] Like AT 4, its trinitarian structure closely resembles that of the Apostles' Creed.[72] As already noted, its structure is "undifferentiated," mingling praise and thanks, remembrance and oblation, throughout, and the same may be said for its theology: the flow and context of the prayer provide no ammunition for theological polemics. After thanking and praising God for creation and salvation and everything that was done for us (1–19), we turn to praise again in the *Sanctus* (20–22). In the postsanctus (23–31) we commemorate again the Christ-economy (26–31), especially the Last Supper (28–31). In the anamnesis we recall once more what was done for us and the command to repeat it (35), and then proceed to obey this command, offering the oblation to God (36) and giving praise and thanks again (37–38). Finally, we express the offering a second time (40), asking the Father to send his Spirit on the offered gifts to fructify them unto salvation for those who receive them worthily (40–45). The institution narrative is part of the account of salvation history, and nothing in the text warrants isolating it as a special "formula."[73] But it would be equally anachronistic to argue from the text that at the oblation (36), before the epiclesis, the gifts are still unconsecrated, so that what we offer is mere bread and wine.[74] The entire anaphora

---

(Moscow: Izd. "Nauka," 1977) 221–36, 317–9. See also Ledogar, *Acknowledgment*, 32 n. 7.

[71]Easily the best interpreter of the theology of CHR is H.-J. Schulz, "Ökumenische Aspekte der Darbringungsaussagen in der erneuerten römischen und in der byzantinischen Liturgie," *Archiv für Liturgiewissenschaft* 19 (1978) 7–28; idem, "Das frühchristlich-altkirchliche Eucharistiegebet: Überlieferungskontinuität und Glaubenszeugnis," *Internationale kirchliche Zeitschrift* 70 (1980) 139–53; idem, *Ökumenische Glaubenseinheit*, esp. 48–53 (see the lengthy critique of this work by B. Schultze, *OCP* 44 [1978] 273–308). Schulz, *The Byzantine Liturgy*, passim, esp. 10ff., 142–5, 154–9; idem, "Patterns of Offering and Sacrifice," *SL* (1982) 34–48; and esp. idem, "Liturgischer Vollzug und sakramentale Wirklichkeit des eucharistischen Opfers," *OCP* 45 (1979) 245–66; 46 (1980) 5–19. See also B. Schultze, "Die patristiche Eucharistielehre im Gespräch evangelischer und orthodoxer Theologen," *OS* 28 (1979) 97–144; idem, "Die dreifache Herabkunft des Heiligen Geistes in den östlichen Hochgebeten," *OS* 26 (1977) 105–43.

[72]Schulz, *The Byzantine Liturgy*, 142–5; idem, *Ökumenische Glaubenseinheit*, 48–53.

[73]Schulz, "Patterns of Offering," 35–6.

[74]On the relationship between institution narrative, oblation, epiclesis, see most recently H.-J. Schulz, "Hochgebet und eucharistische Darbringung. Das wiedererschlossene Zeugnis der Liturgie in seiner ökumenischer Bedeutsamkeit," in E.

is just that, an "anaphora" or sacrifice of praise and thanks, and attempts to divide it into discrete theological "moments" and exploit them for special dogmatic concerns has no hermeneutic legitimacy.

In a word, CHR provides a superb example of the sane, balanced, eucharistic theology of the undivided church of the first millennium.

Renhart & A. Schnider, eds., *Sursum Corda. Variationen zu einem liturgischen Motiv. Für Philipp Harnancourt zum 60. Geburtstag* (Graz/Budapest: Akademie-Verlag, 1991) 140–6.

Index

Gregg, Robert C., 136
Gregory of Nazianzus, 120, 122, 126
Gregory of Nyssa, 88, 120, 122, 211
Gregory Thaumaturgus, 120–2
Gregory the Illuminator, 111
Gregory, Anaphora of St., 57, 144, 159, 210, 219, 221
Gregory Abul Farag, Anaphora of, 215
Gregory John, Anaphora of, 215
Griggs, C. W., 81–2

Hamm, F., 219
Hanson, R.P.C., 8, 67, 211
Hanssens, J. M., 115, 154
Hardy, E. R., 176
Heiming, O., 155
Heinemann, Joseph, 52–3, 54
Hiba (Ibas), 19
Hippolytus, 10–12, 35, 45, 62, 64, 174
Houssiau, Albert, 113, 116–17
Hudra, 20, 24

Ignatius of Antioch, 105
institution narrative, 3, 11, 13, 14, 16, 20, 21, 23–6, 32–4, 40, 43, 49, 52, 56, 59, 69, 70, 72, 74, 75, 83–6, 101–2, 106–7, 113, 115–17, 125, 127, 129, 137–9, 142, 145–8, 151, 158, 163, 167–70, 179, 204, 217–19, 222, 225
intercessions, 5, 6, 7, 16, 20, 21, 23, 39, 40, 41, 42, 49–50, 52, 54, 60–6, 70–2, 74, 75, 113, 115, 117, 121, 130, 139, 140, 142, 145, 147, 159–63, 165, 167–70, 176, 177, 181, 203–4, 217, 223
Irenaeus, 49, 64, 67, 101–2, 220

Jacob of Edessa, 154
Jacob, A., 196
Jacobite, 154, 204–6, 217, 221
James, Anaphora of St., 35, 41, 43, 46, 57, 60, 64, 65, 66, 70–2, 75, 87, 110, 112, 116–18, 128, 138, 140, 150–1, 153–72, 179–81, 195–6, 204–6, 215, 216, 220, 222, 223

Jasper, Ronald C. D., v, 112, 138, 144, 156
Jedlicka, J., 155
Jerome, 96
John, Acts of, 51
John the Scribe, Anaphora of, 15
Johnson, Maxwell E., v, 3, 6, 17, 74, 92, 209, 210
Johnson, Todd, 118–20
Jungmann, Josef A., 7, 52, 155, 158, 161
Justin Martyr, 1–2, 49, 62, 64, 67, 72, 101, 102, 104, 105

Kannengiesser, Charles, 90
Kelly, J.N.D., 166
Khouri-Sarkis, G., 197
Kilmartin, Edward, 40, 84–5, 103–4
Kohler, Kaufmann, 174–5
Kopecek, Thomas, 182–3, 185
Kraft, R. A., 209
Kretschmar, Georg, 79–80, 82–3, 143, 146
kuddasha, 20

LaCugna, C. M., 93
Lanne, Emmanuel, 111, 114–16, 118, 218, 219, 221, 223
Ledogar, R., 218, 219, 225
Lefort, J., 59
Leontius of Byzantium, 109, 197, 206, 217
Leontius of Caesarea, 111
Leroy, F. J., 114, 197
Lietzmann, Hans, 72, 87, 164, 176
Ligier, Louis, 7, 10, 13, 40, 51, 63, 158, 177, 215, 217
Logos, 17, 74, 86–92, 95–107, 135, 137
Lyman, Rebecca, 136

Macomber, W. F., 24–5, 33–4, 36, 79, 220, 223
Magne, Jean, 36
Malabar, 20–1
Mango, C., 221
Manichees, 135–8, 143, 148